Gender Power and Mediation: Evaluative Mediation to Challenge the Power of Social Discourses

Gender Power and Mediation: Evaluative Mediation to Challenge the Power of Social Discourses

By

Jamila A. Chowdhury

CAMBRIDGE SCHOLARS

PUBLISHING

Gender Power and Mediation:
Evaluative Mediation to Challenge the Power of Social Discourses,
by Jamila A. Chowdhury

This book first published 2012

Cambridge Scholars Publishing

12 Back Chapman Street, Newcastle upon Tyne, NE6 2XX, UK

British Library Cataloguing in Publication Data
A catalogue record for this book is available from the British Library

ISBN (10): 1-4438-3983-3, ISBN (13): 978-1-4438-3983-9

DEDICATED TO

My dearly loved parents:
Saleh Ahmed Chowdhury, my father
Jahanara Begum, my mother
&
My benign, compassionate husband *Mohammod Lutful Kabir*

TABLE OF CONTENTS

LIST OF ACRONYMS

ABS	Australian Bureau of Statistics
ACAS	Advisory Conciliation and Arbitration Service
ADB	Asian Development Bank
ADR	Alternative Dispute Resolution
AG-AGD	Australian Government-Attorney General's Department
ASK	*Ain o Shalish Kendra*
BBS	Bangladesh Bureau of Statistics
BDT	Bangladesh Taka (currency)
BLAST	Bangladesh Legal Aid and Services Trust
BNWLA	Bangladesh National Women Lawyers' Association
BRAC	Bangladesh Rural Advancement Committee
CPC	Code of Civil Procedure
DLR	*Dhaka* Law Report
DMC	*Delhi* Mediation Centre
FCO	Family Courts Ordinance
FLA	Family Law Act
GOB	Government of Bangladesh
ICDDR, B	International Centre for Diarrheal Diseases Research, Bangladesh
ISDLS	Institute for Study and Development of Legal Systems
IVAWS	International Violence against Women Survey
IWRAW	International Women Rights Action Watch
LCB	Law Commission of Bangladesh
LJCBP	Legal and Judicial Capacity Building Project
MFLO	Muslim Family Laws Ordinance
MLAA	*Madaripur* Legal Aid Association
MMC	Malaysian Mediation Centre
NADRAC	National Alternative Dispute Resolution Advisory Committee
NAVSS	National Association of Victim Support Schemes
NCBPF	NGO Committee of Beijing plus Five
NFCC	National Family Conciliation Council
NFM	National Family Mediation
NGO	Non-Governmental Organisation

NMAS	National Mediation Accreditation System
PDI	Power Distance Index
PMC	People's Mediation Committee
PML	People's Mediation Law
PRC	People's Republic of China
PSA	Personal Safety Australia
RAM	Reformed ADR Movement
SMC	Singapore Mediation Centre
UK	United Kingdom
UNDP	United Nations Development Programme
USA	United States of America
WHO	World Health Organisation
WSA	Women's Safety Australia
WSS	Women's Safety Survey

LIST OF STATUTES

Name of Statutes	**Country**
Administrative Dispute Resolution Act 1990	United States of America
Administrative Dispute Resolution Act 1996	United States of America
Arbitration Act 1940	British India
Arbitration Act 2001	Bangladesh
Chowkidari Act 1870	British India
Civil and Commercial Code, BE 2468	Thailand
Civil Procedure Law 1991	China
Code of Civil Procedure 1908	British India
Code of Civil Procedure (Amendment) Act 1999	India
Code of Civil Procedure (Amendment) Act 2002	India
Code of Civil Procedure (Amendment) Act2003	Bangladesh
Code of Civil Procedure (Amendment) Act 2006	Bangladesh
Contracts of Employment Act 1963	United Kingdom
Courts of Conciliation Act 1892	Queensland, Australia
Family Courts Ordinance 1985	Bangladesh
Family Law Act 1975	Commonwealth, Australia
Family Law Act 1996	United Kingdom
Family Violence (Prevention & Protection) Act 2010	Bangladesh
Guardianship and Wards Act 1890	Bangladesh
Income Tax (Amendment) Ordinance 2011	Bangladesh
Industrial Relations Act 1971	United Kingdom
Labour Act 2006	Bangladesh
Legal Aid Act 2000	Bangladesh
Money Loan Courts Act 2003	Bangladesh
Money Loan Courts (Amendment) Act 2010	Bangladesh
Negotiated Rule Making Act 1990	United States of America
Rudimentary Payments Act 1965	United Kingdom
Trade Union and Labour Relations Act 1974	United Kingdom

LIST OF TABLES

List of Boxes

LIST OF FIGURES

PREFACE

The book is an excerpt of my PhD thesis, which was undertaken at Sydney Law School, the University of Sydney, Australia. The PhD degree was awarded in 2011 and no emendation of the thesis was required. The text deals with the practice of family mediation and some of the challenges that may hinder its effective use by marginalised groups in a society. Those challenges include gendered power disparity and family violence, especially towards women, and the discussion extends to how the challenges can be overcome through a practice of evaluative mediation to provide fair outcomes for women.

While other contemporary texts on mediation focus on Western style facilitative mediation and its limitations in attaining fair justice for women suffering gendered power disparity and family violence, this text emphasises an evaluative mediation style that is embedded in Eastern social practices. Instead of focusing on gendered power disparity and family violence as limitations on the practice of facilitative mediation, this book will detail the practice of evaluative mediation which can provide fair justice to women despite the presence of gendered power disparity and family violence in a society.

This single authored book has some unique features that distinguishes it from, and makes it complementary to, other books on mediation in the market. One of the book's most distinctive features is that unlike other conventional books, which focus on Western style facilitative mediation, this book pays particular attention to evaluative mediation and its practice that may solve many unresolved challenges for facilitative mediation. Also unlike other contemporary books on mediation, this book not only discusses different theories of power and equity in mediation, it also includes a number of verbatim quotes from different mediation sessions to demonstrate how those theories are operationalised in a real life context. This is in sharp contrast with other available books on mediation in the market, which are written in the context of Western industrial societies.

Though not explicit from its title, this book deals with the issues in the context of Eastern developing countries, particularly in Bangladesh. The material relates not only to Bangladesh but also other Eastern developing countries where the practice of facilitative mediation is criticised or even opposed by many scholars on the grounds of gendered power disparity and family violence. Thus, this book could serve as a core text in many developing countries' law school graduate courses on family dispute resolution. Some of its chapters could also serve as important reference material on the evolution and development of mediation in many developed and developing countries.

It would be my immense pleasure if the book can satisfy the need for students, scholars, and practitioners concerned in the effective use of evaluative mediation as a means to promote access to justice for marginalised groups in our society, especially for women.

Dr. Jamila A. Chowdhury

ACKNOWLEDGEMENTS

Since many of the materials incorporated in this book were nurtured by my PhD thesis conducted at the University of Sydney, Australia, I owe an enormous debt of gratitude to my PhD supervisors: Emeritus Professor Dr. Hilary Astor, Commissioner, Law Commission, New South Wales (NSW), Australia and Associate Professor, Dr. Belinda Smith, University of Sydney, Australia. Their careful reviews, thoughtful responses and insightful supervisions have been wonderfully motivating.

I shall take this opportunity to express my gratitude to those who assisted me vigorously in getting permission to conduct my study at different governmental and non-governmental levels including family courts and NGO mediation centres. I especially owe thanks to Mr. Zakir Hossain, Director, Judicial Academy for Training Institute (JATI) and former Additional District & Session Judge, *Narayanganj* District and Mr. Shahjahan Kabir, Additional Chief Judicial Magistrate, *Dhaka* district of Bangladesh, who supported me by facilitating access to different official records concerning ADR and by providing suggestions to join up my endless questions in this field.

My gratitude must be extended to Ms. Rokeya Rahman, Senior Assistant Judge, *Mymensingh* District and Ms. Farida Yeasmin, Deputy Director (Legal Affairs), Bangladesh Legal Aid and Services Trust (BLAST). Without their sincere cooperation and wholehearted support, I might not have been able to retrieve many important data on in-court and out-of-court NGO mediation within a short time.

Special recognition also goes to many other individuals without whom this work would not have been possible. In this respect, I would like to acknowledge all the mediation participants. Further, especial thanks go to all the family court judges, NGO mediators and lawyers who were all busy people, but who were very generous in giving up some of their valuable time to be interviewed during the study. This book also acknowledges its debt to the thoughts of other scholars who have contributed to the field of mediation as it is today.

I would like to extend my special thanks to *Cambridge Scholars Publishing* for bringing out this book. Particularly, my heart-felt acknowledgements go to Carol Koulikourdi and Amanda Millar for their sincere cooperation in this regard.

Finally, writing this book would have been tedious at best without the love and patience of all of my family members. With a special mention, I am indebted to my husband, Mohammod Lutful Kabir, who, though away from me during this publication and engaged with his own PhD, inspired me relentlessly and gave me the strength to accomplish this task.

CHAPTER ONE

INTRODUCTION: ACCESS TO JUSTICE, MEDIATION AND ITS FUNDAMENTALS

1.1 Understanding Access to Justice and Mediation

Justice delayed is justice denied. Justice should not only be speedy, "but above all things, [it should be] cheap" (Estey 1985, 1076). The decisive factors for effective justice are those which "make justice easier to access, simpler to comprehend, quicker to deliver, and more certain" (Atkinson 2004, 6).[1] Because of delays in justice, the system affords those who are "economically stronger retain[ing] possession of the subject of the dispute over a longer period of time," who are "least liable to injustice" and denies the rights of those who are "most exposed to oppression" (Estey 1985, 1072–76). In fact, "[t]o render the expense of legal process exorbitant, is not delaying—it is absolutely denying justice to all but the rich" (Estey 1985, 1076). Therefore, access to justice should be expeditious and less expensive to be inclusive of the economically disadvantaged.

Access to justice, in its narrower sense, means access to formal adjudicative process in the court system or access to litigation (AG-AGD 2009, 5). The problem of access to justice through adjudicative process or litigation was identified in the extract of *The Black Book* as early as 1820. But "things seem to have changed little since [then] in relation to the speed to which the litigation process can resolve civil disputes" (Fulton 1989, 40). Further, access to justice, in its narrower sense, echoes the doctrine of "social exclusion" in the society, which has been defined as "limited

---

[1] See also, Wilfried Scha'rf, *Report on the Proceedings of the Consultative Group Meeting on Access to Justice and Penal Reform in Africa*, 18–20 March 1999.

access to the full range of social citizenship rights, which precludes the poor from exercise of such rights" (Sommerlad 2004, 349). As revealed through the criteria of Atkinson (2004), it is not necessary that accessible justice is delivered only through formal adjudicative process. In its broader sense, access to justice, therefore, may be enhanced through some informal non-adjudicative processes. That is to say, access to justice includes justice delivered to all, especially the poor, through formal or informal non-adjudicative processes (Zander 2000, 5; AG-AGD 2009, 3). As is discussed throughout this book, there are different alternative modes of justice, as complementary for the existing formal adjudicative process that can be used to accelerate access to justice to those who would otherwise be deprived of it through formal judiciary due to their economic vulnerability.

The next question inevitably arises regarding the purpose of access to justice. Though scholars have defined "justice" from different viewpoints (Kelsen 2000), justice generally has the inherent meaning of being "fair." Therefore, access to justice is served when it satisfies mainly the following two purposes:

- ensuring that people have physical access to the existing justice delivery system (AG-AGD 2009, 3), such as court, tribunal, or any other informal forums delivering justice; and

- equally importantly, ensuring that the justice delivery system accessed by people provides a fair justice (Boulle 1996, 55). If the justice delivery system is not fair, mere physical access to court, tribunal or any other justice mechanisms may not ensure "real" access to justice.

However, there are two contesting views regarding the fairness of justice. While many scholars are concerned about "procedural" fairness or fairness in the grievance handling process (Landis & Goodstein 1986; Tyler 1988; Carney 1989), others are concerned about the "quality" of the outcome (Beauchamp 1980; Buttram, Folger & Sheppard 1995). Those who support procedural fairness argue that fairness in a grievance handling process leads to a greater satisfaction for the aggrieved person and also a fair outcome. Nevertheless, supporters of the latter view show their concern that a fair process may not end up with a fair outcome (Menkel-Meadow 1991, 220).

The idea of all these different views on access to justice has been categorically compiled by Lord Woolf (1995) in his *General Principles to Access to Justice* report. According to him, to ensure access to justice in a civil justice system, the system should:

- be fair and be seen to be so by:

  ensuring that litigants have an equal opportunity regardless of their resources to assert or defend their legal rights

  providing every litigant with an adequate opportunity to state his or her own case and answer his or her opponents

- be just in its outcome
- deal with cases with reasonable speed
- be understandable to those who use it
- provide as much certainty as the nature of particular cases allows, and
- involve procedures and cost that are proportionate to the nature of the issue.

Throughout this book, these criteria will be used to determine and compare access to justice delivered by different modes of justice with particular reference to mediation and litigation. However, before moving on to a detailed discussion on access to justice through mediation, the next section elaborates on the barriers to access justice through formal adjudicative process or litigation. Subsequently, this chapter answers whether mediation can be used as a better alternative means to fill the vacuum of litigation and uphold the notion of access to justice.

1.1.1 Barriers to Access to Justice

Available means of justice may not ensure its accessibility. To make a clear distinction between "availability" and "accessibility," Hutchinson (1990, 181) rightly linked availability "to the question of whether a service exists" and access "to the question of whether a service is actually secured." Therefore, the mere availability of justice carries only a little meaning to justice seekers if it is not accessible to them. In other words, even when justice is made available in state courts, people may not have required access to it. Hutchinson (1990, 181) argues that "[t]he difference between availability and access is caused by 'barriers'," which Rhode (2000–01, 1787) calls "procedural hurdles" that "may prevent the have-nots from translating formal rights into legal judgment."

Scholars have identified various factors as "barriers" to access to justice through litigation. When discussing barriers to access to justice, Macdonald (1990, 298–300) broadly identified two different types of barriers: "subjective barriers" and "objective barriers." Subjective barriers relate to intellectual and physiological barriers including "age, physical or intellectual deficiency … the attitude of state functionaries such as the police, lawyer and judges" (Macdonald 1990, 300). The "objective barrier" relates to "purely physical barriers" including geographic dispersion of courts, availability of claims officers and lawyers etc., while other objective barriers are "cost of obtaining legal redress," "delay in legal proceedings" and "structural complexity of the legal system" (Macdonald 1990, 300). According to Macdonald (1990, 299–300):

> Because psychological and intellectual barriers go to the very substance of what we mean by justice, the metaphor of barriers is inapt to describe them … For obvious reasons, it is these objective barriers, which most conveniently fit the instrumental metaphor of barrier, and hence are on the agenda of reformers.

Others scholars also identify the most important objective barriers as delay and cost (Tate 1979; Dickson 1989; Rhode 2003–04). The predominant problem of delay in litigation vividly persists in many developing countries (Chowdhury 2005; Agarwal 2009). The "existing judicial system cannot ensure justice for the poor; many people are never produced before the court because of their poverty and the loopholes in [the judicial] system"[2] (Asian Development Bank 2003). As women are the poorest section of many developing countries, they have particular problems of

[2] The Minister of Law Justice and Parliamentary Affairs, Bangladesh, Barrister Moudud Ahmed addressed as chief guest at the inaugural function of a division-level training workshop on "Mediation techniques: Alternative Dispute Resolution (ADR) in the civil justice delivery system in Bangladesh" held at a city hotel on July 24, 2003.

access because of their reduced ability to bear the costs of justice (Golub 2003, 6; Asian Development Bank 2004; Meene & Rooij 2008, 16). Therefore, "the formal legal system has no attraction for the people especially women" (USAID 1995). The following sub-sections discuss in more detail the objective barriers which limit access to justice through a system of trial.

(a) Backlog of Cases and Delay in Disposal

The trial system takes a long time to make final settlement of disputes (Pearson & Thoennes 1984, 498). Access of the poor and disadvantaged to the formal justice and legal entitlements in courts is limited in many developing countries because of a huge backlog of cases, consequent delays in the disposal of cases, and high litigation costs (Asian Development Bank 2002; Ameen 2005a; Agarwal 2009). For example, in 2006 only 148,563 cases were disposed of from a total of 617,059 placed before the district courts of Bangladesh and therefore 468,496 cases were left pending for disposal at the end of the year (Supreme Court of Bangladesh 2008, 85). Similarly, in 2010, 31 million cases were pending in different Indian courts, amounting to a case load of 2,147 cases for each of the 14,576 judges available in the Indian judiciary at that time (Russo & Katzel 2010, 87). The backlog situation is even more serious in other developing countries. For instance, as reported by Calleros (2009, 172), the volume of total case backlog in Brazil once reached an unmanageable level of 4,850 cases per judge. The situation was even worse in Egypt where nearly 8,000 cases were pending per judge in 2000. Due to such a high case load, clearance rate of pending cases was only 36 percent in Egypt, compared with 80 to 100 percent attained by other developed countries (Ikram 2009, 299). Similar problems of case backlog also exist in Tanzania, Pakistan, Sri Lanka, and many other developing countries (Cheema 2005, 171; International Monetary Fund 2010, 158; Freedom House 2010, 577; Rios-Figueroa 2011, 313). If the current rate of disposal through a system of trial continues, many developing countries cannot expect to mitigate this backlog and resulting delays.

Delays in litigation not only retard justice to those in the trial process, but such delays even discourage two-thirds of the plaintiffs from entering the formal court process (UNDP 2002, 9). In some developing countries, delay in the trial process "[h]as reached a point where it has become a factor of injustice, a violation of human rights. Praying for justice, the parties become part of a long protracted and torturing process, not knowing when it will end" (Alam 2000). Sometimes delay in courts is coupled with uncertainty. Of those interviewed in a survey conducted by Transparency International, Bangladesh (2004), 53.9 percent of plaintiffs/defendants were uncertain about when their cases might be resolved. As stated by a former Chief Justice of the Supreme Court of Bangladesh:

> Our legal system has thus been rendered uncaring, non-accountable and formalistic. It delivers formal justice and it is oblivious to the sufferings and woes of the litigants, of their waste of money, time and energy and of their engagement in unproductive activities, sometimes for decades. (Kamal 2005b, 137)

Delay may also have an impact on outcome. When people are finally granted a hearing, the end result may not be just because "the longer the period from the time of the events which are the subject matter of the action to the time of the trial, the harder it may become to prove the facts of the case" (Astor & Chinkin 1992, 33). Therefore, due to delay, the existing trial systems in many developing countries fail to provide justice to their citizens within a reasonable range of time and quality of outcome.

(b) Exorbitant Cost and Exclusion of the Poor

Apart from case backlog and delay, the high-cost of litigation also restrains access justice for the poor (Tate 1979; Dickson 1989; Asian Development Bank 2002; Rhode 2003–04). As the disposal of cases is delayed in many developed countries, total charges paid to the lawyers increase with consecutive court appearances (Chowdhury 2011). As indicated by Bergoglio (2003, 49), there is a negative relationship between judicial costs and rates for eviction in Argentina. The extent of such negative relationship is higher for cases where a large number of litigants represent the ordinary people of the society (Bergogilio 2003). All these judicial costs pose an additional burden and may cause economic hardship to the poor. As cited by Khan (2006, 64):

> The high cost of litigation is a challenge, which judiciary has made attempts to meet without any spectacular success. Even after decades of independence, the poor, backward and weaker members of society feel that they do not have equal opportunities for securing justice because of their socio-economic conditions.

Sometimes, the cost of litigation is further increased by the cost of bribes. For instance, in Bangladesh, most parties (63 percent) have no option but to bribe court officials to accelerate the disposal of their cases (Hasan 2002, paragraph 7; Huq 2005, 102–03; Transparency International 2007, 181). During interviews conducted by Transparency International in Bangladesh, 88.55 percent of respondents agreed that it was almost impossible to get quick access to justice from the courts without using financial incentives or some other forms of pressure (Hasan 2002, paragraph 10). In fact, particularly in developing countries "increasing expenses of litigation, delay in disposal of cases and huge backlogs" in the legal system may have "virtually shaken the confidence of people in the judiciary" (Hasan 2008a). Therefore, even if formal judiciary is literally open for every citizen who may seek justice, a hidden barrier of exorbitant cost may keep the access to formal justice out-of-reach for the poor and disadvantaged section of the society.

(c) Inadequate Availability of the Formal Justice-Providers

Though many of the developing countries struggle against an acute backlog of cases and a delay in the delivery of justice, poor financial capabilities may limit their ability to engage more judges to clear such backlogs. For example, at present, there are only 77 Supreme Court [justices], and 750 other judges to dispense justice to a population of nearly 150 million people in Bangladesh (Transparency International 2007, 181). Therefore, only 5.5 judges in the lower judiciary serve a million people. This is still below the rate attained by other neighbouring countries like India. In 2008, India had fourteen judges per one million people. In 2001, the number of judges per one million people was 0.6 in Peru, 0.5 in Chile and 0.36 in Brazil (Calleros 2009, 170). The scarcity can be better understood if we compare the figure with the judges to head of population ratio of some other developed countries like Australia, the UK, and the USA. For example, the USA and the UK have 160 and 110 judges per one million of population respectively (Singh 2002, 155). Therefore, the situation of under-staffing in many developing countries is severely restricting ordinary citizens from accessing justice from their formal judiciary.

(d) Procedural Complexities and Large Contingent of Illiterates

Among the barriers to access to justice identified by scholars, sometimes the complexity of the legal process gets special mention (Macdonald 1990). Literature shows that litigation follows a much more complex procedure than mediation (Ruth 2006). The complexity of the formal court system makes its procedure most difficult to comprehend for poorly educated, illiterate women who are ignorant of this system due to their lack of experience beyond the four walls of their home. It has been shown that women in many developing countries do not understand what is happening inside the courtroom and therefore do what their lawyers tell them to do (Roger 1990; Wisconsin Lawyers 2009).

For instance, in Bangladesh, procedural complexity in dealing with civil disputes severely affects a large number of plaintiffs who do not have sufficient literacy to have the minimum understanding of this process (Chowdhury 2005). Complexity in litigation goes one-step further because witnesses are sometimes hired to fabricate cases. In one survey conducted by Transparency International, Bangladesh,[3] hiring of witnesses was reported by 19.8 percent of the respondents involved in litigation. The 28.6 percent of urban households who reported about hired witness was markedly higher than the 18.9 percent of rural households. This type of fabricated witness can destroy any remnant of faith and honour remaining between the parties. The primary objective appears to be simply to champion their opponent rather than making any amicable or fair settlement of their dispute.

The extent of the complexity extends even further when litigants have to go back and forth to different courts to settle different facets of a single dispute. For instance, in Kenya, cases on the distribution of marital property is dealt with by High courts and Magistrate courts for Christian marriage, by High and Islamic courts for Muslim marriage, and by District Magistrate courts for conventional marriages (Ellis 2007, 65). These complexities may lead to further delay and promote a high cost of legal

---

[3] "Survey on Corruption in Bangladesh" conducted for the Transparency International Bangladesh by the Survey and Research System, *Dhaka*, Bangladesh, with the assistance of the Asia Foundation, Bangladesh. The survey was divided into two phases: Phase I consisted of a "pilot study" to ascertain the nature, extent and intensity, wherever possible, of corruption, and the places where corruption occurs. In the pilot study, a small-scale national household survey was undertaken to obtain information on public delivery services and their corruption in providing those services. This study was performed in six different public sectors among which the judiciary deserve a particular mention. Phase II was a large-scale survey to provide baseline information on corruption in a sample of 2,500 households.

representation, without which it becomes virtually impossible for ordinary people to afford court processes.

(e) Limited Access to Legal Aid

Legal aid can help to resolve disproportionate access to justice based on economic power (Tate 1979; Mayer 1987; Dickson 1989; Neumann 1992; Mack 1995; Rhode 2000–01). The practice of government legal aid programmes dates back to fourteenth century Europe when Henry VII waived court fees for poor litigants, and empowered courts to provide "legal representation" by appointing lawyers for poor clients (Johnson 1994). In 1960, the United States of America experienced a new concept of legal aid funding which included not only provision of legal advice and legal representation in the court but also provision of legal information and education to make people more informed about their rights. Similar concepts were later introduced in Australia, Canada and other parts of Europe (Blankenburg 1997). Whatever form a legal aid may take, its availability affects the ability of poor people to access justice through litigation (Tate 1979, 906; Dickson 1989, 3). Further, adequacy of legal aid is also important because otherwise many litigants who are theoretically entitled to service from state appointed lawyers, may not get quality service or suffer long delays if "court appointments are [considered as] a financial loss for lawyers" (Mansnrus 2001, 102). Thus, availability of adequate legal aid may help to relieve a part of the cost burden from the shoulders of the poor by enabling them to get free services from lawyers and subsidies to cover other court charges (Mayer 1987; Neumann 1992; Mack 1995).

However, the main problem relating to legal aid remains in its limited access to the poor due to its scarcity, and the ignorance of the poor about its availability. Such scarcity of legal aid funding from many developing country governments make access to justice extremely difficult for the poor (UNDP 2002, 43; Siddiqua 2005, 71). Though the situation and the nature of cases dealt with vary in different countries, the situation is worse in most of the developing world. For example, in 2005 the Chinese government funded legal aid was sufficient to serve, at best, only one-third of the total population who were in need of it (Hualing 2010, 172). In Bangladesh, only 5 percent of the family cases have access to government provided legal aid (Chowdhury 2011). Similarly, the demand for legal aid far outweighs its supply in many developing countries like Brazil, Vietnam and other Central Asian countries (Mariner, Cavallaro & HRW

1998, 67, Joseph & Najmabadi 2003, 373). Scarce legal aid may substantially increase the number of unrepresented litigants at courts or cause that "some people suspected of committing serious criminal offences may not face trial" (Aldous 2008, 403). Therefore, in many developing countries, formal courts remain only as a means to ensure justice for the affluent members of society.

As formal court procedures remain inaccessible to many poor and disadvantaged people of the developing world, they could easily be deprived of justice altogether. Thus, the need to find alternatives which provide access to fair justice for the economically vulnerable is evident. Given all the major limitations of the formal court system, mediation could be a good "complementary method" for ensuring access to justice in poor developing world countries which commonly face huge backlogs in their judiciaries and can only provide limited access to legal aid. The following section elaborates on how scholars observed the importance of mediation over trial in dispensing justice and why they have argued for mediation as a better alternative for access to justice by the poor and disadvantaged.

1.1.2 Mediation: An Efficacious Means of Access to Justice

Mediation is an alternative dispute resolution method adopted in many jurisdictions in which an impartial third party helps individuals to resolve their disputes, without having any power to impose a binding solution (LeBaron 2001, 121). One of the benefits of mediation is that it addresses court backlogs by providing cheap and accessible methods of dispute resolution for the poor (Folberg 2004, 20; Stockdale & Ropp 2007, 37; Gold 2009, 224). "It is estimated that one dollar spent on mediation will cost three for arbitration and fifteen for litigation," thus, "[a] consensus base[d] process is proving to be cost effective" (Hoffman 1993, 12). Mediation in community dispute centres may even be provided free of cost (Folberg 2004, 20; Chowdhury 2011, 229). This is in sharp contrast with the barrier to access to justice in terms of the high cost of litigation. Other scholars have also demonstrated the cost advantage of mediation in terms of litigation (Crosby, Stockdale & Ropp 2007, 37). As shown in Table 1.1, a survey of 1,884 mediation clients of Singapore Mediation Centre (SMC) indicated that mediation provides substantial cost and time savings in comparison with litigation (Lee and Hwee 2009, 15).

Table 1.1. Clients' perception on cost and time savings through mediation

	All parties surveyed	Parties who settled through mediation	Parties who did not settle through mediation
Cost savings	81%	93%	52%
Time savings	85%	96%	59%

Source: Lee and Hwee 2009, 15.

As indicated in Table 1.1, more than 90 percent of the clients of SMC who resolved their disputes through mediation thought that they were able to minimize both time and cost to resolution by using this process. Though the statistics in Table 1.1 did not indicate the percentage of cost and time that clients may save through mediation in comparison with litigation, another comparison of cost and time made by Chowdhury (2011, 201–5), for court-annexed family mediation and litigation in Bangladesh, indicated that clients can save a substantial percentage of their cost and time by resolving family disputes through mediation. Results from empirical study (Chowdhury 2011, 201–5) also indicated that under mediation procedure, party consensus not only accelerates the resolution of disputes but also enhances its execution. Results from a questionnaire survey among lawyers conducted by Chowdhury (2011) indicate that in the case of litigation, more than 50 percent of the clients have to pay lawyer's fees exceeding BDT 10,000, while none of the cases resolved through mediation required lawyer's fees of more than this amount. On the other hand, 95 percent of in-court mediation can be resolved with lawyer's fees less than BDT 5,000, whereas in the case of litigation, only 23 percent of cases can be resolved with the lawyer's fees not exceeding BDT 5,000. A more than 50 percent cost savings in mediation in comparison with trial cases has also been acknowledged by Gold (2009, 224).

Table 1.2. Cost and time savings in mediation in comparison with litigation

	Average Cost (BDT)	Average Time
Litigation	10000	17.1 months
Mediation	5000	10.3 months
Percentage Savings in mediation	50%	39.8%

Source: Chowdhury 2011, 201–5

However, cost and time savings from out-of-court mediation in comparison with litigation would be much higher as the cost of out-of-court family mediation in Bangladesh remains nil, and the average time to resolution for out-of-court resolution is only 1.96 months, in comparison to 17.1 months for litigation (Chowdhury 2011).

In addition to the cost and time savings, another benefit of mediation indicated by scholars include the simple and easily comprehensible method of dispute resolution through mediation. One study conducted by Chowdhury (2005) in Bangladesh indicates that all of the female mediation clients surveyed well understood the court-annexed mediation process used to resolve family disputes. This was in sharp contrast to only 10 percent of female clients who clearly comprehended the trial process in family courts (Chowdhury 2005). Understanding the process also increased client satisfaction on the dispute resolution method. As indicated by Gold (2009, 224), couples attending mediation remain more satisfied with the process and tend to recommend mediation to others on more than 90 percent of cases.

1.2 Approaches to Mediation: Beyond Facilitation

Generally, it is argued by Western scholars that the objective of mediation is the mere facilitation of parties to resolve their disputes through negotiation (Menkel-Meadow 1995; Kovach & Love 1998; Stitt 2004). Such facilitation through mediation may be provided in four different settings, such as: (a) court-annexed mediation (b) mediation by private mediators (c) mediation at mediation agencies and (d) community mediation provided at community or neighbourhood justice centres (Folberg 2004, 10). However, irrespective of the place where mediation is conducted, the objective of mediation varies both historically and in contemporary practice. Different approaches to mediation may be practised by mediators based on different theoretical justification (Boulle 2011, 46). The nature of dispute and desire of parties also affect the approaches of mediation used in a dispute (Spencer 2011, 50).

Scholars and practitioners have identified different types of mediation based on the objectives of mediators and how they intervene in a dispute resolution process. Watnik (2003, 144) divided mediation into two types: facilitative mediation and evaluative mediation. Folberg (2004, 14–17) identified three different types of mediation based on the type of interventions made by mediators: facilitative mediation, evaluative mediation and transformative mediation. Boulee (2011, 44–6) discussed a fourth type of mediation, which he termed "settlement mediation." The desired objectives of mediators also affect the types of interventions applied by them. Based on these varieties of objectives and methods of interventions used by mediators, the four different approaches of mediation identified by scholars are:

(1) Facilitative mediation

(2) Evaluative mediation

(3) Transformative mediation; and

(4) Settlement mediation

However, the approaches to mediation are archetypical in nature because any particular mediation that starts with a facilitative approach may end up with an evaluative mediation.

1.2.1 Facilitative Mediation

Facilitative mediation is a dispute resolution process in which a neutral third party makes procedural intervention to help parties to identify their interest in a dispute that facilitates their negotiation (Boulle 2011, 44–5). Facilitative mediators also ensure procedural equality between parties by creating a level playing field for both of the parties to negotiate their interests (Folger 2004, 15). Mediators may ask questions to clarify their positions and interests in mediation (Zumeta 2001, 1; Gaffal 2010, 202). According to Folberg & Taylor (1984, 8), "the most useful way to look at mediation is to see it as a goal-directed, problem-solving intervention." Therefore, facilitative mediation is also known as problem-solving or interest-based mediation (Boulle 2011, 44). However, a facilitative mediator will not make any evaluative statement on the merit of a dispute nor provide any evaluation on the content or outcome. It is assumed that parties will act in their best interest (Gaffal 2010, 202). Therefore, facilitative mediation may not attain a fair outcome for both of the parties if one party remain silent or bargains inefficiently in mediation due to some cultural barrier, ignorance of rights, or in fear of the other party attending mediation (Zumeta 2000; Chowdhury 2011).

1.2.2 Evaluative Mediation

Evaluative mediation is a rights-based approach (Folger 2004, 15). An evaluative mediator may facilitate bargaining between parties; however, in addition to facilitation, an evaluative mediator may provide his or her advice or suggestion to parties and may help them understand their legal and social position in a dispute (Folger 2004, 15). Mediators may assist parties to settle according to law, social norm or other industry standards, therefore it may be referred to as advisory or normative mediation (Boulle 2011, 45–6). Evaluation may be provided on the content of a dispute (Riskin 1996; Rifkin & Cobb 1991). However, there is an existing debate on whether mediators limit their evaluation only on the content of a dispute or extend it towards the outcome of a dispute. As observed by Lowry (2004, 84–5), the degree of evaluation may vary depending on the need of the parties attending mediation. Though some scholars have argued that evaluative mediation is "wrong" (Alfini 1997), as observed by Riskin (1995, 101) mediation standards and codes do not necessarily restrict evaluations but circumscribe them in some way. To provide informed evaluation, an evaluative mediator needs to be an expert on the area in dispute.

1.2.3 Transformative Mediation

In contrast to the facilitative and evaluative approaches of mediation, transformative mediation does not focus on the enhancement of bargaining capacities of the parties (Gramberg 2006, 70). A transformative mediator is more involved with the psychological aspects of a dispute and provides counselling or therapy to resolve disputes by improving relationship between parties and making each more sympathetic to the position of the other (Harvey 2006, 561; Gramberg 2006, 70). As transformative mediation may involve therapy and always attempts to improve the relationship between parties, it is also termed as "therapeutic mediation" or "reconciliation mediation" (Boulle 2011, 44). As observed by Folger (2004, 16), the main purpose of a transformative mediation is to change the relationship between parties while settlement of disputes remains as a secondary issue. In a transformative mediation, a mediator does not have any directive role. To apply this technique, mediators need to be adept at counselling, therapy, or dealing with other emotional issues involved in a dispute (Boulle 2011, 45–6). Therapeutic or other forms of transformative mediation may be used to improve continuing relationships, such as matrimonial issues, workplace disputes or a victim-offender relationship in community mediation (Boulle 2011, 45).

1.2.4 Settlement Mediation

In settlement mediation, mediators encourage parties to make a compromise at a mid-point between their initial positions. A settlement mediator makes minimum intervention in the mediation process and does not help parties to identify their genuine interest in a dispute, but allows parties to make a compromised decision on the basis of their positional arguments (Boulle 2011, 45–6). The objective of a settlement mediator is to identify the individual settlement ranges for both of the parties, identify the overlapping settlement range and encourage parties to negotiate and settle at a point somewhere within their overlapping range of settlement capability (Cooey 2006, 240). Therefore, depending on their negotiation capacity, each party attending settlement mediation may not be able to participate equally. Sometimes it is synonymous to "compromise mediation," "distributive mediation" or "positional mediation" (Boulle 2011, 45). This type of mediation may be used in settling industrial disputes or insurance claims, etc.

1.3 Dynamics of Mediation: The *Modus Operandi*

A third party is indispensable in mediation; however he or she may serve to mitigate or accelerate the dispute. Whatever approach mediators use, if they want to mediate effectively, they need to be adept at many dispute issues and understand third party intervention dynamics. For example, scholars identified how the roles of conflict, negotiation, emotion and culture may determine how an intervention by a mediator may change the mediation dynamics.

1.3.1: The Role of "Conflict" in Mediation

Mediation is essentially a conflict resolution process. Therefore, mediators need to understand conflict, and how it arises and evolves in interpersonal relationship requiring mediation. Conflict is state of antagonistic human relationship that may begin from a difference of opinion. As explained by Simpson (1998, 2), a conflict may arise because of opposing views on three different issues: material assets, psychological needs for control or recognition, and conflict of value. Conflict may also be evident in different spheres. While intrapersonal conflict is a person's disharmony with his or her own morality, interpersonal conflict is between two people, intra-group conflict is between group members while inter-group conflicts are between groups. Therefore, differentiation itself may be the cause of interpersonal or family conflict (Christner, Mennuti & Mennuti 2008, 255). According to Nichols & Schwartz (2000, 123):

> The goal of Bowen's[4] therapy became the differentiation of self of key family members, so they could help the whole family differentiate. This emphasis on differentiation, meaning control of reason over emotion, betrays Bowen's psychoanalytic roots.

Though Bowen (1978) developed this concept from a family relationship perspective, it is equally applicable in other inter-personal conflicts. Thus, the level of differentiation of each person's "self," "full-self," or "half-self" is an important factor in mitigating or accelerating conflict. When a person's ability is esteemed with "full-self" (i.e. a self-esteem vigour with capability and separateness independent from the feelings of others), in contrast to "half-self" (i.e. a "symbiotic relationship" when "one feels angry and upset, the other becomes equally upset and angry"), he or she will have an advantageous position in mediation. However, whether the conflict in mediation accelerates or mitigates due to a person's differentiation depends on the level of such differentiation. In other words, if both parties in mediation are of "full-selves," the conflict will be much higher when either or both parties are of "half-selves" (Taylor 2002, 35–7).

[4] The concept of differentiation was first proposed by Bowen in 1978.

Since mediation is an empowering process (Davis & Salem 1984, 18–19; Neumann, 1992, 231–32), a dynamic mediator tries to take a holistic approach by combining the concept of differentiation and conflict so that half-self parties will be empowered and differentiated in this process and conflict will not be escalated.

Sometimes triangulation escalates conflict. Family members generally try to maintain harmony and a good dyadic relationship. Each dyad of a family can maintain a dyadic relationship between and among family members by respecting individual differences and building a positive emotional environment without involving a third party (Fogarty 1976, 150). However, when people in a dyad are in conflict they may try to involve a third party in a dispute to form triangulation by taking support from that third party. In the case of family conflict, this third party is usually the children (Christner, Mennuti & Mennuti 2008, 255). The concept of triangulation is:

> The term given to triads that are formed bringing others into conflict in negative patterns to try gain help and support. Triangulation is done by the parties on an unconscious level rather than as the active step of going to a designated third party. (Taylor 2002, 40)

If triangulation forms an "unhealthy alliance" between family members and if it is not minimized, it might create a further conflict (Taylor 2002, 40–2) which Kreisberg (1998, 25) describes as the "cyclical nature of conflict." In Haley's (1991, 115) view, such a "perverse triangle" gives continuing conflict. However, a dynamic mediator's role as a third party in a dispute is positive and not as negative as triangulation. According to Augsberger (1992, 154):

> In contrast to triangulation, clear triad formation is intentional, methodical, and purposive. The participants know that the triad is a temporary arrangement designed to clarify and strengthen the dyadic relationship through reconciliation of its difficulties so that a third party will be unnecessary and undesirable. The third person of triad is committed to neutrality, to availability to each person, to flexibility in offering interventions, and to equal justice for all concerned. Effective mediators, who can form triads without triangulation, are recognized by disputants in every culture. The wise person who can maintain a median position and mediate from the centred stance is prized, honoured and trusted, whether in Asia or Africa, Australia or the many cultures of Latin America.

Thus, a careful mediator will endeavour to mitigate the impact of negative triangulation in a dispute so that the conflict does not exacerbate or create another conflict. An intervention mitigating the negative triangulation "at the right time and in the right way can speed the process of de-escalation" (Taylor 2002, 65).

1.3.2 The Role of "Negotiation" in Mediation

Mediation is assisted negotiation where the parties of a dispute are encouraged to negotiate effectively to determine the outcome of their consensual settlement. The objective of a mediator, especially mediators from low-context cultures, is to assist interest-based negotiation between parties who might have tried to negotiate from a fixed and rigid position (Taylor 2002, 99; Strasser & Randolph 2004, 69). Mediation is "conducted under the umbrella of principled negotiation." The major difference between mediation and principled negotiation is that, in a principled negotiation negotiators have to think about "what to do" to get a win-win solution, whereas in mediation, a mediator has to think about "how to do it" by making parties negotiate for their win-win interest (Spencer 2002, 59). The concept of principled negotiation was first introduced by Fisher and Ury in 1991. Under this new concept of negotiation, the objective of a mediator is four-fold: to help parties to separate from the problem, to focus on interests rather than on position, to invent options for material gain, and to insist on using objective criteria (Strasser & Randolph 2004, 70). Due to gender role ideology in the society, women may not be as tough negotiators as their male counterparts, especially when husbands are involved in family mediation (Nyquist & Spence 1986). As mediation is an assisted dispute resolution process where parties need to negotiate with each other to attain a better outcome, a mediator also needs to be conscious about factors which may hinder effective negotiation between mediating parties.

1.3.3 The Role of "Emotion" in Mediation

Proper handling of the emotions of mediating parties remains a challenge for effective mediators (Strasser & Randolph, 146). Giving parties' time to relieve their emotion may help them to proceed with substantial issues. If a mediator ignores emotions, this may further frustrate emotional parties who will eventually lose trust in the mediator (Weinstein 2001, 35). However, bringing great emotion to mediation may hamper the essential dispute resolution process (Spencer 2011, 29). It is important that while showing empathy to a party's emotion, mediators maintain their unbiased and impartial position and not show favouritism simply because one party becomes emotional. Showing empathy in mediation is possible without taking sides (Weinstein 2001, 34).

Without losing focus on substantial issues, a mediator may show empathy with an emotional party and lead him or her to focus on the cause of emotion and how to resolve it (Spencer 2011, 29). Another problem is created when a pre-determined or calculated emotion is displayed by any party into mediation simply to get sympathy (Weinstein 2001, 36). Therefore, mediators need to be aware of these emotional issues.

1.3.4 The Role of "Culture" in Mediation

Culture may bring an important component into mediation. The culture of dispute resolution affects the mode of mediation (Adamopoulos & Kashima 1999, 184). A mediator also needs to be aware of the meaning of culturally located responses which parties may make during mediation. Response of parties to negotiation and mediation may vary according to culture, and if a mediator cannot appropriately recognise and interpret such responses, it may create confusion (Boulle 2011, 133). For instance, anthropologist Edward Hull distinguished between high-context and low-context cultures, and understanding such differences in cultures is important for a mediator (Samovar, Porter & McDaniel 2010, 215).

In high-context (Eastern) cultures such as Japan, Korea, China or African America, people may not express all their feelings and emotions through words, and inference, gesture, or even silence may have a specific cultural meaning which warrants a culturally specific response (Samovar, Porter & McDaniel 2010, 215–6). In low-context (Western) cultures such as Australia, Canada, Germany, Scandinavia and North America, most interaction is expressed verbally and very little is embedded in the context or explained through body language (Samovar, Porter & McDaniel 2010, 217). High-context cultures are motivated by the principles of "indirectness as part of the forms of politeness" and "shared values of esteem for others." The approach of low-context cultures is direct, as indirectness is thought of as cowardly and lacking in self-esteem (Taylor 2002, 99), and principled negotiation is conducted by separating people from the problem (Strasser & Randolph 2004, 70). However, in high-context cultures, people and problems are deemed to be interrelated and thus inseparable. According to Augsberger (1992, 91):

> The low-context cultures tend to view the world in analytic, linear, logical terms that allow them to be hard on problems but soft on people, focused on instrumental outcomes but easy on affective issues; while high-context cultures perceive the world in synthetic, spiral logic that links the conflict event and its impact, issue, actors, content, and context.

Therefore, a cultural understanding is important for a mediator to comprehend the desire, anger and emotion of parties attending mediation, particularly in a high-context culture. Before simply transferring critiques which are relevant in one jurisdiction and culture to another, it is important to have a cultural understanding between the two.

1.4 Perspectives of Mediation: Differentiation between Low-Context and High-Context Cultures

Mediators use four basic models of mediation. While the objective of transformative and settlement mediation is either to maintain or improve the current relationship between parties, facilitative and evaluative mediation involves the attainment of a consensual solution to a dispute without giving primary importance to the maintenance or improvement of a relationship. A strong debate in the literature concerns the legitimacy of the facilitative and evaluative model (Boulle 2011, 46). As observed by Lim (1996, 363), Western or Eastern cultures may have an important impact on the mediation process. A mediator does not need to switch from one model of mediation to another depending on each case because the mediation model can be pre-set to suit the cultural practice of a society (Lim 1996, 196). Therefore, a historical perspective on mediation is discussed to understand whether a facilitative or evaluative mediation model would be more appropriate for Western or Eastern societies.

1.4.1. Western Mediation

Developed countries like the USA, the UK and Australia have a very high judge to population ratio as well as a developed court infrastructure. Nevertheless, to maintain their speedy trial process, these countries are diligent users of mediation. This section provides a brief history of the practice of mediation in the in-court and out-of-court settings of a few developed countries. The objective is to link their current practice of mediation with their historical perspective on dispute resolution culture.

(a) Mediation in the United States of America

The United States of America (USA) is one of the front-runners in the institutionalized practice of mediation in in-court and out-of-court settings. ADR movement in the US started in the 1970s, and the year 1976 deserves a special mention due to the Historic Pound Conference.[5] At that conference, Chief Justice Warren Burger expressed his dissatisfaction with litigation, acknowledging that trial is "too costly, too painful, too destructive, and too inefficient for a truly civilised people." As observed by the USA's Supreme Court Justice Sandra Day O'Conner, "courts should be the place of last resort, rather than the place of first resort" (cited in Zondervan 2000, 112). This view suggests the importance of community mediation and other out-of-court forms of Alternative Dispute Resolution (ADR). The practice of community mediation started in the USA from the early 1970s (Zondervan 2000, 111). Community mediation resolves disputes on a variety of issues including arguments between neighbours or disputes of students at school. It can also resolve disputes of citizens with medical practitioners, local councils or with their employers and co-workers (Alexander 2006, 153).

In 1978, the USA's Department of Justice initiated an experimental project on community mediation in three neighbourhood justice centres. In a survey, 88 percent of the service receivers from community mediation expressed their satisfaction with it (McCold 2006, 25). Though the community mediation programme in the USA practises different forms of ADR, including arbitration, mediation and conciliation, mediation remains a cornerstone of community mediation (Zondervan 2000, 112). As American society is individualistic and competitive in nature, and individuals seek to pursue their individual rights, the mode of mediation in the USA reflects this view (Hall 2002, 35). According to a report from the National Institute of Justice (1997), mediation in community justice centres is practised as:

> An effort by a neutral party to assist disputing parties to resolve the conflict through the conduct of face to face meeting. In such meetings, the

[5] See Frank Sander, "Varieties of Dispute Processing," in *The Pound Conference: Perspectives on Justice in the Future*, edited by Leo Levin and Russell Wheeler. St Paul: Minnesota, 1979.

> third party is not authorized to impose a settlement on the parties, but rather seeks to assist them in fashioning a mutually satisfactory resolution to the conflict.

In the USA, the concept of a "neutral party" implies a third party whose role in mediating the disputes/conflicts is confined to mere facilitation, rather than any evaluation on the content of dispute. According to Taylor (2002, 99):

> In low-context cultures, like mainstream North American society, members of the culture who are in conflict tend to adapt to and adopt Fisher and Ury's four part formulation … of separating people from the problem, focusing on interests rather than positions, inventing options for mutual gain and insisting on objective criteria.

North American society focuses on an interest-based approach, in contrast to a rights-based approach of evaluative mediation. The definition of mediation expounded by Folberg & Taylor (1984, 7–8), one of the most commonly accepted not only in the USA but also by other Western authors, did not use the term "facilitative"; but its essence can be found as they state mediation as a process:

> By which the participants, together with the assistance of a neutral person or persons, systematically isolate disputed issues in order to develop options, consider alternatives, and reach a consensual settlement that will accommodate their needs. Mediation is a process that emphasizes the participants' own responsibility for making decisions that affect their livers.

Since the eighteenth century, mediation has been a core element of dispute resolution theory and practice in USA (Wing 2008, 93), and the success of mediation outside USA's courts is worth mentioning here.

By 1997, more than 550 community mediation centres were active in the USA which were dealing with over 45,500 cases each year (Ray 1997, 73). Community justice centres in New York were so successful in diverting cases from formal courts, that the state funded a network of community dispute resolution centres, expanded its network to sixty-two countries and is now serving as the world's largest unified mediation programme (New York State Unified Court System 2003; McCold 2003). According to a report of the National Association of Community Mediation (2004), community mediation centres are currently working in every state of the USA.

Because of the success of community justice centres in the quick resolution of disputes with high client satisfaction, the federal government chose to use ADR to resolve more than 155,000 cases in 1989, in which either the federal government was a party or some federal questions were involved (Susskind 1989). Therefore, in 1990 the *Administrative Dispute Resolution Act 1990* and *Negotiated Rule Making Act 1990* was passed in the USA. The objective of the *Administrative Dispute Resolution Act 1990* was to authorize different federal agencies to resolve their disputes with citizens through informal dispute resolution processes: conciliation, mediation, fact-finding, mini-trials, and arbitration (Breger 2001, 1). The *Administrative Dispute Resolution Act 1996* replaced the earlier Act and broadened the scope to practicing ADR by USA agencies in resolving their disputes.

The use of court-connected mediation proliferated in the USA in the 1980s and 1990s (Hall 2002, 35). In some cases, parties were required to mediate before proceeding through to trial while in other cases, courts were given the discretion to decide which cases should go to mediation (Alexander 2006, 396). As observed by Alexander (2006, 393):

> Hundreds of court [annexed mediation] programmes exist in general jurisdiction state courts throughout the nation. Additional mediation programmes exist throughout the federal system at both the trial and appellate court levels. Mediation also takes place in small claims, as well as specialized courts such as housing courts.

(b) Mediation in the United Kingdom

The legislative mandates to conduct mediation/conciliation in different types of employment related litigations were also recognized in the United Kingdom (UK). A series of Acts including the *Contracts of Employment Act 1963*, *Rudimentary Payments Act 1965, Industrial Relations Act 1971,* and the *Trade Union and Labour Relations Act 1974* had different provisions for conciliation or mediation and were in operation from the early 1970s (Liebmann 2000, 19). The Advisory Conciliation and Arbitration Service (ACAS) formed under the *Trade Union and Labour Regulations Act 1974* has defined mediation in a way that is more akin to non-binding arbitration defined later in this chapter. According to ACAS, mediation is a dispute resolution process where a "mediator hears the evidence and arguments of both sides, and makes recommendation that is not binding over parties" (ACAS 1995). However, it also had a provision for conciliation that was the same as mediation practised in Western countries where a third party facilitates disputing parties to reach their agreement without playing an advisory role (Liebmann 2000, 20).

An initiative for out-of-court mediation for families was taken in 1978 when the first Family Conciliation Service was established in Bristol. The number of these services increased gradually over the year, and in 1981 twenty local services jointly formed the National Family Conciliation Council (NFCC) (Liebmann 2000, 21). In 1988, Lisa Parkinson, one of the co-founders of the Family Conciliation Service in Bristol established the Family Mediators' Association (Parkinson 1997). Though initially family mediation services dealt only with child related issues, in 1989 a report from the Conciliation Project Unit recommended that family mediation should not be restricted to child related issues. Later, recourse to a mediator at the pre-trial state was made mandatory in the *Family Law Act 1996* before applying for legal aid (NFM 1996). Besides the family mediation services provided by a different partner organisation of National Family Mediation (NFM), family mediation in the UK is now available from barristers who are qualified in family mediation (Liebmann 2000, 22). Despite the variation in practitioners, in the UK the term "mediation" is usually given a narrow meaning and is associated almost exclusively with the facilitative approach (ICE 2007, 877).

The movement of community mediation in the UK initiated in 1980s was followed by some promotional activities from the USA and Australia. In early 1980, several mediation experts from the USA and Australia visited the UK and discussed with different groups of people regarding the potential of mediation in the UK (Liebmann, 17). The primary impetus for community mediation in the UK came in the victim-offender mediation field with the first victim-offender mediation project initiated in South Yorkshire in 1983. Following this, four other mediation projects were funded by the Home Office between 1985 and 1987 (Reeves 1987). One report published by the National Association of Victim Support Schemes (NAVSS 1984) indicates that by 1984, twenty-five mediation centres were active in the UK, with twenty-three involved in victim-offender mediation and only two involved in other community issues (Marshall 1984). However, gradually the scope of mediation at community mediation increased to varieties of disputes. In 1989, the Forum for Initiatives in Reparation and Mediation published a list of forty-five running or proposed mediation centres of which fifteen were involved in victim-offender mediation, fifteen in community mediation and the rest in school conflict, racism, cross cultural issues and commercial issues.

(c) Mediation in Australia

Alternative forms of dispute resolution, bypassing the formal adjudicative system, have been practised in Australia since time immemorial. Aboriginal people in Australia have long had a well-developed community based, non-adjudicative system to mitigate disputes (Astor & Chinkin 1992, 5). The British colonial government imported some non-litigious dispute resolution systems based on English Law. The passing of the *Courts of Conciliation Act* at Queensland in 1892 and provision for informal conferences in Arbitration and Conciliation Court in 1904 for the Commonwealth of Australia can be regarded as initial legislative changes in Australia to accommodate ADR in its formal justice system (Condiffe 2000).

Subsequently, different legislations have been passed to popularize the use of ADR all over Australia. However, it was not until 1975 that the ADR movement achieved momentum when the *Family Law Act* was passed for the use of mediation in family dispute trials in formal courts all over the Commonwealth of Australia.

The National Alternative Dispute Resolution Advisory Committee of Australia (NADRAC) developed a definition of mediation that identifies the four different steps to resolution of disputes. As defined by NADRAC (2002, 34):

> Mediation is a process in which the parties to a dispute, with the assistance of a neutral third party (the mediator), identify the disputed issues, develop options, consider alternatives and endeavour to reach an agreement.

As mentioned in the definition provided by NADRAC, a mediator is a "neutral third party." To explain what is meant by the term "neutral," NADRAC states (2002, 34):

> The mediator has no advisory or determinative role in regard to the content of the dispute or the outcome of its resolution, but may advise on or determine the process of mediation whereby resolution is attempted.

Therefore, the mediation practised in Australia is facilitative one, where mediators do not have any directive or interventionist role in mediation. According to the Joint Select Committee of the Family Law Act in Australia, by August 2004, mediation has been included in 190 various Acts, rules, and regulations all over the country (NADRAC 2004). At present, four different forms of court-connected mediations are practiced. These include: informal referral to mediation where a court encourages parties to recourse mediation; formal referral by a court after considering the suitability of a dispute for mediation and willingness of parties to attend mediation; formal referral by a court to attend mediation when a court considers a dispute suitable for mediation, irrespective to the desire of the parties; and mandatory referral by a court to mediation irrespective of the nature of a dispute or desire of parties (Alexander 2004, 6).

Further, according to a report prepared for the Commonwealth Attorney-General of Australia, by 2001 all States of Australia had community justice centres to resolve disputes at the local level. Furthermore, Western Australia has a community justice centre to resolve disputes among the Aboriginal people through mediation. Australia also has Administrative Appeals Tribunals and public policy ADR to resolve public disputes over policy issues relating to environmental matters, land usage, and resource management and planning.

1.4.1 Eastern Mediation with Particular Reference to Asian Countries

(a) Mediation in the People's Republic of China

Chinese mediation has developed from a unique historical social and cultural background that promotes the Confucian philosophy of maintaining peace and harmony in a society. Mediation in the People's Republic of China (PRC) promotes socials values of selflessness and promotion of social harmony rather than individualism and personal justice promoted by the West (Jia 2002). The PRC has a long history of community mediation. While it is not possible to pin-point the time period in which the practice of mediation started in the PRC, a rich practice of community mediation can be found in Confucianism. The lesson of Confucius (551–479 B.C.) is to forgive, tolerate, and cooperate with others rather than making complaints. More pertinently, one should "persuade" the other person to get his or her cooperation. In short, Confucianism highly values compromise and persuasion, as well as the intermediary who was able to secure them (Cohen 1966; Chen 1996). The success of Chinese mediation largely lies on this principle of social harmony. As observed by Triandis (1989, 80):

> In a society where harmony is the ideal and "doing the right thing" is essential for good relations, one often does what one believes to be socially desirable even if one's attitudes are inconsistent with the action.

Following its rich culture of mediation, in the PRC during the nineteenth century the unofficial mediators tended to dominate the dispute-resolution arenas, settling disputes within families, clans, and villages (Huang 2005). The disputes were taken to a formal authority only when informal mediation failed. However, community mediation in the PRC became more institutionalized after the Chinese revolution in 1949. In 1954, People's Mediation Committees (PMC) were formed in almost every neighbourhood of the PRC, and comrades from the Chinese Communist Party were involved in PMCs to resolve local disputes. It is argued that the PMCs' resolutions of disputes are not only based on local values but also reflect party policies (Halegua 2005, 715).

There are about one million mediators in the PRC (Laden 1988) — about one for every one thousand people. As indicated by Ren (1997), the number of mediators per 100 people of the PRC exceeds the number of judges per 100 people in the USA. This indicates a great commitment to the practice of community mediation in the PRC.

As observed by Jia (2002), in contrast to USA mediators, the Chinese mediators' knowledge about disputants is a major asset which enables them to determine who is right or wrong in a dispute. To a Chinese mediator, the major goals are eliminating the dispute and defusing anger. No one expects the mediator to be neutral, and most mediators and citizens think that the mediator's determination on who is correct simply expedites resolution of the dispute. Unlike mediators in the West, Chinese mediators do not wait for the parties to initiate the process. Rather, they promptly find and insinuate themselves into the dispute before positions become harden (Jia 2002; Chen 2002).

In addition to community mediation, the PRC also has a practice of court-connected mediation. According to Articles 85 and 87 of the *Civil Procedure Law* (1991) of the PRC, courts invite parties to resolve their disputes through mediation. Though participation in mediation is voluntary, any agreement reached through this process becomes as legally binding as court judgements (Moser 1997, 81). The PRC also has a practice of mediation in international trade disputes. In these situations, parties may attend mediation under mutually agreed rules or procedures before attending trial or arbitration. Any agreement reached through mediation is considered as private contract between the parties (Moser 1997, 82). In August 2010, legislators in the PRC first considered a law to provide a legal basis to community mediation. It recognised the PMC as a legal authority to resolve community disputes and specified its legal structure (Liew 2011, 532). By doing so, the PMC got formal authority to conduct mediation under the purview of the People's Mediation Law (PML) of the PRC. According to this law, PMCs are formed to resolve local disputes. According to Article 17 of the PML, parties have autonomy to accept or reject the invitation to attend mediation and, according to Article 21 of PML, "in the process of mediating disputes among the people, people's mediators shall stick to principles, make legal reasoning and do justice to the parties concerned." Therefore, the practice of mediation is evaluative though participation remains voluntary.

(b) Mediation in Thailand

Like mediation in the People's Republic of China, mediation in Thailand is also a part of the indigenous culture where people used to submit their dispute to the respected elderly people of their society (Suvanpanich 1997, 271). As indicated by Limparangsri and Yuprasert (2005, 199), mediation was even practiced in Thailand 700 years ago during the era of King *Ramkamhang* who used to act as mediator to resolve disputes among his subjects. However, mediation in Thai society was practiced without an institutional mandate and without specific rules or guidelines (Limparangsri & Yuprasert 2005, 199). In traditional Thai mediation, initially the mediator tried to attain a consensual decision between parties, and if this failed, mediators provided their evaluation on the dispute. Though mediators' evaluation was not binding upon parties, they usually abided by it to avoid social sanction (Srvanpanich 1997, 272). Moreover, according to Section 850 of the *Civil and Commercial Code of Thailand* (BE 2468), a mediation agreement would be binding upon parties if they wrote a document outlining their compromise agreement and signed it (Suvanpanich 1997, 272). To illustrate the evaluative nature of Thai mediation and its acceptance in Thai culture, Pryles (2006, 431) explained:

> In earlier times, disputing parties would submit their dispute to an elder person whom both parties respected … The method by which the elder person would resolve a dispute was very simple. Simple negotiation was usually tried first. If the parties could not resolve their problem, the elder person would make the decision … At present, though Thai society has changed dramatically, such a method of resolving disputes is still prevalent.

Despite the sporadic practice of mediation in Thai society over centuries, it was not until the beginning of 1990s when an increased number of case loads in Thai courts, followed by a financial crisis, made the policy makers think about mediation as a cost effective alternative for litigation (Limparangsri & Yuprasert 2005, 199). In 1994, mediation was first introduced in Thai Civil Courts under the slogan "convenient, quick, economical and fair." Under this scheme, judges were encouraged to resolve cases at the pre-trial stage (The Civil Court Act 1995; Suvanpanich 1997, 273). To facilitate court-annexed mediation during trial, further amendment was made in the *Civil Procedure Code* of Thailand in 1999. This amendment allowed Thai judges to appoint third party mediators at any stage of a trial and also to conduct *caucus* to resolve cases through mediation (Section 183). All civil court proceedings in Thailand need to be conducted in public. However, before the enactment of this amendment, there was confusion as to whether judges could hold *caucus* to conduct court-annexed mediation once a trial begins (Limparangsri & Yuprasert 2005, 200).

In a court-annexed mediation, judges in Thai civil courts try to create an informal environment by holding the mediation session outside the courtroom, by not wearing gowns, and by serving drinks (Suvanpanich 1997, 273). Further, the historical mediation practice has an influence on the mode of mediation practiced by judges in court-annexed mediation. As stated by Suvanpanich (1997, 274):

> The civil court has guidelines for judges who act as mediators. For example, they have to read a case accurately and seek the real need of both parties and ascertain a satisfactory resolution which may lead the parties to end their case.

Therefore, from the practice of mediation in both in- and out-of-court, it can be reasonably concluded that a practice of evaluative mediation persists in that society. As discussed below, a similar observation can be made in India and Bangladesh.

(c) Mediation in India

From time immemorial, various forms of informal justice systems prevailed in the Indian sub-continent and have been governed by the religious and cultural norms of the society (Kamal 2002; Siddiqui 2005). It is said that the "villages' self-governance is as old as the villages themselves" (Siddiqui 2005, 29). *Rig Vedas*, the oldest Hindu religious script, dating from 1200 BC, mentions the existence of village self-governance in India. Some historical basis for the resolution of disputes by the heads of neighbourhoods is also found in the work of Sen (1984, 17) who claims the existence of dispute resolution at the village level during the period of the *Dharmashastra* (Hindu religious mandate). At that time, the terms *Panchayet*, later *Shalish*, were used to indicate informal justice systems that were very similar to current day concept of evaluative mediation (Chowdhury 2011).

It is generally assumed that this kind of local government was the basic form of government until the sixth century BC when large kingdoms began to emerge and the role of local government become subject to the central authority (Siddiqui 2005, 29). During 1500 BC to 1206 AD, when Hindu rulers governed the sub-continent, the king was considered the "fountain of justice" and was the highest authority in the Court of Appeal in the state (Halim 2008, 36). Government officials ran other courts and tribunals to administer justice under the authority of a king (Halim 2008), but the central authority left local people to resolve civil and petty criminal matters through their local village councils, i.e. *panchayets* (Siddiqui 2005, 38). Village *panchayets* were made up of a council of village headmen, the composition of which varied depending on the economic and social structure of the villages being governed. As noted by Siddiqui (2005, 31–2), *panchayets* resolved different forms of disputes. Sometimes they were formed to ensure that the members of a caste adhered to the religious and social norms of their caste and to settle disputes among members. *Panchayets* also maintained public order and inter-caste relationships among the villagers. Additionally, *panchayets* served to resolve labour disputes, such as those among servants and farmers or among the servants of different farmers. Village *panchayets* were also responsible for resolving civil disputes within the area (Rahman 1997, 47; Ameen 2005a, 110). As *panchayets* were the local bodies for resolving disputes among people in a locality, justice administered by this indigenous system was very much influenced by the custom and religion of that locality. As Siddiqui (2005, 33) observed:

> Custom and religion made the *panchayets* so important that they often had an almost sacred status—although they could hardly be described as unbiased and objective. The *panchayets* never made their decisions by voting, but by a "consensuses" arrived at by the upper caste members of the *panchayet*, and this was generally accepted by the lower castes. This method well suited the purpose of the conservative village leadership, which wanted to maintain the status *quo* in society.

Because of the high impact of customs and religions on the decision of *panchayet/shalish*, these qualities are often found in present day evaluative mediation. Further, the effectiveness of *panchayet* can be seen in the words of Jain (1999, 61):

> These *panchayets* fulfilled the judicial functions very effectively and it is only rarely that their decisions gave dissatisfaction to the village people. The members of the *panchayets* were deterred from committing an injustice by fear of public opinion in whose midst they lived.

According to Islam (1997, 22), "the panchayet served civil and policing functions, coordinating rent given etc., while the *shalish* was a village *Sabha* or council that was called on to settle moral and ethical issues." Therefore, *shalish* can be perceived as a variation of *panchayet* that resolved civil issues among local habitants. The term *shalish* is derived from the Arabic word *shalish* meaning "three." It conveys the sense of "middle"—middle man—the third party in a conflict resolution. In traditional villages, *shalish* was generally conducted by a group of the village people, including village headmen and other local elites. Whatever the variation of the terms *panchayets/shalishs*, *t*he central government body did not interfere with the decisions even when they contravened the central administrative laws, and no appeal could be made against their decisions.

The glorious history of the system of *panchayets/shalishs* during the *Mughal* period (1526 AD–1756 AD), however, was drastically curtailed by the advent of the British in the sub-continent. The East India Company started to intervene in the administration of justice in British India under a Royal Charter in 1726 (Halim 2008). Later, with the decline in *Mughal* rule, the East India Company controlled the administration of the Bengal province. Initially, the company adopted a new *Zamindari* system to administer justice by curbing the authority of the deep-rooted indigenous *panchayet* system (Siddiqui 2005, 39). However, the *Zamindari* system proved inefficient as the *Zamindars* (landlords) were usually biased, oppressive and concerned with profit (Jain 1999, 31). Realising the importance of the long-adopted *panchayet* system, the British revived this indigenous system of administering justice by promulgating the *Chowkidari Act 1870*. Though the village *panchayet* system was revived as *Chowkidari Panchayet* under the *Chowkidari Act 1870*, it remained mostly unpopular (Datta & Datta 2002, 94). After the independence of India in 1947, many *Naya* (New) *Panchayets* were formed all over India under its constitutional mandate (Sinha 2004, 22).

In addition to community mediation, the possibility of mediation of court intervention in civil cases settled outside the court was introduced through Section 89[6] of the *Code of Civil Procedure (Amendment) Act 1999 (*Act XXXXVI of 1999).

It was not until an amendment of the Code, namely the *Code of Civil Procedure (Amendment) Act 2002* (Act XXII of 2002) that the court-connected mediation was incorporated in Indian courts. The first initiative was taken through a pilot project at the *Hazari* Court complex in *Delhi* in August 2005 to train judges to provide judicial mediation at their chambers (Liew 2011, 539). Further, the *Delhi* Mediation Centre (DMC) was established at the *Hazari* Court complex in October 2005. Though the *Civil Procedure (Amendment) Code 2002* did not provide a definition of mediation, as referred by the DMC, explaining mediation in CPC, Justice Sharma adopted a definition given by International Labour Organisation as follows:

> Mediation may be regarded as a half way house between conciliation and arbitration. The role of the conciliator is to assist the parties to reach their own negotiated settlement and he may make suggestions as appropriate. The mediator proceeds by way of conciliation but in addition is prepared

[6] Section 89 dealt with settlement of disputes outside the Court. It runs: "(1) Where it appears to the court that there exist elements of a settlement which may be acceptable to the parties, the court shall formulate the terms of settlement and give them to the parties for their observations and after receiving the observation of the parties, the court may reformulate the terms of a possible settlement and refer the same for-(a) arbitration; (b) conciliation (c) judicial settlement including settlement through *Lok Adalat*; or (d) mediation. (2) Where a dispute had been referred (a) for arbitration or conciliation, the provisions of the Arbitration and Conciliation Act, 1996 shall apply as if the proceedings for arbitration or conciliation were referred for settlement under the provisions of that Act. (b) to *Lok Adalat*, the court shall refer the same to the *Lok Adalat* in accordance with the provisions of sub-section (1) of section 20 of *the Legal Services Authority Act 1987* and all other provisions of that Act shall apply in respect of the dispute so referred to the *Lok Adalat*; (c) for judicial settlement, the court shall refer the same to a suitable institution or person and such institution or person shall be deemed to be a *Lok Adalat* and all the provisions of the *Legal Services Authority Act 1987* shall apply as if the dispute were referred to a *Lok Adalat* under the provisions of that Act; (d) for mediation, the court shall effect a compromise between the parties and shall follow such procedure as may be prescribed."

> and expected to make his own formal proposals or recommendations which the family court judge may be accepted.

Following the success of the pilot programme at the *Hazari* Court, judicial mediation was initiated and another mediation centre was established at *Karkardooma* Court complex in December 2005 and May 2006 respectively. By June 30, 2010, more than 28,000 cases of a different nature were referred to DMC that attained a success rate ranging from 60 to 79 per cent during the same period (DMC 2010).

(d) Mediation in Bangladesh

Though Bangladesh emerged as an independent country in 1971, it got its legacy from the British ruled Indian sub-continent. Like India, the history of *panchayet/shalish* also plays a pivotal role in governing informal and traditional dispute resolution system in this region. It is already indicated that the practice of evaluation in a traditional dispute resolution system in the form of *panchayet/shalish* was a common phenomenon in this region. It is not a recent phenomenon in Bangladeshi culture, rather a customary practice of the informal justice system that has a history of more than thousand years (Kamal 2002; Siddiqui 2005). Thus, it is not unlikely that the evaluative nature of traditional dispute resolution system conducted in out-of-court settings also might have some influence on our current-day practice of court-annexed mediation in Bangladesh. The justification of practising evaluative/directive mediation in court-connected mediation can be observed in the words of Hasan (2001, 14), the former Chief Justice of Bangladesh:

> We found that for the present, pure mediation in every case is not really suitable for our legal system. It took many years for the USA to reach the present stage through trial and error. Our experience is only a few months old. Slowly it dawned on us that instead of pure mediation if it is combined with a little bit of directive method, to which our judges, lawyers and litigants are familiar with, the judges would be more successful in their efforts.

This is further reverberated by Kamal (2002, 6), the former Chief Justice of Bangladesh, and the pioneer of court-connected mediation in Bangladesh:

> Learn from the pilot courts and the lawyers involved in mediation and other methods what practical problems they encounter, adjust and re-adjust your programme accordingly, so that what finally emerges is not a foreign

> model, but an indigenous Bangladeshi model, suited to the legal culture, ethos and traditions of this country.

Unlike its people's long acquaintance with traditional practice of evaluative mediation in out-of-court settings in Bangladesh, the court-connected mediation was unknown to them till 1985. There was no court-annexed mediation scheme in Bangladesh until separate family courts were establish to deal with family disputes under the *Family Courts Ordinance (FCO) 1985*. It states under Sections 10 and 13 of the FCO that any family court shall exercise ADR in the form of mediation in resolving family disputes pending before it. The provisions for "pre-trail mediation" under Section 10[7] of the FCO 1985 provides that the court shall try to make reconciliation between the disputant parties just after its pre-trial hearing or before going to any formal trial. However, if any or both of the parties do not agree to make compromise, the family court judge,[8] who is also a mediator in family cases conducted in the family court, shall proceed to the formal trial and at the end of trail and before making judgment the concerned judge will again try to make a compromise/reconciliation between the parties under Section 13 of the FCO.[9]

However, because of the lack of motivation of the concerned judges to conduct mediation at family courts, inadequate training to judges and

[7] A provision for pre-trial mediation has been delineated in Section 10 of the *Family Court Ordinance 1985*: "(1) When the written statement is filed, the Family Court shall fix a date ordinarily of not more than thirty days for a pre-trial hearing of the suit. (2) On the date fixed for pre-trial hearing, the Court shall examine the plaint, the written statement (if any) and the summary of evidence and documents filed by the parties and shall also, if it so deems fit, hear the parties. (3) At the pre-trial hearing, the Court shall ascertain the points at issue between the parties and attempt to affect a compromise or reconciliation between the parties."

[8] All Assistant Judges are *ex-officio* presiding judges of the family courts in Bangladesh (Section 4 [3] of the FCO 1985). In family courts, judges act as mediators and take attempts for pre-trial mediation. However, if his or her attempts for mediation fail, the same judge conducts the case in trial.

[9] Provision of pre-judgement mediation as laid down in Section 13 of the *Family Court Ordinance 1985*: "After the close of evidence of all parties, the Family Court shall make another effort to affect a compromise or reconciliation between the parties."

lawyers, and the non-existence of any uniform method to practice mediation in family courts, the practice of mediation did not reach its desired level until the Reformed ADR Movement (RAM) in 2000 (Hasan 2002). Under RAM 2000, several steps were taken to improve the practice of court-connected mediation under the auspicious of the Institute for the Study and Development of Legal Systems (ISDLS)[10] of the USA. Judges and lawyers of family courts were trained on mediation and proper incentive mechanisms[11] were established to motivate judges to settle more disputes through pre-trial mediation.

Finally, after necessary adjustments and amendments to the initial model of mediation, family court mediation began to achieve good results. By the fall of 2000, the reformed model was deemed successful with 40 percent of total cases resolved through mediation (Kamal 2002, 12; Hasan 2005, 133): "Mediation has flourished in the country against the backdrop of a logjam of cases, leading to unacceptable delay and expenses in the adjudication of disputes and stagnation of civil litigation."[12]

---

[10] ISDLS initiatives seek to help the foreign country-partners to address the problems of the formal judicial system and to make procedural reforms with the help of their models that have been successful in other parts of the globe. ISDLS base most of the study components of its civil justice reform collaborations on studies of the California civil court system where, due to the practice of mediation and case management, only 1 percent of civil cases goes to full-trial and thus is considered at the forefront of procedural civil justice reform. In all ISDLS projects, foreign legal groups study the techniques and litany of the alternative to litigation utilised in California. Not only this, ISDLS visits the foreign country-partners to observe what they learned or to assist their reform proposals. At this point, the ISDLS successfully reforms civil justice system in many countries in the world.

[11] For encouraging mediation in family cases, a government decision was reached that for every successful family mediation case, the judges concerned would get two credits, i.e. equivalent to the holding of two litigation cases; and for every two failed mediation cases, they would get one credit. Accordingly, a government circular to that amendment was issued (Circular no: 6; dated on May 31, 2000).

[12] The former Chief Justice, in a workshop on "Mediation Techniques-Alternative Dispute Resolution in the Civil Justice Delivery System in Bangladesh," organized by the Legal and Judicial Capacity building Project (LJCBP), financed by World Bank, held at Chittagong, Bangladesh on July 17, 2003.

As stated by Kamal (2002), the former Chief Justice of Bangladesh, and one of the pioneers of RAM 2000:

> The "reform movement of [mediation]" started at the beginning of 2000 in Bangladesh has thus far made exciting progress in exercising [mediation] in a more methodical way in the family courts by decreasing its judicial backlogs on one hand, and getting enormous support from the legal community at large, on the other.

Following the success of mediation in family courts, court-annexed mediation is also now introduced in civil disputes[13] and other different forms of disputes[14] in Bangladesh. In fact, justice through in-court mediation was popularised in Bangladesh to solve the backlog problem under a World Bank project in 2000. The primary motivating factors for the policy makers promoting mediation in the Bangladesh family courts in 2000 was to provide quicker access to justice for the poor, especially to women (ADB 2002).

Though a development of in-court mediation in family courts improved the situation, those unable to access courts remained out of the sphere of the formal justice system. Thus, different Non-Governmental Organisations

---

[13] Section 89A and 89B were inserted to introduce mediation and arbitration under the *Code of Civil Procedure (Amendment) Act 2003 (Act IV of 2003).* To motivate judges to resolve disputes through mediation, similar circular like family cases also came into effect which provided that for one successful civil mediation case, the judges concerned would get two credits, i.e. the equivalent to the holding of two litigation cases, and for every two failed civil mediation cases, they would get one credit (Circular no 59(KA)G dated June 23, 2003). In addition, by insertion of section 89C through the *Code of Civil Procedure (Amendment) Act 2006 (Act VIII of 2006),* mediation can even be practised in civil cases at the stage of appeal.

[14] The provision of conciliation has been introduced in the *Money Loan Courts Act 2003* (Act VIII of 2003) and the *Money Loan Courts (Amendment) Act 2010* (Act XVI of 2010) *to* resolve commercial disputes relating to financial institutions under Sections 21 and 22. The *Labour Act 2006* (Act XLII of 2006) also inserted ADR provisions to resolve labour disputes under Section 210. The *Arbitration Act 2001* (Act I of 2001) (later amended in 2004) has been introduced to resolve commercial disputes relating to domestic and international trade issues through arbitration. Recently, mediation is also incorporated in the *Income Tax (Amendment) Ordinance 2011* (Sections 152F to 152S) to resolve income tax disputes.

(NGOs) emerged to fill up this vacuum and to provide informal justice in a more meaningful way than it had earlier through *panchayet/shalish* practised in the country. The NGOs movement started in Bangladesh just after its independence in 1971 to rehabilitate the war torn people and has now attained worldwide recognition. For example, the Bangladesh Rural Advancement Committee (BRAC) was established as a small local NGO in 1972 to aid and rehabilitate the war torn people, but is now one of the largest NGOs in the world, having seventy million beneficiaries. Although *Grameen* Bank, BRAC, etc. are world famous NGOs in Bangladesh, they are famous especially for the micro-credit and different social mobilisation programmes, such as primary education, health care, etc. A different set of NGOs initiated another silent revolution, and considered by the local people as their trusted friend in attaining more equitable access to justice, especially to women, includes *Madaripur* Legal Aid Association (MLAA), *Bachte Sekha*, Bangladesh Legal Aid and Services Trust (BLAST), *Ain-o-Shalish Kendro* (ASK), and many others.

MLAA, established in 1978, is considered as the pioneer of NGO-based out-of-court mediation in Bangladesh. To provide mediation services, MLAA formed a committee with the Chairman and Member of the Union *Parishad* (Council) which included other local elites, such as teachers of primary school, *madrasa* (religious school), other influential local leaders, etc. to form a mediation body that could ensure more equitable justice. Since its establishment, it has not only resolved local disputes through mediation but also trained local leaders and elites to change their knowledge and attitude towards the use of law while making mediation at the local level (The Asia Foundation 2002a, 18; MLAA 2004, X; Khair 2008, 103). Like MLAA, *Bachte Sekha,* another NGO established in 1982 and working in the *Jessore* and *Khulna* districts of Bangladesh, practices another variation of mediation that gives maximum emphasis on strengthening women's voices during the process. To ensure this, *Bachte Sekha* formed an eleven-member village mediation committee which included seven women (World Bank 2001).

Another human rights NGO, ASK, not only provides the service of mediation but also, through its "Gender and Social Justice Project," sensitizes the local government bodies and law enforcement officials to the violation of women rights. It also strengthens the ties among local people, including journalists and lawyers, to monitor human rights enforcement mechanisms. Therefore, ASK is working towards changing societal knowledge so that women may benefit more from the implementation of law over time.

BLAST started its operation in 1993 and now has a network covering all nineteen greater districts of Bangladesh. BLAST runs legal awareness programmes and public interest litigation to establish rights in various sectors including labour law, family law and state abuse of prisoners (The Asia Foundation 2002a). One of the popular services of BLAST is to provide a legal aid and advocacy service to its clients if their mediation effort to resolve a dispute fails: "BLAST utilizes a people-oriented model for mediation which also adheres to the jurisprudence principles of the country" (The Asia Foundation 2002a, 26). Therefore, it seems that BLAST conducts its mediation under the shadow of law and uses law to legitimize its mediation efforts.

According to the contemporary literature, NGOs are now providing pro-women out-of-court mediation services to millions of women in Bangladesh by ensuring their greater participation and promoting their voice in the society (Casper & Kamal 1995, 35; Gulab 2000, 139; The Asia Foundation 2002c, 21; Siddiqi 2006a, 48—50): "Under NGO administered mediation, disputants are encouraged to express their views without bias or fear" (Khair 2004, 64). As these rule-based NGOs provide low-cost informal justice, "poor people, particularly women feel comfortable and pleased about the easy access to local dispute resolution mechanisms" (UNDP 2002, 93). Therefore, both court-annexed and out-of-court NGO mediations in Bangladesh are promoting a rights-based mediation which upholds legal rights.

The discussion so far on development and historical perspectives of mediation in the West and East indicates that the practice of court-annexed mediation in the East is still at the preliminary stage in comparison with court-connected mediations in the West. However, countries at the East do not lag behind the West in the practice of out-of-court mediation. The East has a rich culture in which to practise mediation in their out-of-court settings where mediators have considerable power to intervene in disputes in order to attain a fair and amicable solution. The indigenous and traditional practice of mediators' evaluation in community mediation also has an influence in the current development of court-annexed mediation in the East. Such practice suggests an evaluative approach of mediation, in contrast to Western mediation, where the mediators follow a facilitative approach, take a non-interventionist role and focus on interests rather than rights. The interventionist and legally informed role of mediators in the East contributes more on rights/positions of the parties, rather than on their interests. Further, while the Eastern cultures view the "people and the problem as inseparable and interrelated," the Western cultures see their relation as separate (Taylor 2002, 99). Since the social and cultural context of East is more "widely diverse" than Western liberal democratic countries (Taylor 2002, 257), approaches and critiques relevant to Western societies may not be applicable in Eastern societies. Thus, an unsuitable transfer of knowledge and ideas without considering the context could lead to cultural imperialism. Such cultural imperialism may involve "the use of economic and political power to exalt and spread the values and habits of a foreign culture at the expense of a native culture" (Bullock & Stallybrass, cited in Tomlinson 1991, 3). If action is taken on the basis of research and critique from one culture into another, it may fail to achieve positive change in that society (Tomlinson 1991). For example, LeResche (1992) observed that Korean Americans with Asian heritage follow a process of dispute resolution that is very different from the American problem-solving style in terms of their starting assumption and process dynamics (LaResche, cited in Taylor 2002, 258–9). Therefore, the contextual and cultural differences are considered carefully while discussing other traits of mediation throughout this book.

1.5 Defining Mediation: An Eastern Context

Western scholars consider mediation as a process of dispute resolution where two parties negotiate to find a consensual outcome with the help of a neutral third party mediator who facilitates and controls the process. Such Western-fashioned facilitative mediation fosters greater cooperation among parties to resolve their disputes, without any primary concern about the content (Fisher & Ury 1991; NADRAC 2002, 34; Tillett & French 2006, 147). The reason for a dispute could emanate from a past event. For example, a marital dispute may arise when a husband fails to pay proper maintenance to his wife, or a work place dispute may arise if an employer discharges one of his employees without showing proper grounds for doing so. According to the definition of facilitative mediation, mediators should not make deterministic statements about "what should or should not" have been done by either of the parties to avoid the dispute.

However, the nature of assistance that a mediator may provide to its parties is still a debated issue. As indicated earlier, the nature of assistance of mediators in Western society cannot be straightforwardly adopted in an Eastern one. Rather, it should be carefully handled due to the cultural variations in different jurisdictions (Augsberger 1992; Taylor 2002; Christner & Mennuti 2008). More particularly, as discussed under the history of mediation in the East, this Western concept of facilitative mediation and the neutrality of mediators may not fit well in every culture: "In many cultural contexts, neutrality might be neither a recognized nor a desirable attribute for mediators" (Boulle 2011, 79). Rather, some advisory or evaluative role of mediators is appreciated. For example, as identified by Palmer (1987, 244):

> The Chinese mediator does not merely act as a channel of communication between the disputants; he is expected to propose possible solutions, to explain the framework of law within which the agreement must be reached, and to take an important part in the parties' negotiations.

Suvanpanich (1999) in Thailand, Boo (1999) in Singapore, and Chowdhury (2011) in Bangladesh all observe the need for the advisory role of mediators and evaluative mediation. As cited by Spencer (2011, 81):

> Because of the community ownership of disputes, mediators are assumed to have an opinion on the dispute, even if they are not personally involved in it. Tribal elders, who are not expected to take on the role of resolving disputes, have preconceived ideas about the dispute because of own kinship ties and family networks.

An advisory or evaluative role is generally applied to the content of a dispute. An evaluative role means that advice is given, or comment is made, from a mediator about what should or should not have been done, or what could be done to avoid conflict when one party is legally obliged to pay to the other, or advising the other party on what to do to resolve the dispute. Such an advisory role may even exist among in-court mediators (Boo 1999; Chowdhury 2011). In many cases, such an advisory or evaluative role is played under the shadow of a law (Chowdhury 2011).

Though it is argued by many Western scholars that an advisory role or an evaluative role of mediators affects the process of self-determination and the parties' autonomy in mediation, these roles entail parties taking an active part in discussion, developing options for settlement and controlling the final outcome (Alexander 2006; Cooper & Field 2008). Sometimes such an evaluative role helps to attain some "higher good" (Taylor 1997, 222).

Therefore, an alternative definition of mediation, contrary to the definition of mediation in Western societies, may allow mediators to provide advice which would help parties to reach an informed and a mutually favourable solution. For example, a mediator may inform parties about legal provision on any issue of their dispute, evaluate the legal standing of each party to a dispute, and advise about the extra time and cost that a party may need to involve in getting such an outcome through litigation. The National Mediator Accreditation Scheme (NMAS) of Australia explains a mediator's advisory role:

> Some mediators may also use a blended process that involves mediation and incorporates an advisory component, or a process that involves the provision of expert information and advice, where it enhances the decision-making of the participants provided that the participants agree that such advice can be provided. Such process may be defined as "evaluative mediation."

This evaluative process of mediation is sometimes termed as "substance-oriented mediation" (Sourdin 2008, 54). In a substance-oriented mediation, "the mediator is often an authority figure who evaluates the case based on experience and offers recommendations on how the case should be resolved." Therefore, for the purpose of this text, evaluative mediation is a dispute resolution process where a third party mediator takes an interventionist role, controls the process of mediation and may also provide his or her evaluation on the content of a dispute and advises parties regarding alternative available remedies and probable court outcomes. However, evaluative mediators do not determine the outcome for the parties and let parties determine it for themselves. The rationale and importance of the practice of evaluative mediation in Eastern developing countries are discussed in the following chapters.

1.6 Assumptions Built into Evaluative Mediation

As discussed earlier, evaluative mediation is a process where a mediator not only facilitates the process but also intervenes on the content of the dispute and assists parties in making informed decisions by promoting self-determination of parties over the outcome of mediation. This definition of evaluative mediation implies the following assumptions are built into it.

1.6.1 Win-Win Approach

Mediators endeavour to ensure a consensual solution between parties which would ensure a win-win solution. Unlike litigation, one party in evaluative mediation does not win outright with the other vanquished. Evaluative mediation ensures a win-win solution which gives both parties a winning feeling which is not experienced when compared to the best outcome they may attain without mediation (Abramson 2004, 4). Though the objective of evaluative mediation is to attain a consensual settlement of a dispute, the objective may not extend to the continuation of an existing relationship by resolving a dispute from its root (Council of Europe 2000, 27; Boulle 2011, 26): “The strongest effort using a win-win approach may realistically only yield, and agreement to disagree and a set of measures by which the parties can live with their differences” (Hoffman1993, 13). Therefore, unlike litigation, a consensual settlement through evaluative mediation may ensure a minimum level of post-mediation relationship between parties.

Though critics may argue whether a win-win approach may work when people strive to realise their rights, for their self-interest, and use their power to attain these objectives, mediators deal with different aspects of rights, interest and power simultaneously to attain the win-win goal (Hoffman 1993, 13). Due to conscious self-interest, parties may not get the same win-win outcome if they negotiate privately; however, the great skill, understanding, and innovation that a mediator devotes into evaluative mediation may make this win-win solution a reality (Hoffman 1993, 13).

A consensual win-win settlement may be attained by comparing the competitiveness of an evaluative mediated outcome with the outcome of a contested trial. During evaluative mediation, mediators may make clients aware of the time and cost of alternative court-room solution, the emotional issues involved in such a process, and other benefits of consensual resolution including a quick realisation of outcomes without further delay by making appeals against court decisions (Folberg, Milne & Salem 2004, 77; Boulle 2011, 45). Parties may make a consensual win-win decision to settle their dispute after considering all these benefits of evaluative mediation, even when they are not willing to continue their existing relationship.

1.6.2 Assisted Dispute Resolution Process

Evaluative mediation is a process of negotiation (Cross 2007, 66). Unlike negotiation, evaluative mediation does not fully rely on the negotiation skill of the parties but on a third party facilitator who assists parties to negotiate effectively (Spencer 2011, 49). A mediator may not be a lawyer but rather a para-legal who is expert in the issues of a dispute, like a medical practitioner in a medical dispute or an engineer in a construction dispute, or even a volunteer from the community (Cross 2007, 66). In addition, the role of an evaluative mediator is not limited to the facilitation of a mediation process and in keeping his or her position on the surface of a dispute. It allows a "knee-deep" exploration into the content of a dispute and extends their evaluation on its substance (Folberg Milne & Salem 2004, 73). However, it is not like the "muscle," "rhino" or "rambo" mediation process in the United States which places mediators in a directive role to control the process and the outcome of mediation (Sourdin 2008, 55).

Therefore, while featuring evaluative mediation as an assisted negotiation process, we need to identify the motive of a mediator behind such assistance. Bush & Folger (1994) identified four different motives of mediators under the oppression story, the satisfaction story, the social justice story and the transformation story. Under the oppression story, assistance from a third party mediator may re-establish the existing power disparity and oppression against the disadvantaged (Picard 2002, 21). As discussed under the definition of evaluative mediation, use of facilitative mediation in developing countries by a neutral third party mediator may be criticized under this view. Under the satisfaction story, a mediator tries to attain a consensual outcome to attain a win-win situation between the parties of mediation. While doing so, a mediator may explain to the parties how mediation can reduce the individual and social cost of a dispute and motivate them to attain a consensual solution (McGillis 1997, 15). This story may work when Western style neutral mediation is conducted between parties who are equally valued in a society, and may not bring about a substantial power disparity in mediation.

Under the transformative story, a mediator tries not only to attain a consensual outcome of a dispute, rather making the parties more understanding and sympathetic to each other's position (McGillis 1997, 15). The objective of mediators' assistance under this story is to change the quality of social interaction. Illustrating this view, Bush & Folger (2005, 14) explain that:

> Consumer mediation can strengthen the confidence of and evoke recognition between merchants and consumers, transforming the character of commercial transactions and institutions. Divorce mediation can strengthen and evoke recognition between men and women, changing the character of male-female interaction generally.

As discussed later in this chapter, the objective of the transformative mediation model is to attain such an objective (Grambaarg 2006, 70). Under the social justice story, a mediator tries to organize and build a coalition among "have nots" to enhance their bargaining power (Bush & Folger 2005, 18). Though this social justice story of mediation was discussed by scholars from the perspective of community mediation (Wahrhaftig 1982; Shonholtz 1987; Moore 1994), currently the social justice mediation model is also being applied to resolve interpersonal disputes. As explained by the Social Justice Mediation Institute of the University of Massachusetts (UMASS 2012):

> Despite the demonstrated success of mediation, recent research shows that it also routinely reproduces privilege both structurally within the institution and interpersonally between disputing parties … After having considered challenges facing conflict resolvers by racism, classism, sexism and other forms of social inequities, [social justice mediators are] trained to mediate using a social justice lens while helping disputing parties reach mutually agreeable solutions.

The mode of evaluative mediation discussed in this text (see chapter two) endeavoured to establish this social justice view on mediation. However, the means through which social justice may be attained through evaluative mediation is not to create stronger social tie and thereby empowering the "have-nots." A mediator rather challenges the social discourses that creates race, class or sex in a society and defuses the power that a party from privileged social group may bring into mediation. As explained by Folberg (2004, 84–5), even the facilitative mediators make some internal evaluation. However, as mentioned earlier, to what extent or how mediators may express their evaluation depends on the need of the parties attending mediation.

1.6.3 Consensual Outcome

Evaluative mediation promotes consensual outcome. Unlike litigation, where the major emphasis is on the settlement of a dispute but is similar to the objective of any other mediation, the objective of evaluative mediation is to reach a consensual decision to settle a dispute (Council of Europe 2000, 27). However, a consensual decision should not be confused with coercive compromise. By providing each party a fair chance to share their views and express his or her evaluation on the merit of the claim from each party, an evaluative mediator tries to ensure that a consensual outcome in mediation is not attained through gross compromise made by one party due to his or her lesser power or inability to effectively participate in the decision-making process (Waldman 2011, 95). Further, to ensure an integrative win-win solution, an evaluative mediator provides expert opinion or evaluates a legal outcome, but shall not urge parties to accept any specific settlement (Boulle 2011, 46). Therefore, consensus in evaluative mediation is not earned in an authoritative or suppressive environment rather in a controlled facilitative environment where both parties may think about their best interest before making any consensual agreement. However, consensual decision-making does not mean a unanimous decision. In a consensual decision-making process, each party need not necessarily think that the decision attained is the best for his or her interest, rather for all of them to "accept and support consensus as a reasonable compromise to address the issue at hand" (Termini 2007, 250). The value of the outcome attained through mediation may remain better than the value of their best possible alternative outcome through trial or otherwise.

1.6.4 Voluntary Process

Evaluative mediation does not create any binding decision. Though in many court connected mediations, an agreement is signed between parties after settlement, like any other mediation, evaluative mediation is also a voluntary process and parties may withdraw from mediation at any time before a settlement has been reached (Spencer 2011, 72). Sometimes the degree of the voluntary or non-binding process of evaluative mediation is described under four different stages, namely: voluntary entry into mediation; absence of settlement pressures; free choice of outcomes; and abidance or non-abidance of any outcome reached through mediation (Singer 1994, 20; Sourdin 2008, 64).

Entry to an evaluative mediation may remain voluntary or the law may require parties to try mediation before contesting their cases through trial. Irrespective of whether entry to mediation is voluntary or not, in evaluative mediation a mediator may not pressure parties to reach a solution, or urge to accept any specific solution (Riskin 1996, 25; Cooley 2006, 34). Finally, consensual decision through evaluative mediation may remain non-binding upon parties (Chowdhury 2011). However, non-abidance of the mediation decision may have some legal and social consequences (Moser 1997; Chen 2002). Therefore, evaluative mediation may promote abidance of mediated outcomes either through direct contact between parties or through fear of social sanction if outcomes of evaluative mediation conducted by any socially respected mediator are not followed by the parties. More reasons for abidance are discussed in chapter two.

Moreover, while in evaluative mediation a third party mediator may provide his or her advice, predict legal consequences or not settle a dispute and may provide their evaluation on the content of a dispute, a process of evaluative mediation does not exclude facilitation (Sourdin 2008, 149; Boulle 2011, 46). In practice, it is possible that a mediator starts mediation with a more facilitative environment and then applies evaluative techniques if parties fail to attain a consensual solution with this initial facilitative attempt, or fail to respond to a facilitative technique (Folberg 2004, 85; Cooley 2006, 34). Therefore, an evaluative mediator needs to think about the maximum limit of his or her evaluation. However, the use of that maximum limit of evaluation does not apply to every individual case as a rule, but rather depends on the context of a dispute and disputants (see chapter two).

1.6.5 Confidential Process

Like any other forms of mediation, one core advantage for which parties may prefer evaluative mediation in comparison with court proceedings is its confidential nature (Boulee 2011, 669). As observed by the High Court of Australia in *Field vs. Commissioner of Railway* (NSW) (Cited in Crosbie 1995, 53):

> The purpose [of confidentiality] is to enable parties engaged in an attempt to compromise litigation to communicate with one another freely and without the embarrassment which the liability of their communication to be put in evidence subsequently might impose upon them.

It is worth noting here that confidentiality is a broader concept than privacy. Mediation may remain private to any person other than the parties (Cooley 2006, 445), and such privacy may enable parties to discuss their private issues freely in mediation. However, privacy does not ensure confidentiality if it is not assured that issues discussed and evidence adduced in mediation shall not be used as evidence for further court proceedings or shall not be disclosed to others without getting prior permission for the parties to a mediation (Cooley 2006, 445–6).

Further, confidentiality in mediation may also exist inside the mediation room. For example, when a party shares his or her feeling or some strategic point with an evaluative mediator during private sessions, the mediator shall not disclose that information in the joint sessions between parties (Doherty & Guyler 2008, 42). The code of mediators' ethics may prohibit mediators to share confidential mediation content even to their friends and family members (Rovine 2009, 275). Furthermore, the agreement attained through mediation shall also be limited to the parties and mediators, and it shall not be treated as a public property (Doherty & Guyler 2008, 42).

1.7 The Current Dilemma of Mediation: Neutrality of Mediators vs. Gendered Power Disparity and Family Violence

Though evaluative mediation has the potential to overcome many limitations of facilitative mediation as well as the formal justice system that may hinder poor people in accessing justice through trial, and provide low-cost, quick access to fair justice, procedural incompetence of the mediators may make this consensual dispute resolution process ineffective under certain contexts.

Firstly, the major dilemma that exists in the field of mediation, and widely debated under contemporary literature, is the nature and extent of neutrality that should be followed. As already introduced in this chapter, while Western societies generally adhere to and advocate for facilitative mediation and strict neutrality of mediators (Kovach & Love 1996; Alfini 1997), contrary opinion suggests an evaluative method to better cope with the impact of gendered power disparity and family violence in mediation (Cobb 1993; Pinzon 1996; Bagshaw 2001). As will be discussed in more depth in chapter two, strict neutrality permits mediators only to make even-handed intervention in to the process of mediation, while in evaluative mediation, a mediator can provide their evaluation on the content of disputes and provide their expert opinion or suggestions to help parties reach a consensual settlement of their dispute.

Secondly, mediation may not work under extreme power disparity (ABA 2004, 105). Mediation is criticised and even opposed by many scholars on the grounds of gendered power disparity which may exist in a society (Neumann 1992, 227; Kelly 1995, 85; Mack 1995, 125). Scholars who have an orientation towards Western style facilitative mediation identify such power disparity as a hindrance to effective negotiation in mediation and a barrier that may cause inequitable outcomes for them as a consequence (Bryan 1992; Cobb 1993; Astor 1994b; Mack 1995; Field 1996). However, this text argues that the critiques of mediation and power disparity are themselves culturally located and thus they may not all apply in every context. The critiques of power in mediation by Western scholars are critiques of facilitative mediation, whereas in cases of evaluative mediation, mediators may play a much more extensive and interventionist role to manage power relations between the parties.

Further, mediation is sometimes criticized on the grounds of referral of family violence cases to mediation (Hart 1990; Gagnon 1992; Astor 1995; Mack 1995; Field 1996). It is also criticized for the "decriminalisation of offences" in a society (Siegal 2010, 436; Scheb & Scheb 2012, 161). The violence exacerbates any existing gendered power disparity that women face in their family and consequently may compel women to be acquiescent to their perpetrator husbands and in-laws. As a result, in contemporary literature it is argued that the likelihood of violent consequences may make it impracticable for women to negotiate with their husbands and in-laws (Neumann 1992; Astor 2002). However, as mentioned above, this argument does not have practical significance in the context of many developing countries where the ability to access formal litigation is very poor and accessible to only a limited percentage of high-income people. For example, though there are many criminal laws in Bangladesh that impose stringent punishment for different types of family violence and public violence, because of limited access to the formal justice system mentioned earlier, at present a large majority of the poor population, especially women, cannot benefit from such legal provisions. Without an alternative, these women would be excluded from the formal justice system.

Therefore, sometimes a practice of evaluative mediation under the shadow of law is considered as a better alternative that may provide fair justice despite the presence of family violence. However, even evaluative mediation may not work when "silence" and "fear" exist in mediation due to such violence (see chapter five).

1.8 Conclusion

A practice of evaluative mediation may enhance access to justice in many developing countries by providing a low-cost, quick means of justice. Evaluative mediation conducted under the shadow of law has a special potential to provide fair outcomes when lack of financial capability, substantial power disparity and other social discourses may hinder access to justice through litigation or facilitative mediation. The following chapter discusses different theories of neutrality and how the contemporary development of the concept of neutrality under the post modern view supports the practice of evaluative mediation. Chapters three, four and five elaborate evaluative mediation by identifying two factors—gendered power disparity and family violence in the society, which may hinder its potential and therefore access to fair outcomes through evaluative mediation. Using Foucault's (1980) post-structural notion of power, chapter three firstly explains how society creates gendered power disparities, and how these may restrain women from attempting to negotiate with their counterparts in mediation. It then argues that mediation is a forum that can, to a significant extent, neutralise the effect of power disparity among parties. It is further argued that, though women in many developing countries have fewer sources of power than men, it is the law which might create discourses of equality and for the protection of women, and it is these discourses which may be deployed by mediators to assist women in mediation. Mediators' practice of evaluative mediation acts to defuse the effect of power disparity and ensure effective participation of women.

Chapter four explains empirical observations on how evaluative mediation is conducted in practice, and Riskin's (1996) grid is adopted to analyse the practice of evaluative mediation. Chapter five critically analyses the impact of family violence on women's effective participation in mediation. Contrary to the arguments predominant in contemporary literature on facilitative mediation in Western liberal democratic societies, this chapter demonstrates that a number of factors protect women in mediation in many developing countries. It contends that despite the presence of family violence, the practice of evaluative mediation can provide fair justice if stringent laws against violence, counselling and social awareness programmes of NGOs against such violence, and long separations of victimised women from their husbands before coming to mediation exist. Evaluative mediation, together with these components, can appear to redress the trauma of past violence and help women to negotiate effectively during mediation.

Since the practice of evaluative mediation is not yet well documented in literature, these chapters would be beneficial for the practitioners to get a practical understanding on how evaluative mediators deal with different issues including neutrality, power disparity and the impact of family violence in mediation. Furthermore, by analysing empirical data, chapter six demonstrates that a practice of evaluative mediation may bring fair outcomes in comparison with what can be attained through litigation. Finally, the concluding chapter seven delineates some policy implications that were made in light of the lessons learnt throughout this text and would be beneficial to promote the practice of evaluative mediation even further.

CHAPTER TWO

NEUTRALITY IN MEDIATION: FROM A "STRICT" TO "EXPANDED" NOTION OF NEUTRALITY

2.1 Introduction

Mediation is a process through which a third party "assists" parties to resolve their disputes or to reach a consensual settlement, without imposing a decision on them. However, how far a third party mediator may assist or intervene in the mediation which is a consensual decision-making process is a widely debated issue among scholars (Greatbatch & Dingwall 1989; Piper 1993; Fisher and Brandon 2002; Lucy 2005; Astor 2007). Issues of agreements and disagreements among scholars revolve around what constitutes neutrality: should mediators remain "strictly" neutral by controlling only the process of mediation, or should they use expanded neutrality and intervene in the content and/or outcome of a mediation to make it fair, and how much neutrality may mediators sacrifice while still remain impartial in their conduct. As identified by Douglas (2008, 152), three different types of relationship exist in a mediation process. These are: (a) the relationship between mediators and each of the parties, (b) the mediators' relationship as between parties, and (c) the relationship between the parties themselves. The neutrality and/or impartiality of mediators depend on these relationships. A discussion of the neutrality of mediators therefore needs to consider all three dimensions of the relationship, and to examine how mediators manage all these relationships to maintain their neutral and/or impartial position. However, as discussed in this chapter, the style of mediation varies depending on the nature and extent of neutrality practised by mediators.

Any specific definition of neutrality and a consequent style of mediation, when "looked at closely, reveal[s] deep underlying assumptions or values that may or may not be consistent with a particular practitioner's own worldview, values, and intentions and abilities" (Taylor 2002, 105). As discussed in chapter one, culture and historical practices vary across countries and such variations influence the process of mediation, and how parties and mediators expect to interact with each other during mediation. Thus, the cultural context of parties should be taken into consideration and carefully handled while conducting mediation. As explained by Adamopoulos & Kashima (1999, 184):

> The effectiveness of a third party will depend not only on his or her skills but on the match between the third party's intervention strategies and the disputants' expectations based on their cultural background.

Therefore, before discussing contemporary development of the concept of neutrality in mediation, this chapter focuses firstly on cultural expectations about mediators' neutrality and the relationship which exists between disputants from different Western and Eastern societies before they enter into mediation. These cultural expectations are then used to define the nature and limit of mediators' intervention desired by the parties, and thereby reconstruct mediators' neutrality according to cultural perspectives.

2.2 Neutrality in Mediation: Paradigms and Diversity in Cultural Expectations

Mediation is a problem solving approach: "Problem solving embedded in the context of third-party mediation process was the first wave of mediation practise … Problem solving itself was perceived as an alternative to a retributive and distributive justice system, where people 'placed claim and rights' …" (Taylor 2002, 111). Therefore, people enter into mediation with a specific objective in mind, which is to resolve, or at least find a mutually acceptable solution to their dispute. When people enter into a process they have some "pre-conceived" expectations of what "ought" and "ought not" to be expected from that process (Robbins 2009, 100). Similar expectations may exist when people enter into mediation. The level of fulfilment of these "pre-conceived" expectations affects individual performance and motivation towards that process. As exemplified by Robbins (2009, 100):

> Suppose you enter an organisation with the view that allocating pay on the basis of performance is right, while allocating pay on the basis of seniority is wrong. How are you going to react if you find that the organisation you've just joined rewards seniority and not performance? You're likely to be disappointed—and this can lead to job dissatisfaction and a decision not to exert a high level of effort.

These pre-conceived expectations are affected by individual values. Value governs whether "a specific mode of conduct or end-state of existence is personally or socially preferable to an opposite or converse mode of conduct or end-state of existence" (Robbins 2009, 100). Therefore, the commitment and motivation of parties entering into mediation may also vary depending on where they are able to find a reflection of individual values in the mode of conduct used by a mediator, and an end-state sought through mediation. These individual values are shaped by the socialisation process of the parties, and are mostly learned during their early childhood from their parents, teachers, friends and relatives (Marquis & Huston 2009, 154; Wood 2011, 159). Though the value systems of individuals within a culture may vary, one general notion we may introduce into mediation to accommodate many individual values simultaneously is to embed cultural values.

2.2.1 Cultural Values

Culture can be defined as a set of values or principles commonly shared by people living in a society. Peterson (2004, 22) defined cultural values as "principles or qualities that a group of people will tend to see as good or right or worthwhile." Though cultural practices may be polar opposites in two or more cultures, they are still appropriate in their own context (Rack 1983, 14). For example, the United States may be considered a country of "masculine" culture that makes a clear distinction between male and female while Sweden may be distinguished for its "feminine" culture (Liu 2001, 22). We may have a special preference for a specific type of culture, but we may not make a judgement on whether another culture is good or bad. A clear distinction between "preference" and "judgement" has been demonstrated by Jennifer Nedelsky (1997, 107). As she describes it, we may express our preference by saying "I like this painting"; however, we are expressing our judgement when we say "This is a great painting." Further, despite the fact that there could be thousands of sub-cultures within a culture, it is still possible to generalize cultural values (Peterson 2004, 23; Wood 2011, 148). Though people may not always behave according to their cultural values, such values are reflected through the repeated behaviours made by individuals over a long period of time (Rafael 144, 56). As explained by Peterson (2004, 27):

> There are exceptions to every rule, but generalisation that come from research and from the insight of informed international cultural experts and professionals allows us to paint a fairly accurate picture of how people in a given country are likely (but never guaranteed) to operate.

Therefore, despite the lack of a perfect match in individual behaviour with cultural values, it is better to have an understanding about cultural values because "if [we] can adjust [our] own behaviours to dovetail with [others], [we] are much more likely to find comfortable, compatible, and fruitful ways of working together" (Peterson 2004, 24). As mediators have to work closely with parties to a dispute, the same argument also applies to mediation. Moreover, to suggest a specific type of mediation appropriate for any given culture, we need to identify the cultural root, not its branches. Identifying the root is important because "[b]behaviour that [we] see is a branch; the roots, the part [we] don't see make the branch what it is" (Thomas 1992, 51).

However, identification of cultural roots may not be immediately forthcoming as considerable debate exists on whether cultural values change over time. While modernisation theorists such as Karl Marx and Daniel Bell argue that cultural values change with the socio-economic development of a society, cultural theorists such as Max Weber and Samuel Huntington claim that cultural values cast an enduring and autonomous influence over societies (Inglehart & Welzel 2005, 48). Though paradoxical, it is possible that cultural values may change yet remain inherently identical over time. As expressed by Peterson (2004, 28):

> The trunk and basic form of the tree remain essentially the same over the years, but the leaves change colour every season and are replaced every year … In spite of these changes, though, a willow is always a willow and a redwood remains a redwood.

To differentiate the part of culture that remains static over time from the other part that accepts changes, Peterson (2004, 28) introduced the concept of "big C-culture" and "small c-culture." Peterson (2004) also explained that in every part of a culture, either big or small, only a fraction is visible like the tip of an iceberg and the rest remain hidden.

Table 2.1. Cultural paradigm

	Big C-culture	Small c-culture
Invisible culture	*Example:* Core values, attitudes or beliefs, society's norms, legal foundations, assumptions, history, cognitive process.	*Example:* Popular issues, opinions, viewpoints, performances or tastes, certain knowledge (trivia, facts).
Visible culture	*Example:* Architecture, geography, classical literature, presidents or political figures, classical music.	*Example:* Gestures, body posture, use of space, clothing style, food, hobbies, music, artwork.

Source: Adopted from Peterson 2004, 25.

To choose the nature of mediators' neutrality and determine the extent of their intervention suitable for any cultural context, we therefore need to look at the Big C-culture or enduring part of that culture. For example, to understand the Big C-culture of mediation, in chapter one, we have discussed the historical perspectives of mediation in Western and Eastern societies. As demonstrated in chapter one, respected people in China, India and Thailand have been serving for many centuries as mediators and settling local disputes according to social norms and cultural values (Cohen 1966; Chen 1996; Limparangsri & Yuprasert 2005; Siddiqi 2006a). Therefore, use of evaluation by mediators may remain a cultural expectation for parties of a dispute. This section elaborates further on how cultural expectations might vary among disputants attending mediation across different cultures.

2.2.2 Mediators' Neutrality in High-Power-Distance vs. Low-Power-Distance Culture

A distinction between high-power-distance culture and low-power-distance culture has been suggested by Hofstede (2001). According to Hofstede (2001), high-power-distance and low power distance culture are parallel with the high-context and low-context culture mentioned above. However, a distinction made on the basis of power-distance or hierarchy has a greater implication for mediation and other forms of dispute resolution modelled under different cultural contexts.

As observed by (Lee & Hwee 2009, 115):

> In low-power-distance cultures, there is a greater degree of flexibility, mobility and ambiguity in relationship and status, matched by more direct communication and the avoidance of verbal, communicative ambiguity: directness and avoidance of ambiguity reflect the pattern of low-context communication in which the meaning is almost wholly contained in the words; and
>
> In high-power-distance cultures, the reverse applies; there is less ambiguity in roles, states and hierarchy, matched by a higher degree of willingness and need to use ambiguity in communication: hence the indirect style of high-context communication. Apparent communicative ambiguity reflects the high-context expectation that meaning will be understood.

The distinction between high-power-distance and low-power-distance culture has special significance for the role of a third party involved in a dispute resolution process. As observed by (Adamopoulos & Kashima 1999, 184), disputants in high-power-distance cultures place more reliance on high-authoritative third party intervention in resolving their disputes, than on their own negotiation capabilities. In most of the disputes, there could be an "asymmetry of influence" (Lee & Hwee 2009, 124). While in a low-power-distance culture it is expected that such asymmetry in dispute resolution would be removed by facilitating equal participation and agency of the disputants, in a high-power-distance culture such asymmetry is accepted by the disputants as a "normative feature" of their engagement. As observed by Lee & Hwee (2009, 124):

> Inequality of relationship and decision-making authority in negotiation counterparts is not likely to be mitigated merely through the adoption of a set of process norms that, for example, assume or seek to create equality of participation and voice in any transaction.

Therefore, a more interventionist role of a mediator remains a cultural expectation from the parties attending mediation. As shown in Fig. 2.1, countries coloured deep ash are high-power-distance societies, while low-power-distance societies like the United States and Australia are depicted with a light ash colour.

Fig. 2.1. Power-distance worldview

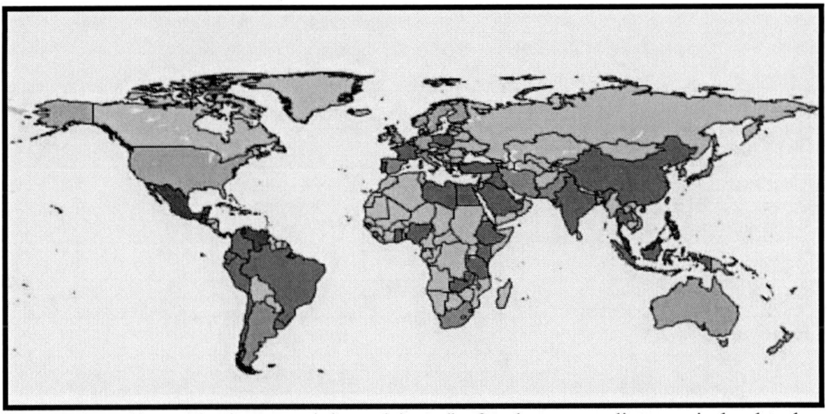

Source: http://www.kwintessential.co.uk/map/hofstede-power-distance-index.html

A comparison of Fig. 2.1 with the discussion of historical perspectives on mediation in Western and Eastern countries in chapter one indicates that high-context eastern countries such as China and India also possess high-power-distance cultures in which mediators historically command higher value in the society and use social and cultural norms to make their evaluations during mediation (Cohen 1966; Triandis 1989; Chen 1996; Siddiqi 2005).

On the other hand, mediators from low-context Western countries such as the USA and Australia, place more emphasis on facilitative process and strict neutrality on their part, rather than on their own evaluation or active intervention in disputes (Cooks & Hale 1994, 64; Douglas 2008, 140; Wing 2008, 95).

Table 2.2. Power Distance Index (PDI)

Country	PDI value	Country	PDI value
Malaysia	104	**Thailand**	64
Philippines	94	**South Korea**	60
Mexico	81	**Pakistan**	55
Venezuela	81	**Japan**	54
China	90	**Italy**	50
Egypt	80	**United States**	40
Iraq	80	**Netherlands**	38
Indonesia	78	**Australia**	36
Ghana	77	**Germany**	35
India	77	**United Kingdom**	35
Singapore	74	**New Zealand**	22
France	68	**Israel**	13
Belgium	65	**Austria**	11

Source: Hofstead 2001:89

As shown in the Table above, countries in the East like Malaysia, the Philippines, China and Indonesia have higher PDI values in comparison to their Western counterparts such as the United States, the United Kingdom, New Zealand and Australia. Therefore, it is expected that mediators from Malaysia or Indonesia would not be as neutral as mediators from Australia, and would bring in more evaluation during mediation. For instance, as explained by Wall & Callister (1999, 344) while defining Malaysian community mediation, "the *ketua kempung* [village head man] usually talked to each party separately, listened to each, and suggested some concessions or relocations." The same strategy is currently being followed by mediators in the Malaysian Mediation Centre (MMC): "The mediator is authorized to conduct joint and separate meetings with the parties and to suggest opinions for settlement" (Ahmed & Rajasingham 2011, 47). The following section will discuss how this cultural diversity in the practice of mediators' neutrality is adopted in contemporary literature on mediation.

2.3 The Rhetoric of "Strict" Neutrality: Towards Possibility or Impossibility?

Most scholars from Western liberal democracies view the neutrality of mediators as a basic safeguard of the parties attending mediation. According to Astor (1997, 221), "The neutrality of a third party who … mediates is central to our ideas of fairness and justice in western liberal democracies." The concept of neutrality in mediation is so inherent that sometimes the terms "mediator" and "neutral" are used interchangeably.

Boulle (2011, 73) explains neutrality with three different meanings. Firstly, neutrality in the form of disinterestedness means that a mediator does not have any personal or commercial interest in the mediated outcome. Secondly, the independence of mediators is another form of neutrality whereby the mediator neither has any prior relationship with nor shows his allegiance to any party who may have an interest in the mediated outcomes. Finally, impartiality of mediators is considered as another form of neutrality whereby a mediator handles disputes from both sides in an even-handed and unbiased manner.

Astor (2007) goes one-step further by extending this view of neutrality into four different aspects. Neutrality, in its first aspect, means mediators will be independent from their "own perspectives, experiences and opinions" and control the process without influencing the content or the outcome of the dispute. The second meaning of neutrality implies the impartiality of the mediators whereby he or she will "treat the parties equally, not favouring one over the other" (Astor 2007, 223). The third component of neutrality signifies that the mediator will not be influenced by any personal or financial connection with the disputants. This criterion resembles the independence criterion of Boulle (2011). As argued by Astor (2007, 222), neutrality in mediation must not only be done, but be seen to be done. In some cases, such as mediations conducted in small towns, a mediator may have some personal acquaintance with the parties; such acquaintance will be revealed at the beginning of mediation so that parties may decide whether they will proceed with such a mediator. A fourth element of neutrality indicated by Astor (2007, 223) is that mediators shall not be influenced by any third party outside the dispute, such as government. This fourth criterion extends the scope of the third by keeping neutral mediators away from the influence of governments, a privilege enjoyed by judges in liberal democratic countries.

As with Boulle (2011) in his third element of neutrality, Astor (2007) also advocates an impartial intervention by a neutral third party mediator. However, she splits the impartiality criterion into two separate elements. Instead of taking impartiality in its ordinary meaning, which is sometimes used interchangeably with the term "neutrality," she firstly imposes a limit on mediators' intervention by asserting that mediators shall not influence the content or outcome of mediation. Further, while intervening in the process of mediation, mediators shall maintain their impartiality by treating both of the parties in an even-handed way (Astor 2007, 222). "It entails allowing each side adequate opportunity to speak and approximate equality of attention" (Boulle 2011, 77).

The "strict" neutrality approach, developed by Western scholars, is more appropriate for facilitative mediation. According to Taylor (1997, 226–27) facilitative mediation defines mediators' strict neutrality by educative and rational-analytic models. With the educative model, the mediator provides information to the parties regarding the mediation process. According to the rational-analytic model, mediators try to bind the parties to a single track and solve disputed issues one by one. To clarify these two models further, mediators act as facilitators. Mediators facilitate parties to negotiate between themselves with the objective of reaching settlement in disputed issues (Taylor, 1997, 221). Thus, models (i.e. the educative and rational-analytic models) which rely on full control of parties over the content and outcome of a dispute would be more suitable for strict neutrality.

Paradoxically, though literature on mediation asserts the importance of maintaining neutrality and mediators claim themselves that they are neutral, empirical evidence does not always go in this direction (Davies 1988; Greatbatch & Dingwall 1989). Rather, it can be shown that mediators function "by directly changing the discourse that the participants are having, and such changes are in fact nonneutral behaviour by the mediator" (Taylor 2002, 171).

For instance, mediators may not restrict them to a strict neutrality view in therapeutic and normative-evaluative models of mediation. While in the therapeutic model mediators concentrate on developing the emotional state of the less empowered party through therapy, and try to make her or him more capable of effectively negotiating with the other party, a normative-evaluative model suggests that mediators tell one or both the parties about their evaluation of the content of a dispute (Taylor 1997, 221). No matter how far they would express their evaluation to the parties, it would be difficult to make progress in mediation if mediators do not have their own evaluation of the content of a dispute. As explained by Lowry (2004, 84):

> Mediators make informed decisions based upon the information presented. They mentally process information, formulate judgements, and respond according to their theoretical framework. They even decide what they think of the parties involved and what the outcome should be. If mediators did not evaluate (at least internally), it would be difficult to move the parties toward a settlement.

Apart from identifying a departure from strict neutrality in practice, even scholars from Western liberal democracies have identified a need for departure from strict neutrality in practice. Scholars have also explained other reasons for which mediators may sacrifice their strict neutrality and strive to maintain their impartiality instead. Cobb & Rifkin (1991) note that mediators' neutrality is widely assumed to exacerbate power disparity in mediation: "Neutrality in mediation has been shown to function as a rhetorical device that obscures the operation of power in mediation" (cited in Astor 2007, 226). A similar argument is provided by Taylor (1997). Thus, by adhering to strict neutrality, mediators may not be able to ensure a fair outcome through mediation, especially where power disparity exists between parties.

Moreover, as discussed earlier, the neutrality of mediators is not equally valued in every culture. For example, mediators' neutrality may not be either a recognized or an acceptable criterion in Aboriginal culture (Boulle 2011, 79). As observed by Kelly (2009, 198), "the best mediator for an Aboriginal dispute may be an Aboriginal person who is connected to the dispute." Therefore, though mediators are independent from the parties they mediate, when the context of mediation demands it and the culture of disputants supports it, mediators should not maintain "strict" neutrality. Furthermore, they should not sacrifice and be disinterested on the quality of outcome attained through mediation. As explained by Wing (2008, 96), "dispute resolution must be grounded in and responsive to the larger societal context, and that individuating and privatizing disputes within a so-called neutral setting violates this requirement."

To minimize the gap between theory and practice, and to cater to the needs of disputants, some scholars suggest an "extended" view of neutrality which permits mediators intervention in the content of disputes in an impartial and unbiased manner, treating parties equally, instead of being neutral on the content and outcome of a dispute (Fisher & Brandon 2002). To them, neutrality means "impartiality," which Cobb & Rifkin (1991) define as "equidistance"; this is a broader definition of what Boulle (2011) calls his third element of neutrality. As a means of maintaining impartiality, while mediators make their intervention on the content of a dispute, Cobb & Rifkin (1991, 44) advocate a principle of "equidistance" so that mediators of the content of a dispute may reconstruct it in such a way that "neither side is favoured or disfavoured." According to the principle of equidistance, a mediator may favour one party in one instance and favour the other party in another. Despite a series of biased interventions throughout the mediation process, mediators can still maintain their overall unbiased and impartial position by applying bias symmetrically to parties attending mediation (Cobb & Rifkin 1991, 44). Extended neutrality through equidistance therefore refers to the idea of an "even playing field" whereby an ideal of fairness through equal intervention in the mediation process is upheld. The ideal, "after all, is not particular to mediation but is foundational to most dispute resolution mechanisms in Western liberal democracies" (Astor 2007, 222). However, the notion of equidistance brings two challenges into the paradigm of mediators' neutrality. Firstly, the perspective that mediators bring to mediation may reflect their own values and may contravene the values of parties attending mediation. Secondly, it fails to identify how much new perspectives mediators may bring into mediation (Astor 2007, 226).

One suggestion sometimes used to address the first challenge is to use objective legal standards that would be equally applicable for all. As observed by Astor (2007), even judges may determine who is right and who is wrong on the basis of an objective legal standard. Therefore, mediators can also conduct mediation and make their evaluations under the shadow of law (Mnookin & Kornhauser 1979). However, problems persist as parties may compromise legal standards in mediation or even abandon such standards altogether in an attempt to uphold their present or future needs (Astor 2007, 223; Boulle 2011, 81). Therefore, mediators may not always be able to maintain their extended neutrality by upholding objective legal standards in mediation. Abandoning an objective criterion such as legal outcome as a standard for mediators' neutrality also poses the risk that mediators will bring their own perspective into mediation (Astor 2007). "When strong feelings and values cannot be denied, dismissed, or separated from the mediation, these function as warning signals that mediators may 'lose their neutrality'" (Cobb & Rifkin 1991, 42).

2.4 The Notion of "Expanded" Neutrality: What Matters Most?

One alternative solution suggested by Astor (2007) to determine the nature and extent to which mediators may bring their perspective into mediation is determined by the "principle of empowerment and self-determination" of the parties. A similar view has been suggested by other scholars (Field 2007, Cooper & Field 2008). As contented by Field (2007, 181):

> Self-determination is the "justifying good" of the mediation profession; just as, for example, the Rule of Law can be argued as the justifying good of the legal profession. This is because it is self-determination that grounds every model of mediation, from the facilitative to the transformative, and even to the evaluative. Whether a mediator controls the process only, offers information, provides a view as to the merits of the parties' arguments or positions, or proffers possible options for consideration, it remains fundamental to any mediation process that it is the parties who determine the consensual resolution of their own dispute. The mediator's role in any of the incarnations of the process can be seen then as preceding the self-determinant decision of the parties.

To promote self-determination by the parties, Astor (2007) suggests two improvements in the contemporary practice of expanded neutrality. Firstly, while bringing any perspective into mediation, mediators need to practice reflexivity to their own perspective and should remain open to other perspectives that parties may bring. According to the "reflexivity principle," mediators need not remain "value-less" in mediation; rather they should remain aware of their own values and of how they may affect mediation (Astor 2007, 229). As explained by Swain (2009, 322):

> Self-reflexivity in practice demands awareness and control of one's own professional, personal and cultural biases in order to hear and understand the standpoint of the other.

As explained by Astor (2007), a practice of openness to other perspectives allow mediators to see the contested views of a dispute presented by both of the parties simultaneously and to examine the validity of arguments presented from two different perspectives. Mediators may also encourage parties to remain open to the perspectives of the other party.

Mediators may bring in perspectives of law that would empower parties and enhance party self-determination on the outcome of mediation. For example, in divorce mediation, a mediator may explain the laws on divorce and other matrimonial issues. As observed earlier in this chapter, parties in a high-power distance culture may take power disparity as a normative value of their interaction and may rely more on intervention by mediators rather than their own efforts to negotiate for a fair outcome in mediation. Due to such pre-conceived cultural expectation by the disputants, it may be desirable and acceptable in the East that mediators may intervene on the content of a dispute in an effort to reach a fair outcome through mediation. While making such an evaluation, mediators shall remain impartial or try to uphold the marginalized discourse that would otherwise be unheard in mediation (Astor 2007, 232).

However, even when mediators try to uphold marginalized discourse in mediation, evaluative mediators in the East may not expect to attain a fair outcome through mediation by making their intervention according to the principle of equidistance. Wing (2008) has asked a series of probing questions to clarify why mediators may need to sacrifice the principles of neutrality as well as equidistance in order to attain fair outcomes thorough mediation. As propounded by Wing (2008, 96):

> What are the consequences when a mediator treats equally those who are on an uneven playing field? and when differing experiences of violence and of access to power, decision making, and respect impact the lives of the participants, who is better served when power inequities are attended to by symmetry and neutrality?

Therefore, evaluative mediators may not provide their evaluation following the principle of equidistance, and follow rather the principle of equity (see chapters three and five for more on the impact of power and violence in mediation). While defining the term equity, as explained in the World Development Report (World Bank 2006, 19), "societies may decide to intervene to protect the livelihoods of its neediest members (below some absolute threshold of need) even if the equal opportunity principle is upheld." To ensure fair justice for the parties of a dispute, evaluative mediators may follow the principle of equity while making their intervention in mediation. Mediators may need to intervene more to uphold the discourse of a marginalized party who otherwise would not be able to obtain a fair outcome through mediation.

However, as mentioned earlier, even when mediators make evaluations to reach a fair outcome, they may not contribute a new perspective to mediation without exercising reflexivity (Astor 2007, 233). To set a limit for mediators' evaluation, Astor (2007, 233) has proposed a test for mediators:

> What the mediator should insert into the mediation should be guided, not by pretence of neutrality which must necessarily be constantly flouted, but by the principle that the parties should have the maximum control possible given their context and situation.

Therefore, mediators may suggest new perspectives and enable parties to judge those suggestions and make their informed decision by accepting or rejecting those perspectives shared by the mediators. In other words, evaluations made by mediators will empower parties to understand the issues and decide fair outcomes for themselves. However, mediators should not bring in new perspectives or make evaluations if it seems that one or more of the parties is not able to examine options, or unable to judge his or her own position in mediation. An evaluative mediator should not determine the outcome for the parties.

2.5 Avoiding Perils through Expanded Neutrality: The Connection between Purpose and Practise

Since in a high-power-distance culture mediators face a culturally defined expectation to bring norms and values to bear on the content of a dispute, ambiguity may arise as to whether such intervention can be legitimized under the contemporary paradigm of mediator neutrality. As discussed in this section, mediation under a post structuralist view allows for consideration of the context of the dispute and enables a mediator to challenge the dominant discourses that may contribute to the power disparity between parties in mediation[15] (see chapter three). Maintaining procedural equality in mediation may not ensure effective participation of women when widespread gender disparity in the society places them in a more subjugated position. One of the clearest presentations of this

---

[15] However, a mediator should not assume power disparity between parties at the inception of mediation by looking at their outlooks only (Davis & Salem 1984, 18). Power in family mediation may arise simply from a sense of entitlement while others may not be able to negotiate effectively even if they bring a substantial amount of income, education or self esteem to mediation (Astor 2005, 31). Therefore, "[t]throughout the mediation process, mediators must observe how power is asserted; note whether and how the assertion tilts the participatory and negotiating power of the parties" (Kelly 1995, 88).

argument is in the work of Astor (1994, 153) who elegantly argued that "the consequence of treating unequal parties with equality is inequality."

In a related vein, Bagshaw (2001, 217–18) suggests that mediators should not define their role as "neutral." Rather, they should see that their role is to challenge the dominant discourse that may subjugate the voice of indigenous people, women, or children in mediation whenever possible. Cobb & Rifkin (1991, 49) also emphasise that the "traditional notion of neutrality" in mediation may uphold power imbalance and result in "unjust agreements." Depicting an empirical study, they further affirm that mediators can ensure fair justice through mediation by actively participating in the determination of issues and settlement of disputes. Cobb & Rifkin (1991) describe a form of neutrality that allows mediators to use their procedural power not only to assist parties in telling their stories positively but also to take part in "discursive formation" that protects the voice of parties with marginalised discourse in mediation. Therefore, mediators may take part in framing the content of disputes but such intervention is not possible if the mediators adhere to the strict meaning of neutrality.

As will be discussed while describing mediators' power and the process of conducting mediation in chapter three, family mediators in Bangladesh commonly use their procedural power and power of law, i.e. prerogative power, to intervene in the content of a dispute and challenge dominant discourses of husbands during mediation. According to the notion of post-structural power, they are enabled to do so by dominant cultural discourses (see chapter three). However, power created through cultural discourses does not remain constant: "Power is always a definite form of momentary and constantly reproduced encounters among a definite number of individuals" (Foucault, cited in Grosz 1990, 87). Therefore, following the result of such encounters, there is always a possibility for change in existing power relations between parties. The next chapter further elaborates on this issue.

2.6 Does Evaluative Mediation under Extended Neutrality Attain Party Satisfaction?

As discussed in chapter one and further reaffirmed earlier in this chapter, evaluative mediators in high-context, high-power-distance Eastern culture have historically resolved community disputes according to their cultural norms and values (Cohen 1966; Chen 1996; Suvanpanich 1997).

Nevertheless, because disputants in high-power-distance cultures tend to accept the intervening dispute resolution practised by authoritative figures of their society, a further concern may remain as to whether those authorities also remain unbiased and impartial in delivering their justice through evaluative mediation. While observing the quality of justice delivered by the *panchayet* or indigenous dispute resolution system in the Indian sub-continent, Jain (1999, 61) commented:

> These *panchayets* fulfilled the judicial functions very effectively and it is only rarely that their decisions gave dissatisfaction to the village people. The members of the *panchayets* were deterred from committing an injustice by fear of public opinion in whose midst they lived.

A similar observation has been made by Alford, Winston & Kirby (2010, 99) regarding the quality of traditional Chinese mediation. As observed by Alford, Winston & Kirby (2010, 99):

> The King's Tribunal focuses on mediation … with "three members" (*san yuan*), "four hearts" (*sin xin*), and "seven methods" (*qifa*). The "three members" refer to the three types of personnel involved in the mediation-people's judges, people's assessors, and people's mediators. The "four hearts" refer to "a just heart" (*gong xin*), "a sincere heart" (*cheng xin*), "a patient heart" (*nai xin*), and "a persistent heart" (*heng xin*). Obviously these are values of fairness.

While describing mediators' neutrality in Aboriginal culture, Behrendt & Kelly (2008, 64) explained:

> In Aboriginal communities there is a recognition that certain people are reputed for their impartiality within the community, and may be suitable to deal with some disputes … The fact that the mediators have an indirect involvement in the dispute, but are nevertheless trusted by the disputants, can be seen as an advantage, not a disadvantage.

Though in some cases the practice of traditional mediation by village headmen is contaminated by politics and they are lose their century-long pride as a last resort for local justice, new forms of community organisations are emerging to fill this vacuum (Chowdhury 2011). Therefore, it can be expected that a practice of evaluative mediation in the East will be able to provide fair justice to disputants with the assistance of impartial and unbiased mediators.

2.7 Conclusion

Discussion so far reveals that the practice of neutrality and its extent—from strict to expanded neutrality—may vary across cultures with different jurisdictions. Despite the variations, the bottom line is that we can appreciate the use of "extended" neutrality if such a form is accepted and respected by disputants attending mediation in any specific culture, and if it also suits the needs of the parties attending mediation. Because parties may have pre-conceived expectations of the role of mediators and the practice of expanded neutrality based on their cultural values, they may face a power disparity that restricts their effective participation in mediation (see chapter three). A practice of evaluative mediation may therefore become more highly valued by the society. However, to achieve such a higher value, evaluative mediators need to understand the perspectives of the parties attending mediation and to limit their evaluation to the point beyond which their intervention may seize a party's self-determination at the outcome of mediation. To assess whether a practice of evaluative mediation can create real value in the society, chapter six provides a quantitative analysis on fairness of outcome attained through evaluative mediation in comparison with that of trial. Chapter four demonstrates with empirical evidence how evaluative mediators in the East, with particular reference to Bangladesh, may attain a fair justice through mediation while maintaining a position, as defined in this chapter, which is not strictly neutral but at the same time impartial and fair.

CHAPTER THREE

GENDERED POWER DISPARITY: A BARRIER TO ATTAINING FAIR OUTCOMES THROUGH MEDIATION

3.1 Introduction

The potentiality of mediation is questioned due to some quandaries and dissonances. Power disparity, as indicated in chapters one and two, is one of such dilemmas that impede the worth of mediation for "the relatively powerless—ordinary people who could not afford, or were otherwise alienated from, the formal justice system" (Astor 2007, 226). Mediation of family disputes is criticised and even opposed by many scholars on the grounds of gendered power disparity that may exist in a society (Neumann 1992, 227; Kelly 1995, 85; Mack 1995, 125). Scholars who have an orientation towards Western style facilitative mediation and "strict" form of neutrality of mediators (see chapters one and two) identify such power disparity as a hindrance to the capacity of the less powerful (e.g. in the case of family mediation, generally women) to negotiate effectively in mediation, and a barrier that may cause inequitable outcomes for the disadvantaged and vulnerable in consequence (Neumann 1992, 231; Kelly 1995, 85; Mack 1995, 124). Because women in Eastern developing countries are generally a less powerful section in the society compared with their male counterparts it is claimed that "the subordinate position of women in … society is prevalent in every sphere of their lives … Diverse cultural factors support and encourage the accentuating of sex differences and discrimination" (Ameen 2005b, 4). A similar disparity of power between male and female also exists in mediation. This chapter implicates power theories in the conduct of family mediation. The same theoretical understanding can be replicated in resolving other types of disputes in which considerable power disparity exists between parties.

Many scholars have identified power as being the possession of factors such as education, income, occupation or wealth (Fisher 1983, 153;

Haynes 1988, 278; Hughes 1995, 574; Babcock & Laschever 2003, 23–27). Therefore, women are identified as less powerful because of lower possession in terms of income, education, wealth, etc. As mediators cannot equalize these factors in mediation, mediation is discouraged when substantial power disparity is measured in terms of these factors. However, using the post-structural notion of power developed by French Philosopher Michael Foucault (1980), this chapter explains that power remains in social discourses and so cannot be possessed by individuals. It is argued that "gender" created through social discourses may remain as an even more dominant factor in mediation which can undermine the negotiating capacity of women despite their possession of superior income, education or employment status compared with their male counterparts. Though Foucault (1980) did not refer directly to "mediation," his theory of power can be used to explain:

- how social discourses create gendered power disparity and disempowered women in a society

- that power is not directly linked with the possession of income, education or occupation and how it may therefore be possible for a mediator to address gendered power disparity in mediation without making any effort to equalise the possession of these factors between the parties attending mediation, and

- that even when considerable gendered power disparity exists in a society, mediators may help to attain fair outcomes for marginalized groups (usually women in family mediation) attending mediation by: (a) challenging dominant social discourses that might undermine the voice of the marginalized group in mediation; (b) conducting mediation under the shadow of law, or by applying gender equalising legal discourses that are "legally binding" for all parties attending mediation; and (c) using gender equalising religious norms which are "morally binding" on the parties and so could be helpful in upholding the marginalised voice of women in mediation.

Nevertheless, even when power is defined under a post-structural notion as mentioned earlier, Western style facilitative mediators adhering to strict neutrality may not be able to challenge the dominant discourses to control power disparity in mediation. However, following the discussion in chapter two, this chapter argues that the critiques of power disparity in mediation are themselves culturally located and thus may not apply in every different context. While the critiques of power in mediation by Western scholars are those of facilitative mediation, evaluative mediation is practised in many developing countries of Asia, including China, Thailand, India and Bangladesh where "law" plays a major role and forms the basis of mediators' interventions to manage the power disparity between the parties (Pryles 1997; Chowdhury 2011) (see chapter four).

By combining the post-structural theory of power with the process of evaluative mediation, it can be explained how mediators can ensure effective participation of women in mediation despite their greatly disadvantaged position in the society—a scenario that represents the context of the life of women in many developing countries in the East (Pryles 1997). The remaining part of this book implicates power theories in "family mediation." Because, in general, women in Eastern developing countries are the least powerful section in the society compared with their male counterparts, it is claimed that the high-cost and other barriers of litigation, as discussed in chapter one, has a more negative impact on access to court for women than it does for men (The Asia Foundation 2002c; Asian Development Bank 2004). They say this is because "the subordinate position of women in ... society [like Bangladesh] is prevalent in every sphere of their lives ... Diverse cultural factors support and encourage the accentuating of sex differences and discrimination" (Ameen 2005b, 4). Therefore, the poverty gap between males and females has been rising over the years in many developing countries and women are the poorest of the poor. Women are thus less able to bear the costs of access to justice in many developing countries (Khair 2001a; Ameen 2005a).

While following the above mentioned objective, this chapter initially discusses the notion of power and its characteristics under the post-structuralist theory, followed by a discussion on how social discourses create gender power disparity in a society. Later, it delineates the negative effect of gender role ideology on the negotiating capacity of women. However, this chapter further clarifies that such a critique relates to facilitative mediation in which mediators take a "strict" neutral role and parties are responsible for negotiating for themselves. Finally, it explains how a practice of evaluative mediation and use of gender equalizing legal discourses create the possibility of effectively controlling the impact of gendered power disparity in mediation.

3.2 Power as a Post-Structural Notion: Foucault's Theory of Power and Its Operation to Create "Gender" in a Society

Power has sometimes been described as "the ability to influence or control others' (Davis & Salem 1984, 18), "the ability to get what one wants" (Neumann 1992, 229) or "the possibility of imposing one's will upon the behaviour of others" (Webster 1954, 323). Haynes (1988, 278) observed that power arises from the "control of or access to emotional, economic, and physical resources desired by the other party." Hughes (1995, 574) also defines power as the "ability to control resources, or the access to resources that the other wants or needs." These authors define power as "possession" of resources such as income, education and employment status, which enable a person to influence or control others (Davis & Salem 1984; Bryan 1992; Neumann 1992; Kelly 1995; Mack 1995). However, as is discussed in the next section, under the post-structural theory power is not something which can be possessed by any person. It is rather a "social construct" that remains in a society and flows with social discourses and other cultural practices of that society (Bagshaw 2003, 207; Astor 2005, 34). Before discussing power under the post-structural notion, this section provides a brief account of post-structuralism and how it differs from earlier views of modernism and structuralism.

3.2.1 From Modernism to Postmodernism

In the sixteenth and seventeenth centuries, Europe experienced the emergence of modernism, a philosophy which attempts to discover an objective and rational explanation of all human experiences. Its endeavour is to seek out universally applicable knowledge which can explain such experiences irrespective of time and space (Bagshaw 2003, 130). "There is also a desire for what is usually referred to as 'closure,' that is completeness in the philosophical system - it must have no gaps, and be a final account of the world" (David 2002, 300). However, many postmodern thinkers such as Hegel (1770–1831), Nietzsche (1844–1900), Heidegger (1889–1976), and Foucault (1926–1984) subsequently challenged the notion of "universal truth" in modernism. Postmodernism, stated simply, is the philosophical ideology that denies any truth that may remain valid universally irrespective of time and space. What is true in one society at a given time may not be true for another society or for that society at a different time period (David 2002, 297–98, 300). While accepting the existence of "multiple truths", Foucault developed his philosophy with a close linkage to the structure of society (Hauggard 1997, 51; Bagshaw 2003, 132; Gutting 2005, 30). The philosophy of Foucault is therefore discussed under post-structuralism.

3.2.2 From Structuralism to Post-Structuralism

Structuralism was introduced by the French linguist Ferdinand de Saussure to understand "how language relates to the world, and how meaning works." According to Saussure (1916), a word does not bear any intrinsic meaning but rather a meaning which is assigned to it arbitrarily. Further, as emphasized by Saussure, the meaning of a word is interrelated with the meaning of other words in a language and cannot be understood in isolation from others (Haugaard 1997, 48; David 2002, 307). For example, cow, goat, lamb, hen, and cock are all animals. If we do not know the difference between the words "cow," "goat," "lamb" and "cock," we might confuse goat, lamb or cock as cow. However, such confusion will not arise if we also know the meaning of the words goat, lamb and cock. Saussure states this system of meaning in a language as "synchronic," or static linguistic. Besides synchronic linguistic, Saussure also observes "diachronic" linguistic which deals with how the meaning of words changes over time. However, Saussure emphasized more the importance of synchronic language because, as he perceived, people in a society at any given time are concerned about the current state of their language, not its history; they are concerned about how contemporary meanings of words are interrelated, not how they evolved over time (cited in Davis 2002, 308).

The arbitrarily assigned meanings to different words and their interrelations as postulated by Saussure in linguistics also exist in other branches of knowledge. Looking at its wider applicability, the structuralist notion was applied by many scholars from other fields (David 2002, 307). Lyotard for instance, indicates that "in fact science must always have recourse to ... 'meta-narrative,' that is, a higher set of principles which are not themselves scientific" (David 2002, 303). Then, one might ask, what these "meta-narratives"? Where do they come from? According to Lyotard, "it is consensus among the community of scientists, not any absolute scientific principle, that forms the basis of scientific legitimacy" (David 2002, 303). Claude-Lévi Strauss, a Belgian anthropologist, made a link between Saussure's linguistic theory and the cultural system of a society. As observed by Strauss, like words in a language, cultural components of a society can be understood only in relation to the other components of the culture. Foucault (1980) also recognizes that in every society there are some historical *a priori* or historically framed cultural codes and, based on these, people understand and explain events in their lives. As cultural practices are interrelated, one cultural practice derives its meaning only in association with others. Thus, to understand the meaning of an event in a certain culture, one has to consider it in the context of a full set of cultural codes which are internally interrelated. Foucault termed such a full set of the cultural codes of a society as "*episteme*"[16] (Haugaard 1997, 51; Paras 2006, 23).

Therefore, *episteme* in Foucault's theory is similar to what Saussure (1916) called synchronic linguistic, or the system of meanings in a language. As a structuralist thinker, Saussure made a rigid separation between object (the meaning of words) and subject (an individual who practises such meaning): "The idea is that as a theorist I simply perceive my object, and then express what I have seen through language. For theory, the subject is an external observer, who just reflects the object" (Davies 2002, 311, 318–319). As such, for Saussure, subjects cannot change objects rather take them as given. However, what causes the basic distinction between the thoughts of Saussure and Foucault is Saussure's challenge against such a clear separation between subject and object. Further, Saussure confines his analysis to the existing set of meanings of words in a society, giving little emphasis to how meanings evolve over time. Unlike Saussure, however, Foucault did not limit his objective to identify that existing social norms are guided by a set of cultural codes. He also explained the dynamics and mechanics of changes in social discourse which occur over time. Therefore, though his theory is related to structures of societies, as is the case with Saussure, Foucault's consideration of the fluidity of social discourses over time and space, elevates his theory of power as a post-structural notion.

[16] An *episteme* is the system of understanding or a body of ideas which give shape to the knowledge of that time.

3.2.3 How Power in Social Discourses May Create "Gender" in a Society?

As a post-structuralist philosopher, Foucault (1980) explained how social discourses (object) create and preserve the power dynamic in a society and how such power may change over time through the discursive practices of the people (subject) in that society. He elucidated how power lies in social discourses (object), identified knowledge as an agent that promotes changes in social discourses and a consequent change in power, and expounded how a dominant group (subject) in a society may change power by the normalisation of knowledge (Gutting 2005, 101). Therefore, unlike Saussure, in Foucault's theory subject and objects are interdependent. Though social discourse may change over time, notions of "truths" or "rights" in a society depend on existing discourses of the society. As observed by Foucault (1980, 85):

> When I see you straining to establish the scientificity of Marxism I do not really think that you are demonstrating once and for all that Marxism has a rational structure and that therefore its propositions are the outcome of verifiable procedures; for me you are doing something altogether different, you are investing Marxist discourses and those who uphold them with the effects of a power which the West since Medieval times has attributed to science and has reserved for those engaged in scientific discourse.

The notion of truth may change as social discourses change. Formation of new truth or change in existing social discourses, on the other hand, depends on the acceptance of a new knowledge by the society. However:

> The formation of truth [knowledge] does not simply happen. It is an outcome of the struggles and tactics of power. This means the disqualification of certain knowledge as idiocy and a fight for others as truth (Haugaard 1997, 68).

Through discursive practices, the dominant group in a society tries to normalize knowledge that can preserve and strengthen their power (Bagshaw 2001, 207).

Similarly, power in social discourses may create "gender" by setting social norms that place men in an advantageous position over women. As observed by Bagshaw (2002, 130):

> Stories and "truths" are inevitably framed by dominant cultural discourses that specify what is normal and what can or cannot be talked about, by whom and in what contexts.

This notion of power suggests that power remains in a social network and so cannot be possessed by an individual (Foucault 1984, 93). When people want to legitimize their own position, they try to do so by using the power of the dominant discourses of a society (Foucault 1980, 85). As revealed in the discussion of chapter four, similar struggles also exist in mediation. Though individuals cannot possess power, they remain as a vehicle of power. Therefore, people who are privileged through dominant social discourses and remain powerful in the society may carry the same dominant discourses into mediation and try to legitimize their own position while marginalizing that of others.

However, an explicit use of dominant discourses may not always be necessary to overpower others. People who enjoy a privileged position in terms of social discourses may remain powerful even without any explicit deployment of such power. For example, a husband who does not want his wife to disclose family violence to others in the society may not need to influence his wife in this regard. Women may remain silent of their own volition if, in a society, disclosure of such violence is considered shameful to women. Further, power is not a commodity and so cannot be measured (Foucault 1984, 93; Mayer 2000, 51; Astor 2005, 32).

Following the same mechanism, social discourses may create a subjugated position for women, framing limited opportunities for them and perpetuating the dominance of men to create gender in the society. According to Neumann (1992, 229), “society grants men greater power than women.” Watson (1994, 118) also argued that the gender role of women does not arise because of innate personal factors but because of the context of their life, that is their family, their work and their society. Careful evaluation reveals that social discourse can create gender disparity in terms of income, education, and the occupation of women relative to their male counterparts. For example, discourses such as “it is useless to spend more on a daughters’ education because they cannot help their parents after marriage,” or that “higher education makes women arrogant” (Blunch & Das 2007, 8), could deprive women of the opportunity to attain a better education and therefore their ability to get better employment outside of the home. A later discussion provides further illustration of how social discourses may cause women’s subjugated position in a society (see section 3.4 below). Before initiating such discussion, the next section presents a brief account of the characteristics of power.

3.3 Characteristics of Power: A Post-Structural Context

It has already been mentioned that, from a post-structuralist view, power is not a commodity like income, education or occupation and so it cannot be possessed and measured. Further, post-structuralism explains power not as generic, but rather as relative and fluid. A person is not equally powerful over each and every other person (Kelly 1995, 87). For example, a man may remain powerful over his female colleague and overpower her by using a dominant social discourse, but he may not use the same discourse against his wife in a similar situation and so remains less powerful against her. Neumann (1992, 229) expressed this idiosyncratic nature of power as situational and shifting. Therefore, power is not determined in a vacuum. It depends on the context and parties to a dispute. The history and dynamics of the disputants' relationship also affects power (Kelly 1995, 87).

Power is therefore contextual. The power of a disputing party may change in relation to the different contexts of the dispute. As mentioned earlier, context may vary depending on the relationship between the parties of a dispute. For example, a Supreme Court judge can be powerful in the courtroom but may not be so powerful when in a dispute with their teenage daughter at home (Astor 2005, 32). The context of a dispute may also vary between the same persons in dispute when the level of dependence between the parties changes. For instance, the power of a father might vary over his daughter depending on whether the daughter is a teenage girl who is economically and emotionally dependent on her father or an adult who can earn a living by herself, and have a boyfriend or husband to share her emotions with. Power under these two contexts varies because the father of a teenage girl is not only a legal guardian but also an economic provider. Therefore, the context of a dispute may change over time as the authority and dependency in a relationship change. As discussed later, a similar change may occur in the post-divorce power relationship between a husband and a wife and this can have an important implication for mediation between them.

Furthermore, as is usually perceived, power may not always be coercive or negative; it can also be positive (Fisher 1983, 152; Mayer 1987, 88; Kelly 1995, 87; Astor 2005, 32). Mayer (2000, 62) appropriately indicated three different approaches to exerting power. These are: persuasion (normative approach), reward (utilitarian approach) and punishment (coercive approach). Although it is possible to use different methods simultaneously, taking more than one method at a time does not usually meet with success

(Mayer 2000, 63). We can change our avenue of exerting power according to how effectively a method works, on whom it works, and under what circumstances. For example, a senior executive can cause a subordinate to work better by persuading them that better work will bring them a better career in the organisation (normative approach); failing that they may reward better performance, for instance by an incentive bonus (utilitarian approach); or as a last resort they may threaten to fire the subordinate if performance is not improved substantially (coercive approach). As will be discussed in chapter four, evaluative mediators may also use different degrees of persuasion or evaluation depending on the nature of power relationship between parties.

3.4 Social Discourses Creating Gendered Power Disparity and Marginalising Women's Status in Society: Experiences from Bangladesh

It has already been discussed that social discourses may create gendered power disparity in a society. This part elaborates on how this occurs in different spheres of women's lives taking instances from Bangladesh, a developing Eastern country in which exists a considerable power disparity between males and females in society. Women in Bangladesh are:

> At a decided disadvantage in this patriarchal society. Having very little access to material resources, women lack autonomy and decision-making power, and are therefore disempowered within the family, community, and society at large. (The Asia Foundation 2002a, 7)

In particular, this section illustrates how social discourses may subjugate women's position in a society in terms of income, education and occupational status. It further analyses how socialisation through gender role ideology makes women more submissive and accommodative, rather than assuming a competitive and decision-making role in their conjugal life.

3.4.1 Social Discourses Causing Lower Income, Education, and Occupational Status of Women in Bangladesh

Because of social customs, many women in Bangladesh have to remain at home to perform household work and are not engaged in outside employment (Haq 1995, 62; Hamid 1996, 32–6). Traditionally, men are engaged in agricultural activities in the field, whereas women are the caretakers of agricultural production through husking, boiling etc., and they also take care of the poultry, livestock, etc. at home (Haq 1995a, 63). Though linked with agriculture, the work done by women at home is taken as their household responsibility and is mostly unpaid. Although a recent labour force survey by the Bangladesh Bureau of Statistics (BBS 2007, 7, 9) indicates that women are increasingly being engaged in the labour force, most women still have to work as unpaid family workers (60.1 percent, compared with 9.7 percent of men), and the incidence of such unpaid female labour is remarkably higher in rural areas (71.8 percent compared with urban women (22.3 percent).

Even when women are engaged in paid employment outside their home, most are employed in low-paid part-time work. For example, wage data shows that in 2005 urban women employed in the readymade garments sector earned 75.9 percent of the earnings of their male counterparts. While as many as 25 percent of male labourers earned more than BDT 5000, only 3.7 percent of female workers reached that level. Twenty-six percent of female workers earned less than BDT 3000 while none of the male workers earned such a low level of income in 2005. Women labourers receive a lower income in comparison with their male counterparts even for performing the same work. For example, for the same hours worked, female machine operators and female helpers in the readymade garments sector earned 71.3 percent and 52.7 percent respectively of the earnings of their male counterparts.

Additionally, in rural Bangladesh, inherited land from their natal family could constitute an important source of wealth for women who in many cases remain housewives after their marriage. However, one earlier case study in rural Bangladesh revealed that, following cultural norms, in 77 percent of cases married women in rural Bangladesh forfeit their legal claim to paternal property (cited in Monsoor 1999, 35; Khair 2008, 39). As observed by Monsoor (2008a, 122), various superstitions are also important impediments to accessing their rights. In one study, 80 percent of the women respondents erroneously believed that their property would be destroyed if taken away from their brothers. One woman told how she took her share from the paternal property and bought three cows which died within a year. Another study by Akhter (cited in Monsoor 2008a, 41) confirmed that 88 percent of married women in *Dhaka*, the capital city of Bangladesh, do not receive any dower during their marital life, even if dower remains a major source of wealth for women, and constitutes a legal claim against the husband of every married Muslim woman in Bangladesh.

Though gradual changes in social outlook are causing the increased involvement of women in income earning activities, gender still pervades in society, as reflected by the pro-male social outlook. As shown in Box 3.1, women still sometimes face social resistance to their working outside the home.

Box 3.1. NGOs facing obstacles to improving women's lives through credit

Mullahs (lit. religious clergy) in the village are opposed to us (Grameen Bank). They (Mullahs) campaign against us. They will tell people that if you are a woman and you are taking Grameen Bank money, you will be expelled from religion. This is against the religion for a woman to take money and enter man's world. We will not put you in a grave in a religious way when you die, if you take Grameen money. That's very scary thing for a woman who has nothing. She thinks, now even if I die, I don't get the last religious rites for my burial. I'd better not take the money.*

* A micro-credit NGO in Bangladesh by Dr. Yunus.
Source: Dr. Yunus, Grameen Bank Experiences and Reflections, 2000.

This could be the reason why women in rural areas constitute a disproportionately high share of unpaid family workers, despite their day-long hard work at home. Statistics gathered under the United Nations System of National Accounts in 1991–92 show that in the rural habitats of Bangladesh, men spend 23 percent of their daily time on marketable work (agriculture or non-agriculture) and only 2 percent of their daily time in performing non-market household activities such as water collection, home care or family care. Women, on the other hand, spend 23 percent of their total time in performing different non-market activities. The remaining time for both men (75 percent) and women (68 percent) is spent as personal time—leisure, study or going to school or to the *Bazaar* [shopping] (Hamid 1996, 28). Another hidden discourse revealed by one recent study indicates that the greater participation of women in the paid labour force may not indicate their economic emancipation, but rather a greater susceptibility to poverty. As observed by Sultana (2004, 77):

> Over the last decades, norms segregating and protecting women have been breaking down. Hence it has been seen that the overwhelming majority of women in Bangladesh are caught between two opposite positions. One is determined by custom, which restricts their activities in private space and the other a crisis from poverty, forcing them in to public spaces for economic survival.

Despite their engagement in the job market, because of a higher engagement in household duties working women lead a very hard life combining their household and family responsibilities. As husbands in Bangladesh do not share household duties due to social norms, these working women have to limit their personal time to cope with their dual responsibilities at home and outside (Nasir 1991, 145; Akter 2000, 236).

Fig. 3.1. Ratio of female to male students enrolled at different levels (2005)

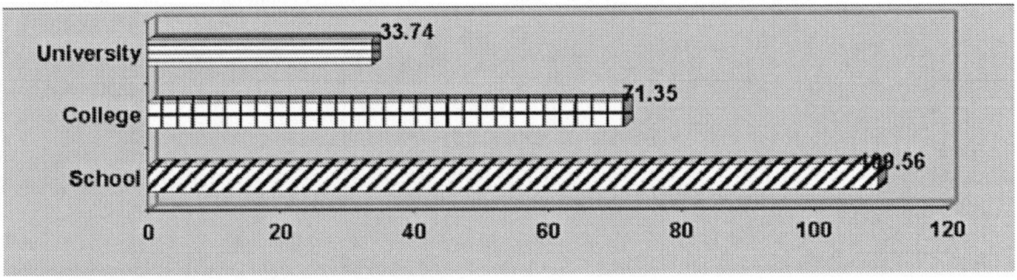

Source: Ministry of Education website: www.moedu.gov.bd/edu_statistics.php

Women also face discriminatory attitudes from society in regard to education. As shown in Fig. 3.1, due to a government subsidy in female education, the net enrolment ratios of females exceeded that of males (109.56 female students enrolled per 100 male students) in primary and secondary (71.35 female students per 100 male students) levels of education. However, the percentage of females in education decreases at higher levels of education where no such subsidy is available for them. Therefore, despite the positive change in women's educational attainments and consequent achievement of gender parity in education, one may not claim that in terms of education women have gained an equal position in the social mindset.

According to a UNICEF study, parents of school-going girls responded that their daughters can learn only a little of their required roles and responsibilities through the school curriculum (Husain 1995, 97). As shown in Table 3.1 below, parents are still placing only a little value on education as a means of enhancing their daughters' knowledge; rather, for most of them, education of their daughters is treated as a means of increasing social status.

Box 3.2. Female students might not get schooling without Food for Education programme

K and his wife M, live with their three children in Kochukata village in Northern Bangladesh. They had four children, but their second child, a boy, died before age four. Both K and M are illiterate. K works as a farm labourer, and M works as a maid servant in a neighbouring house on a part-time basis. Their eldest son, J, about 14, never attended school. He collects firewood, which he sells in the village market. K and M have a nine-year old daughter, A, and a four-year old son, H. A goes to a local primary school. "We would not have sent A to school if we did not receive the monthly free wheat ration from the government's [Food for Education] programme. Instead, she would have looked after H so that her mother could work full time," K said.

Source: Feeding minds while fighting poverty, IFPRI 2001:2.

One remarkable point, however, is that social knowledge about the role of women is changing. As is reflected in Table 3.1 below, the current generation (girls going to school) value formal education more highly than their parents.

Table 3.1. Girls' and their parents' perceptions about benefits of education

Benefits	Girls	Parents
Obtaining job	76%	39%
Enhancement of social status	68%	43%
Better prospect for marriage	59%	21%
Gaining knowledge and skills	62%	8%

Source: Empowerment of Women, Husain 1995a:95.

Therefore, it can be anticipated that when this current generation become mothers, they will place a higher value on education for their daughters. Gender power disparity against women will thus be reduced through education: the normalisation of new knowledge. Though society's view towards female education is changing, responses to the need for educational parity between males and females are still mixed, and some apparent contradictions are still present in the society. A recent World Bank study in Bangladesh demonstrated that although a large majority of respondents believe in the equality of their sons' and daughters' educational attainment, more than half still believe that the groom should have a higher level of education than the bride (Blunch & Das 2007, 6–7). Society believes that if brides are more educated, then they might be less submissive towards their husbands and other elderly in-laws (Blunch & Das 2007, 8). These gendered views of the society are creating a disadvantaged position for many women within it.

3.4.2 Gender Role Socialisation in Household Decision-Making in Bangladesh

It has already been indicated that because of gender role socialisation, women generally have lower social status, "lower reward expectation," and "lower self-esteem," all of which work together to make women less efficient as negotiators (Bryan 1992, 459–87; Neumann 1992, 229; Field 1996, 267). These factors result in gender role socialisation which enables men to be creators of their own fate, while explaining the success of women as an outcome of good luck rather than of their own action. This ultimately creates gender role ideology in the society (Bryan 1992, 472–73). This section elaborates the gender role socialisation of a society, with particular reference to the role of women in Bangladesh.

The role of women in household decision-making has special importance in our discussion of gender roles of women in Bangladesh, as a large majority of Bangladeshi women are housewives and do not work outside the home (Khair 2008, 39). Households are therefore the major area where these women demonstrate their gender role and negotiation capability against their husbands, the parties with whom they have to negotiate during family mediation. Due to the gender role ideology mentioned above, women in Bangladesh are generally not welcome to contribute much in household decision-making (Nasir 1991, 135; Monsoor 1999, 22; Akter 2000, 234; Sultana 2004, 76; Khair 2008, 9). For example, a study conducted by Jahan (1994, 91) on women in Bangladesh, two-thirds of whom were housewives, demonstrated that husbands make the decisions regarding all major household events, such as the purchase of assets and other valuables, the birth of children, schooling of children, etc.

Wives are consulted only in the case of the marriage of children and the purchase of jewellery.

Another study conducted by Nasir (1991, 141–44) on the role of lower middle class urban working women revealed that although participation in household decision-making is improving for them, they only make decisions related to every-day activities with small financial outlay. In a sample of thirty women working in lower grade formal sector employment, twenty-eight responded that although they make decisions on day-to-day household expenditures and also spend for some special occasions such as festivals on their own initiative, the major decisions on expenditure relating to household assets, such as purchase of property or valuables, are made by their husbands. Ironically, even though husbands consult with their male friends, colleagues or relatives when making purchasing such valuables, they never consult with their wives. Again, this occurs because of a social discourse that places less importance on the voice of women in major decision making. Forced intrusion by wives may even jeopardise the marital relationship. Husbands sometimes allow their wives to decide on day-to-day expenditures as they find these daily affairs tedious and complex (Jahan 1994, 91; Nasir 1999, 140–42). Regarding financial matters, women are sometimes used by their husbands as custodians or cashiers rather than as managers of their business. The following cases highlight this issue.

Box 3.3. Women's freedom to make household decisions is subject to male benefits

M, like R, underwent the same experience of facing opposition from her husband when she first disclosed the plan to join BRAC. Her elder son also initially united with the father to dissuade his mother from joining. But the opposition put up by the husband and son did not continue for long as M's son was desperately looking for some capital to start a business and found BRAC as a suitable source for it. Shifting completely from his earlier position, the son rather encouraged his mother to go ahead and obtain a loan for his business.*

* Bangladesh Rural Advancement Committee (BRAC) is an NGO in Bangladesh that provides micro-credit to poor rural women

Source: Marginalisation of women's empowerment and the role of household, 2000, 18.

In the study conducted by Jahan (1994), women are mostly identified as housewives or as being involved in other informal jobs such as part-time domestic workers, hawkers, agricultural workers, or construction workers. In the later study by Nasir (1999), respondents were engaged in formal sector jobs, such as machine operators, tailors, school clerks, family planning field workers, nurses, library assistants, school teachers or even headmistresses. Scholars therefore perceive that employment status could be an important factor for enhancing the voice of women in their families. From the discussion made so far on household decision-making, it seems that women might have better status in their household if they could earn some extra money, hold a prestigious job, and help meet the financial requirements of the family. However, it is usually the case that women are allowed to work outside the home only when their husbands and in-laws feel the need for additional income for the family. This is consistent with the finding that women are not allowed to work outside when their family does not need the money (Kamal 1995, 63, 73). Therefore, though it seems that economic emancipation improves women's voice in the society, working outside the home may not depend on a woman's own choice but rather on the decision of her husband and in-laws. The lower voice of women is also reflected through their marginalized voice in the household decision-making of their day-to-day lives.

Although literature states that women with higher income and better education increasingly have a voice in relation to household decision-making, most decisions are still made by husbands and in-laws who dominate in almost every aspect of their conjugal life. Table 3.2 shows that the rate does not vary significantly between rural and urban areas of Bangladesh.

Table 3.2. Who makes household decisions in Bangladesh?

Nature of decision	Who makes the decision?	Rural%	Urban%	Total%
How much money the household spends on food	Wife only	5.2	6.4	5.4
	Husband only	47.8	44.3	47.1
	Wife and other household member(s) jointly	32.0	34.8	32.6
	Other household member(s)	14.9	14.6	14.9

What food is bought for the household	Wife only	6.2	9.5	6.8
	Husband only	44.8	41.2	44.1
	Wife and other household member(s) jointly	33.8	35.2	34.0
	Other household member(s)	15.3	14.1	15.0
What food is cooked for the household	Wife only	49.5	56.7	50.9
	Husband only	10.6	6.1	9.7
	Wife and other household member(s) jointly	27.5	25.3	27.1
	Other household member(s)	12.3	12.0	12.3
Whether mother attends a health facility for her own health needs	Wife only	5.3	7.1	5.6
	Husband only	38.8	40.3	39.1
	Wife and other household member(s) jointly	40.8	40.5	40.7
	Other household member(s)	15.2	12.0	14.6
Whether the child of a mother goes to a health facility	Wife only	4.7	7.3	5.2
	Husband only	38.8	38.8	38.8
	Wife and other household member(s) jointly	41.5	42.1	41.6
	Other household member(s)	15.0	11.8	14.4

Source: Key findings of Child and Mother Nutrition Survey of Bangladesh 2005, BBS 2005, 3.

It is therefore due to gender role ideology in the society that women in Bangladesh have a lower income, lower education and lower occupational status and are socialised not to make major decisions, even in the family context where they play their major social role. The next concern is how this gender role ideology might affect women's negotiation capacity and disempowering them in mediation. The following section elaborates on this issue.

3.5 Impact of Gender Role Ideology on Women's Capacity to Negotiate: Income, Education and Employment vs. Gender Role Ideology

To explain the disparity between men and women in their capacity to negotiate, some scholars place emphasis on the disproportionate possession of income, education, wealth, employment, etc. between the two groups, without placing importance on gender (Fisher 1983, 153; Haynes 1988, 278; Hughes 1995, 574; Babcock & Laschever 2003, 23–27), while others considered gender as the dominant factor affecting negotiation capacity (Fagenson 1990, 204; Stark 1992, 675). There is yet another group which considers that all these factors operate simultaneously in determining the negotiation capacity of women (Bryan[17] 1992; Neumann[18] 1992; Kelly[19] 1995). However, contrary to the first group which identifies a direct relationship between women's negotiation capacity and their possession of various factors such as education and income, this later group argues that gender bias created through social discourses may affect women's

[17] Bryan has identified a detail list of various tangible and intangible factors that might create power imbalance between parties during mediation and also a detail discussion about how these factors of power might influence the outcome of mediation. The tangible factors identified by Bryan are income, education, occupation etc., while the intangible factors include status, dominance, depression, self esteem, reward expectations, sex-role ideology, and fear of achievement etc (Bryan 1992, 447).

[18] Neumann has also identified ten factors that affect power of an individual. These are: belief system (a belief that one is on the side of right); personality (the image one projects, how powerful one acts); self-esteem (the internalized image of one's self, how powerful one feels); gender (western society grants men greater power than women); selfishness (consistently putting oneself before others is a form of power); force (willingness to use coercion or threats and the fear engendered in others is a form of power); income/assets (power increases with income and the accumulation of assets); knowledge (possessing information is a form of power); status or age (increased status confers increased power, and power usually increases with age); and education (higher levels of education are associated with higher level of power etc (Neumann 1992, 229).

[19] Factors of power identified by Kelly are personality and characteristics, cognitive style and capabilities, knowledge base, economic self-sufficiency, gender and age differences, cultural and societal stereotypes and training, institutionalized hierarchies, and history and dynamics of disputant relationship (Kelly 1995, 89).

capacity to negotiate and that gender acts as a dominant factor which can undermine the negotiating capacity of women despite their possessing superior assets, such as education and income. The following sub-section discusses different theories to illustrate how these factors jointly affect women's negotiation capacity in mediation.

3.5.1 Gender and Negotiation

It is observed that women who are usually accorded a lower return from the society also demonstrate a lower expectation of reward when they attend negotiation. Since mediation is a type of assisted negotiation (Astor 1994, 150), in which two parties negotiate under a neutral third party to reach a settlement, power factors that are important for negotiation may also be important in mediation. Consequently women tend to acquire only a lower distributive share in mediated outcomes because of their lower expectation of reward from the society (Bryan 1992, 475–76). Generally, women are more likely to negotiate for what they think they can get and not for what they think they "should" get (Bryan 1992, 476).

The "traditional sex role ideology"[20] in a society usually leads women to expect minimal returns and so they end up with a lower share of the negotiated outcome. When a woman formulates her expectation, she generally compares what another woman might earn in a similar situation, not what another man might earn in a similar situation. Therefore, in a society in which men usually earn more than women for the performance of identical tasks, the expectation of a woman is usually lower than the expectation of a man in a similar situation (Bryan 1992, 475–76). Besides lower reward expectation, society also has an influence in formulating the

[20] Traditional sex role ideology anticipates a very different marital relationship (from modern or egalitarian sex role ideology): a spousal partnership exists, but equality and role interchange ability do not. Traditional sex role ideology depicts husbands as competent, assertive, and rightfully dominant, and wives as emotive, nurturing, passive, and rightfully submissive. The public domain becomes the husband's proper sphere of action, while the private family domain remains that of the wife. On the other hand, an egalitarian sex role ideology contemplates an equal partnership between spouses, a sharing of roles and equal power in marital decision-making (Bryan 1992, 465).

"lower self esteem"[21] of women which may hinder their confidence in negotiation (Kelly 1992, 229). Lower self-esteem may result from learned helplessness and internalisation of other's reflections about one's ineffectiveness and less worth (Bryan 1992, 481–82). People who have lower self-esteem tend to rely more on their luck and less on their own ability to negotiate. Society sometimes credits the luck of a woman rather the woman herself for doing a better job or attaining better results whereas men's successes are linked with their ability and competence (Bryan 1992, 472–74). However, it is rightly argued, in a later part of this discussion that such belief is not because of their personal attributes but because of their socialisation (Watson 1994, 118).

Studies have examined different theories in attempting to understand the impact that gender role socialisation has on the negotiation capacity of women. Based on those study results, the following discusses how gender may impair the negotiation capacity of women despite their possession of superior income, education, or employment status compared with their male counterparts.

3.5.2 Theories of Gender Role on Negotiation

Scholars have promulgated four different theories to explain how gender may interact with the possession of better income, education and occupational status to determine negotiated outcomes. These are the gender-role socialisation theory, the situational power theory, the gender-plus-power theory, and the expectation status theory (Watson 1994, 119).
According to the gender-role socialisation theory, women are socialised to be soft and co-operative whereas men are socialised to be tough and task-oriented and the respective negotiation patterns of the two groups reflect their pattern of socialisation (Bryan 1992, 482). However, according to situational power theory, no matter what the gender of a person, their capacity to negotiate depends on their possession of income, wealth, and education as well as other factors which may have an impact depending on

[21] Self esteem is the internalised image of oneself; how powerful one feels (Neumann 1992, 229). "An individual's self esteem comes from: (1) self-efficacy, the belief that one's own actions cause one's success in the world and, (2) internalisation of other's reflection regarding one's effectiveness and worth" (Bryan 1992, 472).

the context of a dispute (Watson 1994, 120). The gender-plus-power theory emphasises both gender-role socialisation theory and situational power theory while explaining the role gender plays in the negotiating capacity of women. Therefore, according to the gender-plus-power theory, a male who possesses superior income, wealth, education etc. may become much more competitive and a woman with little income, education or wealth may remain much more submissive in negotiation (Watson 1994, 120).

Although the gender-plus-power theory emphasises the importance of both gender role socialisation and the situational power of women in determining the capacity of women to negotiate, the interaction between gender and situational power and the relative strength of these two factors are not clear. One prediction about their relative strength, however, is made through the expectation status theory. According to this theory, gender creates expectations about the status of a person (Watson 1994, 120). Masculine gender strengthens the force of other factors, such as income, education and higher occupational status held by a man, while feminine gender negatively affects the strength of those other factors. Therefore, according to this theory, a man gets a better outcome when bargaining with a woman from a similar level of power (Watson 1994, 120).

Further, the expectation created through gender is so strong that even women who have higher incomes and better occupational status might not succeed in negotiating effectively with their male counterparts due to their gender (Nyquist & Spence 1986, 87–93). Research data shows that in small mixed-sex groups, women with higher status and power may fail to use their competitive or superior bargaining capacity against males. Women who, due to their higher status, have the potential to exert dominance are deterred from doing so in mixed-sex decision-making groups (Bryan 1992, 465). To test the impact of gender and power on capacity to negotiate, Nyquist & Spence's study (1986) tied one high-dominant person with another low-dominant person and had them work on a gender-neutral task.

As experienced in Nyquist & Spence's study (1986), in same-sex groups, the person with higher dominance took up the leadership in 73 percent of cases. In mixed-sex groups, the result varied considerably depending on the sex identity of the dominant person in the groups. For mixed-sex groups in which the dominant person was a male, the dominant man assumed the leadership in 93 percent of cases. However, in the cases of mixed-sex groups in which the dominant person was a female, in only 35 percent cases did the dominant female assume leadership. The result from the mixed-sex groups with dominant women indicates that, for as many as 65 percent of women, gender role expectation dominates their other means of exerting power in negotiation.

Therefore, when women with higher income, education, and occupational status are compared with their male counterparts, they may fail to attain a better outcome through negotiation. Bryan (1992, 465) has given some explanation of why women with higher status fail to be the leader in mixed sex groups. She explains this situation by using the notion of traditional sex-role ideology. As explained by Bryan (1992), adherence of women to traditional sex-role ideology persuades them to adopt socially acceptable submissive behaviour towards their male counterparts during mediation. Results and explanations from such studies are relevant to mediation because mediation also forms small groups where, with the presence of an unbiased mediator, parties negotiate with each other to settle for an outcome. Furthermore, as explained by the post-structural theory of power, the root of the traditional sex-role ideology which disempowers women lies in social discourses. The submissive behaviour in women has even more relevance to family mediation because research data shows that women face more difficulty negotiating with their husband than with other male persons (Bryan 1992, 464).

Hence, the possibility of women's reduced negotiation capability in family mediation would be more obvious in a society such as that of Bangladesh in which women not only have lower income, education and occupational status, but the dominant social discourses also discourage their equal participation with men. Because of their gender role, women may not become tough negotiators with their husbands during mediation. The poor status of women in household decision-making, as discussed in section 3.4, indicates that although some positive changes in terms of education, income, and occupation have been observed in Bangladesh, these developments are not enough to make women equally capable in negotiation. Therefore, women in Bangladesh might still require extra attention from mediators to bring their issues to the surface during mediation. Similar needs may exist for women attending mediation in other countries, if substantial gendered power disparity prevails in their societies.

3.6 Implications of Foucault's Post-Structural Theory of Power in Mediation: Opportunities for Using Legal Discourses

Mediation is not able to correct basic social ills, create social policy where none exists, or make available resources which do not exist. Mediation is also not optimally designed to change people's personalities, self-awareness, or insight into others' needs (Mayer 1987, 84). However, different scholars have designed varied techniques through which mediators can control gendered power disparity in mediation, including use of legal discourses or other discourses supportive of gender equality in mediation and efforts to restrain or even challenge the use of gender-biased dominant discourses in mediation. Based on the notion of post-structural power discussed earlier in section 3.2, this section explains how mediators can apply this post-structuralist notion of power to salvage women's negotiation capability in mediation.

Some scholars have argued that mediation is a forum in which people try to strengthen their own position and legitimize their own actions by telling positive stories on their own behalf and by discrediting those of others (Cobb 1993, 251). During mediation, the narrative of a party is more convincing when it is complete and culturally resonant (Cobb 1993, 252). Consequently, the understanding and assumptions which are embedded in any culture may act to limit what can or cannot be said and heard, and to make certain claims or stories less credible. This will inevitably have a gendered dimension. Social discourses may restrain women in mediation from forming a complete story, preventing them from telling some parts of it making them less culturally resonant (even when told completely). For example, in Bangladesh it is culturally accepted that a husband has the right to establish a coerced sexual relationship with his wife. Therefore, the claim of a wife against coerced sexual relations in her conjugal life may not be taken seriously as the claim is not culturally resonant. Further, society sometimes blames victimised women for family violence in their conjugal life. Therefore, women who have been blamed for being the victim of violence, or who have seen other women blamed, may decide to remain silent about past violence during their marital life (Astor 1995, 184). However, power created by dominant cultural discourses does not remain constant. As mentioned earlier, it is possible to create new discourses through disqualification of existing knowledge and the establishment of a new knowledge as truth. This process of change is termed as "geneology." As explained by Foucault (2008, 128):

> A geneology should be seen as a kind of attempt to emancipate historical knowledges from that subjection, to render them, that is, capable of opposition and of struggle against the coercion of a theoretical, unitary, formal and scientific discourse. It is based on a reactivation of local knowledges—of minor knowledges.

Though a mediator would not be able to change the social discourse outside the mediation room, the application of the concept of geneology in mediation opens up the possibility that a mediator who knows local culture can contribute to shape a coherent story by considering the marginalized discourse that would not be heard otherwise.

Along with their knowledge of dominant social discourses, mediators should seek some pro-women alternate discourse through which they can challenge gender biased, dominant social discourses and "emancipate" women's subjugated voice as "minor knowledge" in mediation. Without such an intervention, there is a possibility that the discourse of a less empowered party will lack careful consideration from mediators and, in effect, dominant discourses will be upheld in mediation. As mentioned earlier, to make an effective intervention, a mediator has to be aware of many cultural and institutional factors which may create power disparities between parties and, therefore, constrain their participation in mediation (Astor 2005, 35). Therefore, mediation under the post-structuralist view has the potential to consider the context of a dispute and to challenge the power disparity between parties under that context.

Following a post-structural notion of power, feminist scholars also argue that the subordinated role of women can be changed through continual good practice in different social institutions and that such institutional practice may have greater influence on the construction and reconstruction of the social roles of women (White 1991–92, 863–4; Bagshaw 2001, 209). These institutions can normalise new knowledge in the society by defining truth and what is right or wrong, "according to which the true and the false are separated" (Foucault 1980, 132). One of the ways of generating such knowledge can be by the enactment of new laws. This new knowledge through the enactment of progressive law may regenerate power by "detaching the power of truth" from social, economic and cultural hegemony "within which it operates at the present time" (Foucault 1980, 133). The social awareness programme run by different NGOs to uphold women's rights in society, as mentioned in chapter five, may also be able to change social discourses over time.

However, the increased codification of mediation practices in line with Western style facilitative mediation, in which mediators may not provide their evaluation on the basis of legal standards or other gender equalizing principles, will promote the existing power structure by normalizing dominant discourses in mediation (Pinzon 1996, 18; Bagshaw 2001, 206). If we deploy this Western knowledge to the East, without considering the diversity of contexts, the possibility is raised that such specialized knowledge may not be applicable to societies which have different cultural practices, values and power structures. For example, based on the equal standing of males and females in their society, Western mediators usually support facilitative mediation by ensuring "strict" neutrality and maximum party control in mediation. However, a practice of such neutrality in the East could end up with an agreement which reaffirms the existing power disparity in the society (Pinzon 1996, 14), rather minimizing it. Therefore, facilitative mediation with strict neutrality may not ensure fair justice to women in the East where widespread gender disparity in society places them in a more subjugated position in mediation.

3.7 Conclusion

Earlier discussion suggests that two variations of gendered power are at play in mediation. One is the power generated through dominant social discourses which usually favour men over women. This power is demonstrated in the voice of male participants in mediation. The other discourse which can be used to empower women is the discourse of law. This is in many ways a competing discourse because it can be used to challenge the dominant social discourse and uphold women's rights in mediation. As has been observed during mediation sessions in Bangladesh (see chapter four), mediators exercise continual surveillance, not only to maintain a process that ensures equal participation for both male and female but also to challenge discourses that run the risk of subjugating a woman's position in mediation. Although a mediator cannot influence or change the social outlook outside the mediation, under the post-structural view he or she can effectively manage the power play during mediation and endeavour to reach a fair outcome for both parties. Based on empirical observations, the next chapter demonstrates how a practice of evaluative mediation acts as an effective tool in the management of power disparity and ensuring better participation of women in mediation, leading to fairer outcomes for them.

CHAPTER FOUR

EVALUATIVE MEDIATION UNDER THE SHADOW OF LAW: AN IMPASSIVE COMBAT DEFUSING POWER DISPARITY IN MEDIATION

4.1 Introduction

Gendered disparity in power has an impact on mediation. The theoretical premise of the post-structuralist notion of power and impact on gender and mediation has been discussed in chapter three. This chapter introduces the notion of mediators' power during mediation, and links the post-structural notion of "change in power through discourses," with "mediators' power" to demonstrate that a mediator has an opportunity to control the power play in mediation. By uniting theories with practice, this chapter emphasizes the cutting-edge knowledge that, despite the existence of gendered power disparity, evaluative mediation may provide better access to justice for women by challenging the dominant discourses used by husbands to legitimise their own positions and by encouraging women to channel their otherwise hidden and marginalised discourses into mediation. This chapter further incorporates verbatim quotes from the observations of different in-court and out-of-court mediation sessions to demonstrate how those theories are brought to bear in real life mediation.

4.2 Evaluative Mediation: Revisiting the Model

Evaluative mediation is an assisted dispute resolution process with the objective of reaching a settlement according to the legal (or other) rights and entitlements of the parties and within the anticipated range of court, tribunal or industry outcomes (Boulle 2011, 44). Bush & Folger (2005, 44) depict the role of evaluative mediators as being to "steer [the parties] toward outcomes in substantial conformity with legal rights." Thus, evaluative mediation, as discussed so far, is a technique of mediation under which mediators can exercise a "normative" or rule-based evaluative approach to mediation to maintain equity between the parties. For the purpose of this book, evaluative mediation and normative evaluative mediation are terms used interchangeably.

Critics of evaluative mediation sometimes argue that only facilitative mediation can be considered as "pure mediation" (Alfini 1997, 929) and that mediation "should be reserved to the facilitative orientation" (Stulberg 1996–97, 990) and evaluative mediation is "wrong" (Alfini 1997, 928). It is "not mediation" (Feerick 1995, 103); thus it should be "discouraged or prohibited" (Alfini 1997, 927). However, advocates of evaluative mediation reject the idea of the facilitative mediation as "purist" (Putnam 1994, 339). They further argue that it is unlikely even for facilitative mediators "to be able to stand outside time and space and their own culturally and historically located values." Consequently, its content and process cannot be separated (Winslade and Monk 1994, 339). It can be said that evaluative mediation affects the principle of "strict" neutrality in mediation. It is also sometimes claimed that evaluative mediation hinders the principle of self-determination of parties. This is not necessarily true, as is discussed in later part of this chapter.

Advocates of evaluative mediations believe that it helps to attain some "higher good" (Taylor 1997, 222). An evaluative approach is particularly beneficial when substantial power imbalances exist between the parties (Marthaler 1989, 61; Lerman, citied in Astor 1990, 147; Bagshaw 2001, 217–18; Boulle 2005, 222). As discussed in chapters two and three, the neutrality of mediators conducting facilitative mediation between parties with substantial power imbalances may be meaningless because any effort to maintain equality between unequals only results in inequality (Astor 1994a, 153).

However, as discussed in chapter two, considerable debate exists on the nature and extent of evaluation and whether an evaluative mediator can succeed by maintaining party autonomy on the outcome of mediation. Using Riskin's grid on mediators' evaluation, this chapter examines the process of evaluation exercised by mediators both in the in-court and out-of-court mediations observed in Bangladesh. This chapter also demonstrates how impartial evaluative mediators maintain a balance between their level of intervention and party autonomy to ensure party self-determination on the outcome of mediation.

4.3 Understanding Mediators' Evaluative Role in Mediation: An Underpinning on Riskin's Grid

Different interventions made by mediators in practice have been classified by Riskin (1996) in a grid that he termed "Mediator Techniques." Riskin classifies his grid not only on the basis of facilitative mediation, but extends it to include interventions used in evaluative mediation. By incorporating evaluative mediation in his grid, he recognizes the use of the relatively activist and interventionist role of mediators in practice. Riskin therefore clarifies the benefits of using a relatively interventionist role by mediators. According to him, in evaluative mediation, mediators "by providing assessments, predictions, or direction, remove[s] some of the decision-making burden from the parties and their lawyers" (Riskin 1996, 44). Consequently, it can be sometimes easier for the parties to reach an agreement. As discussed in chapter two, in high-power-distance cultures of the East, parties attending mediation may have a pre-conceived cultural expectation that they may get some advice or expert opinion from mediators that would help them to make their decision. Therefore, such an evaluative practice of mediators would be both beneficial to and acceptable by parties attending mediation in the East.

Riskin's grid is sometimes criticised by scholars because they see it as undermining the core norms of mediation—mediators' neutrality and parties' self-determination (Feerick 1995; Kovach & Love 1996; Stulberg 1996–97; Alfini 1997). According to Stulberg (1996–97, 1003), Riskin's grid imposes:

> A pedigree test on ideas: if it comes from the parties, the mediator remains facilitative; if the mediator is the source of an idea, the mediator is evaluative. However, that means that persons are autonomous agents only if they entertain ideas for which they are the source. That vision renders incoherent the notion of personal autonomy and the role of voluntary decision-making that lies at the heart of the mediation enterprise.

However, counter-arguments against such criticisms have been made by a number of scholars (Bickerman 1996; Moberly 1997; Stark 1997; Redfern 1998). Though evaluative mediation, as included in Riskin's grid, is criticised due to the interventionist role of the mediators, such intervention is often deployed by the mandate of the parties themselves (Riskin 1993, 103; Rothfield 2001, 242). That is to say, if the answer to the question of whether parties decide by informed choice that they want the mediator to act in an evaluative role is "yes; the mediator ought to evaluate and it is

Fig. 4.1. Riskin's grid on mediation

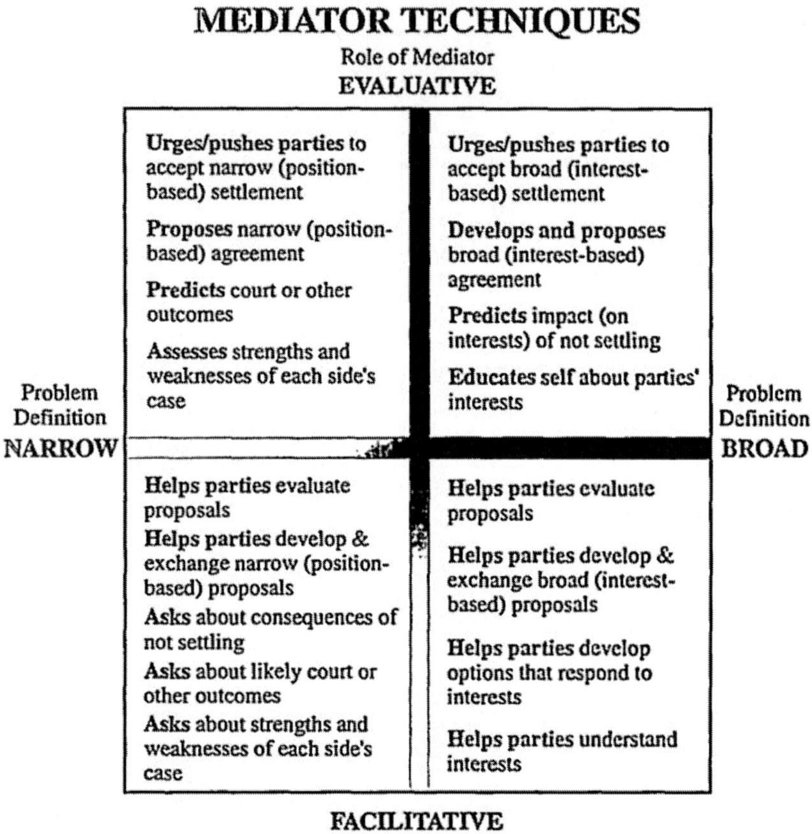

Source: Riskin 1996, 25.

ethical and it is perfectly appropriate" (Riskin 1995, 103). Stempel (1997, 949) also stresses the need for flexible mediation and use of evaluative techniques. Rothfield (2001, 245) notes that when mediators make their evaluation on the basis of a mandate from the parties that he or she can take an evaluative role, the mandate itself implies that the parties' choice is informed and they are self-determined. As explained by King (1999, 67): "The normative-evaluative model may also transgress the rules of neutrality, but in some cases, like the therapeutic model, may be necessary in an educative way at particular times." Therefore, despite the extensive debate around evaluative mediation and its dichotomy with facilitative mediation, its existence will be valid as long as it is "done in a manner that is consistent with the governing aspirations of having parties engage in the settlement-building process" (Stulberg 1996–97, 1004).

As mentioned earlier, according to Riskin's grid, mediation can be conducted broadly in two modes (1) facilitative and (2) evaluative. As shown in Fig. 4.1, both modes of mediation can be used with a broad party interest-based approach, or a narrow rights-based approach. In a rights-based approach, a resolution of dispute is sought only on the basis of the rights of the parties, for example rights that are given in law. In an interest-based approach, a dispute is resolved with the aim of maximising party welfare. However, in reality a solution may be sought with a trade-off between these two continuums. As observed by Riskin (1996, 17):

> At one end of this continuum sit narrow problems, such as how much one party should pay the other. At the other end, lie very broad problems, such as how to improve the conditions in a given community or industry. In the middle of this continuum are problems of intermediate breadth, such as how to address the interests of the parties or how to transform the parties involved in the dispute.

Criteria for broad facilitative mediation are placed in the lower right quadrant of the grid (Fig. 4.1). In broad facilitative mediation, mediators emphasise party interests that increase their welfare. On the other hand, criteria set in the lower left quadrant indicate narrow facilitative mediation, where mediators emphasise a narrow rights-based approach, such as the rights of parties given by law. Criteria for broad evaluative mediation are set in the upper right quadrant where mediators make evaluations about the content and outcome of a dispute and help parties to settle their dispute based on their best interests. The upper left quadrant shows the criteria for a narrow evaluative mediation where parties settle their disputes based on their rights, for example those given by law. However, though mediators may have some preference towards an individual grid, they may not strictly adhere to that particular grid in every situation. As observed by Riskin (1996, 40–1):

> The grid can help us envision an ideal mediator for any individual case. [Mediators] would be sufficiently flexible to employ the most appropriate orientation, strategies, and techniques as the participants' needs present themselves.

Riskin's grid not only helps us to identify whether mediation is facilitative or evaluative, but also to understand whether mediation is being conducted by strictly adhering to the provisions of law or considering party interests. The observations of the features of the in-court and out-of-court mediation process discussed below, together with Riskin's grid which is designed to identify a mediator's procedural orientation, assisted us to define the style of mediation being practised in Bangladesh. The empirical study comprised observations[22] of eighteen mediation sessions[23] (nine in-courts and nine out-of-court) and twelve interviews[24] with mediators (six in-courts and six out-of-court) in three districts[25] of Bangladesh: *Dhaka*, *Mymensingh* and *Narayanganj*.

---

[22] Observations of mediation sessions assisted in cross-checking the assertions made by mediators, for example, for any unconscious exaggeration or misrepresentation made by them during interview (Caspi 1998, 82). However, it was possible that participants would modify their behaviour, words and conduct as a reaction to the presence of a third person during mediation. In all stages of the study, ethical standards were taken into account.

[23] To observe mediation sessions, an observation schedule for both in-court and out-of-court mediation was prepared. Mediation sessions were chosen randomly using the lists of on-going mediations collected from the court registry and NGO registry respectively.

[24] Semi-structured interviews seemed the most appropriate way to access further data about the approach of mediators. Though the interview schedules included open-ended questions, the interviews were focused in nature.

[25] To represent urban, rural and suburban areas, the three districts of *Dhaka* division were chosen under this study were *Dhaka*, *Mymensingh* and *Narayanganj*. The features of urbanisation determining which of these three districts were urban, suburban, and rural are based on the percentage of women living in rural, urban and suburban areas according to the latest Population Census Report in 2007. These districts were chosen in such a way that the difference between rural and urban women could easily be understood from the sample. For example, in aggregate, 77.33 percent of all women in Bangladesh live in rural areas (BBS 2007, 12–14). But the *Dhaka*, *Mymensingh* and *Narayanganj* districts were chosen to represent urban, rural and suburban areas where 9.35, 44.62 and 85.58 percent women lived in rural areas respectively (BBS 2007, 14–15). Thus, the sample districts were not chosen to ameliorate the national average of rural women rather than to make the rural urban difference more vivid in this sample. The choice of sample on the basis of rural, urban and suburban variation of the districts also reflects the difference in the literacy rate of adult women and women's participation in economic activity. For example, among the three districts chosen, the percentage of literate adult women in the *Dhaka* (urban) district was 60.74 percent, compared with 48.10 percent in the *Narayanganj* (suburban) and 34.84 per cent in the *Mymensingh* (rural) districts (BBS 2007, 123). Likewise, regarding the economic participation of women, the rate within the *Dhaka*, *Mymensingh* and

4.4 Process of Evaluative Mediation in Bangladesh: An Empirical Observation

4.4.1 Process of Out-of-Court Evaluative Mediation

In Bangladesh, the most popular and women-oriented, out-of-court mediation providers are Non-Government Organisations (NGOs) when compared with other modes.[26] A number of NGOs[27] provide out-of-court

---

Narayanganj districts was 16 percent, 8.69 percent and 7.77 percent respectively (BBS 2007, 137). As discussed in Chapter three, these factors may affect women's capacity to negotiate in mediation. Moreover, the three districts examined in this study incorporate 11.83 percent of women living in the 61 districts of Bangladesh who attended family courts in 2007 (BBS 2007, 12–15). The sample of these three districts can be considered as representative of Bangladesh as they cover the variation in rural, urban and suburban areas, and are the domiciles of more than 11 percent of the total population of women in Bangladesh. The total number of women in Bangladesh in 2007 was 60,264,000. The number of women in the three districts *Dhaka*, *Narayanganj* and *Mymensingh* was 3,800,000; 1,012,000 and 2,193,000 respectively (BBS 2007, 12).

[26] Another alternative means of out-of-court mediation is village *shalish,* which is generally conducted by a group of persons from the village, including village headmen and other local elites. Village *shalish* is accessible to women without any cost (Harrold 2007); however, "[i]n most of the cases … judgments [of *shalish* fall] harshly on women" (Casper & Kamal 1995, 53). This is a system that has been found to be corrupt and prejudiced against women (Jahan et al. 1995, 77–8; The Asia Foundation 2002a: Siddiqi 2006a, 15; Khair 2008, 115). There are also some other *quasi*-formal bodies, such as Arbitration Councils and Village Courts, which conduct *shalish* to resolve disputes locally. They are formed by the Chairman of the Union *Parishad* (union council—the lowest tier of local government) and two nominated persons from each party; this is commonly known as UP *shalish*. However, these bodies have mostly been found to be non-functional (Ameen 2005a; BLAST 2007).

[27] Amongst different NGO mediation providers, including *Madaripur* Legal Aid Association (MLAA), *Ain-o-Shalish Kendra* (ASK), Bangladesh National Women Lawyers' Association (BNWLA) and Bangladesh Legal Aid and Services Trust (BLAST), Bangladesh Legal Aid and Services Trust (BLAST) was chosen for most of the purposes because it best met the criteria. BLAST operates all over Bangladesh, and like other typical out-of-court NGO mediation providers it conducts mediation informed by law (The Asia Foundation 2002a, 18–26). One of the popular services of BLAST is to provide a legal aid and advocacy service to its clients if their mediation effort to resolve a dispute fails: "BLAST utilizes a

mediation services in Bangladesh. On the day of mediation, a staff lawyer from the relevant NGO usually acts as a mediator and presides over the session maintaining the following steps:

Initiation with ground rules: All of the mediation sessions attended in various NGO registries start with the mediator outlining the ground-rules:

- that both husband and wife have an equal right to participate in the mediation session
- that both will be heard equally
- that one party should not talk while the other is expressing his or her view
- that sufficient time will be given to the other when one has finished his or her part
- that friends, relatives, neighbours and others attending mediation are also called on not to interrupt the parties to express their own grievances.

As was shared by the NGO-mediators during interviews, and also observed while attending mediation sessions, after stating the ground rules, that mediators try to create an informal, congenial and non-confrontational environment so that both parties, especially women, can feel relaxed and express their grievances freely. As observed in Bangladesh, at the beginning of the session the mediators clarify that NGO is not a court, and so parties can express their own choices according to their convenience. As expressed by all of the NGO mediators interviewed for the study, in order to make the environment friendly for women NGOs encourage greater participation by women in their mediation as well as including women lawyers and paralegals as mediators.

Gathering information on the issue of the dispute: NGO mediators usually ask the women to share the facts of their dispute first, then the other parties. Such a strategy is beneficial for women because, as identified by Cobb (1993, 245), the first speaker has an opportunity to tell the story from a positive perspective, i.e. to explain his or her own position positively and put a positive light on the facts (Astor 2005, 16).

---

people-oriented model for mediation which also adheres to the jurisprudence principles of the country." See The Asia Foundation (2002a, 26).

Establishing a positive light at the beginning is important because "once imprisoned in a negative position, few persons are able to construct alternative positive positions for themselves" (Cobb & Rifkin, cited in Cobb 1993, 253). All of the NGO mediators interviewed gave women an opportunity to share their grievances freely when they first came to the respective NGO office to file their complaint. The mediators also stated that about 80 to 90 percent of women speak freely about their claims in mediation.

Mediators' evaluation of the content of the dispute: In all mediation sessions that I observed at NGO offices, mediators challenged the statements made by husbands and other attending family members and friends. For example, in one mediation session observed at NGO in the *Dhaka* district, a husband claimed reconciliation with his wife. Addressing the mediator, the maternal uncle of the husband who was also present at the mediation session said:

Uncle of husband: When she [wife] went to my residence with a complaint against her husband, I asked her [wife] whether your husband tortures her; but she replied "No." If so, why she is not returning to her husband?

Mediator: She might say "No" in your house out of fear, but now she is saying that her husband tortured her and has not paid proper maintenance. Moreover, they made a love marriage. So, if still there is love and affection and the husband provides proper maintenance, why will she not return?

In another NGO mediation in the *Mymensingh* district, the wife demanded her full amount of dower[28] written in the marriage contract, while the husband claimed that he had already paid dower to his wife:

---

[28] A key feature of all Muslim marriage contracts that differs from a standard Western civil marriage is a provision of dower *(Mehr),* a sum of money or any other valuables that the husband gives, or undertakes to give, to the bride upon marriage.

Husband: [to mediators] I have already paid her dower through ornaments and other valuables during marriage.
Wife: Those were my marriage gifts.
Mediator: [to the husband] In your marriage contract have you mentioned the valuables you are claiming now?
Husband: No...
Mediator: Though it is generally believed that anything paid to a bride during marriage will be treated as dower, to claim it legally, one needs to mention it in the marriage contract. Otherwise, it will be considered as a marriage gift, even if you go for litigation.

Similarly, in another NGO mediation session observed in the *Mymensingh* district, a husband claimed that he would not provide maintenance to his wife because she did not carry out his orders. The mediator made an evaluation of the wife's right to maintenance as follows:

Husband: I will not provide maintenance to her because I forbid her to go to my neighbour's house, but she does not care.
Wife: I need to go there to fetch water. How can I run my daily work without water? Why doesn't he [husband] bring water from other places if he does not want me to go there?
Mediator: [to the husband] Why do not you bring water for your wife?
Husband: I have to leave home in the early morning. So I do not have much time to fetch water for her.
Mediator: You should make an alternative source of water available if you do not want your wife to go to your neighbour's house. To get maintenance is her legal right. You cannot stop her maintenance. If your wife claims her right to maintenance in the court, your defence to deny her right to maintenance on this ground will be rejected in court too.

Therefore, as observed during mediation sessions conducted at NGO offices, mediators protected women's rights by emphasising their legal rights while evaluating the content of a dispute.

Assisted bargaining under the shadow of law: At this stage, while mediators help women to negotiate for a better outcome, they advise what women might get if they do not settle in mediation and opt for litigation. At all NGO mediations I attended, I observed NGO mediators using different provisions of law to protect the rights of women. For example, in one particular NGO mediation, a mediator assisted negotiation under the shadow of polygamy law to protect the rights of the woman as follows:

Mediator:	Now what do you want to do? [Asking parties to develop their own proposals]
Wife:	I want to live with my husband, but not with that second wife.
Husband:	I want to live with them both [first and second wives].
Father of the wife:	He has made his second marriage without taking any permission from my daughter. Now we will sue him.
Mediator:	[to the husband] Haven't you taken permission from your wife? [Gathering information about the content of a dispute]
Husband:	No.
Mediator:	[to the husband] The law is now very strict in this regard and you might get imprisoned if they sue. [Assessing weakness of one party's claim]
Mediator:	[to the husband again] What would you do now? According to law, you may pay dower money to one of them and get divorced from her. [Helping parties to develop option].
Husband:	[thinking]
Mediator:	[to the wife] What is the amount of your dower? [Educating self about parties' interests]

Wife: BDT 50, 000

Mediator: Would you consider getting divorced from your husband after getting BDT 50, 000 or do you wish to continue with him?
[Helping parties to develop option]

Wife: I do not want money; I want to get back my husband.
[Wife's strong desire towards restitution]

Mediator: [to the husband] What do you think now? You have already heard what your wife said.
[Though indirectly, the mediator is giving emphasis to the desire of the wife].

Husband: I will divorce my second wife.

However, while protecting the right of one woman in mediation, mediators were observed to be conscious about the non-infringement of any third party interest, especially the interest of any other women who were not attending the mediation session but whose interest would be affected by the outcome. For example, in the mediation session just mentioned, the mediator used legal provisions to protect the rights of the second wife when the husband decided to divorce her and live with the first wife. The mediator replied to the husband:

Mediator: Well, you have decided to divorce your second wife and live with the first one; but in that case you have to wait for a few months. As I have been informed by your father, your second wife is now expecting. According to law, you cannot divorce your wife during her pregnancy.
[Predicting court outcomes]

Mediator: [to the husband again] Moreover, you have to pay her unpaid dower, maintenance up to the delivery of her expecting baby and periodic maintenance to any child born from this marriage.
[Protecting the right of third parties not attending mediation]

Mediator: [to the wife] When claimed, you should not restrain your husband from paying the periodic child maintenance. If the child is a

	boy, maintenance should be paid until his maturity at eighteen, and if the child is a girl, until her marriage. [Helping parties understand interests]
Mediator:	[to the wife again] Do you agree?
Wife:	Yes, I do.
Mediator:	Fine, now we may proceed to draft the mediation agreement. Shall we?

The example mentioned above indicates that although the mediator allowed parties to make their own decisions, by reminding the husband of his legal obligations to pay dower and maintenance to his divorcee wife [and unborn child], he tried to frame a solution under the dictates of law and to protect the rights of third parties, i.e. the divorcee wife and unborn child who, though not present at the mediation session, would be affected by the outcome of mediation.

Attaining fair outcomes for women: When the facts of a dispute and the position of both parties in attaining a solution are clear to mediators, they ask parties to express their desired solution. Women and their guardians are usually given the first chance to share their views. Generally, as observed in NGO mediations, the outcome is reached as follows:

- After hearing from both parties, NGO mediators initially asked them if there is any possibility of reconciliation. However, mediators did not encourage or force parties to reconcile; rather they ensured that any agreed reconciliation was made with the wife's free consent by asking her whether she agreed voluntarily or not. Mediators also stressed the point that the wife is not bound to accept the proposal of reconciliation by the husband and she has a complete right to refuse her husband's proposal. In such a case, NGO mediators helped women to get a fair share of their post-separation entitlements.

- In the case of attaining an outcome for dower and maintenance, NGO mediators tried to ensure that the woman's dower and maintenance as stated in their marriage contract were recovered in the shortest possible time. However, as observed during the mediation sessions and confirmed later through interviews with mediators, NGO mediators did not pressure parties to accept a particular amount of dower or maintenance as outcome; rather they tried to ensure fair outcomes for women by informing them of their legal and religious rights in this regard.

- In the case of custody of children, however, the prime objective of mediators was to ensure the welfare of the children. This motive of emphasising child welfare when determining custody of children corresponds with the legal provisions set out in the *Guardianship and Wards Act 1890*.

Agreement writing and closure: Finally, an attempt is made to resolve the differences between the two sides with terms and conditions which are acceptable to both parties. Mediators summarise the terms and conditions under which the two parties decide to settle and write down those points in a prescribed form. The agreement is then read to the parties and signed by the mediator(s) as representatives of the NGO, by both the parties, and by one guardian as witness from each side. While compiling the agreement, NGO mediators have a final look at the equity of the agreement reached. If any one or more of the conditions seems inequitable for the woman, the mediator explains to the parties its negative consequences and asks the parties to consider revising their terms. According to all of the NGO mediators interviewed, their objective was to ensure that women would obtain fair outcomes in comparison to what they might obtain through litigation.

4.4.2 Process of In-Court Evaluative Mediation

In-court family mediation in Bangladesh is conducted in family courts in two different stages. Firstly, at the pre-trial stage judge-mediators attempt to mediate a dispute before the initiation of trial (section 10 of the *Family Courts Ordinance 1985*). Secondly, mediation at pre-judgment stage may be conducted if the pre-trial mediation effort fails and the litigation begins. For pre-judgement mediation, judge-mediators take a further initiative after the end of the hearing but before the pronouncement of a decree (section 13 of the *Family Courts Ordinance 1985*). It is worth noting that in the family courts of Bangladesh, judges act as mediators both in pre-trial and pre-judgment mediation. It was observed during mediation sessions that the judge-mediators conducted pre-trial mediations in the following manner:

Initiation of mediation: Mediations are held in the Chambers of judge-mediators, which are adjacent to their courtrooms. At the initiation, parties enter the mediation room and take their seats. Generally, in most cases, judge-mediators do not allow lawyers to accompany their clients. However, in around 20 to 25 percent of cases, clients are accompanied by their lawyers at the initiation of mediation. An in-court mediator, who is also a judge of the respective family court, then invites parties to share their grievances. In eight out of nine cases observed, judge-mediators invited the women to express their claims first. Although husbands sometimes tried to interfere when their wives were speaking, judge-mediators played an intermediate role to ensure that the women could continue. Similar activities were observed in all of the in-court mediation sessions attended in Bangladesh. In the one remaining case the husband took the floor first as the mediator invited parties to share their grievances without mentioning who should speak first.

Although it appeared generally that women were able to express their views in mediation, in two cases lawyers were seen to help them in formulating their claims. At this stage, mediators listened to the parties attentively and generally did not allow the other party or lawyers to interrupt. In two out of nine in-court mediation sessions observed, judge-mediators permitted lawyers to attend the beginning of a session, then after an initial hearing from both the parties, lawyers were requested to leave the mediation room.

This might be because in an empirical study made by Zahir (1988, 8) the "judges uniformly held [that] the lawyers of both parties and absence of witnesses [are] responsible for causing adjournments" and the consequent delay in disposal of cases. In most cases, judges blamed lawyers for delaying the disposal of cases. Similarly, all in-court mediators interviewed for this study expressed their reservations about allowing lawyers to attend the full session. In only one of the nine in-court mediation sessions observed were lawyers allowed to attend from the beginning to end of mediation. In addition, all in-court mediators interviewed expressed their reservations about lawyers being permitted to attend the full session. All in-court mediators alleged during interviews that lawyers do not co-operate to achieve a quicker resolution through mediation for the sake of their business interests. Lawyers may prolong a case through lack of co-operation (Menkal-Meadow 1993; Morris 1999) because they can charge the parties for their time for as long as the litigation continues. During interview, one judge-mediator in *Dhaka* district pointed out that:

> Parties settled the dispute at pre-judgement mediation conducted at the 29th court day. In fact, this case could be resolved with the same outcome [BDT 300,000 as dower money] through pre-trial mediation held at the sixth court day. But that was not possible only because lawyers mislead the defendant, saying that he has to pay much less if the case is resolved through litigation.

Setting the ground-rules for mediation: The process of in-court mediation starts with an opening speech by the mediator setting some ground-rules for each party to follow throughout the mediation session. As observed in different in-court mediation sessions in Bangladesh, the ground rules usually stated by the judge-mediators are:

- It is an informal process whereby both of the parties can say anything beyond pliant and written statement; whatever will be said during the mediation sessions cannot be used as evidence subsequently in any court of law. Since it is an informal process and not a court, the mediator shall not pronounce any judgment as a court does after hearing from both of the parties
- Each party is invited to share all of their feelings and demands without any hesitation
- Each party will get sufficient time to express his or her view
- When one party is sharing his or her views, the other party will not interrupt
- If anyone has an objection or constructive suggestion, they may share it when their turn comes or seek the attention of the mediator

The objective of the mediation session is to resolve the dispute, not to lay blame. Though all mediators did not use the same words to state these ground-rules, those mentioned above were the major ones common for all. After setting the ground-rules, mediators start to gather more information on the content of the dispute.

Mediators gather information about the issue of disputes and make their evaluation on the content: It has already been mentioned that women are usually given the first chance to share their views in mediation. In eight out of nine mediation sessions observed in courts, judge-mediators asked women to tell their story first. Mediators, however, were observed to interrupt parties during storytelling and afterwards during negotiation.

Sometimes, they used evaluative statements to cross-check the validity of a claim made by a party. For example, in one in-court mediation the wife was accused of stealing by the husband:

Husband:	She has stolen BDT 50, 000 from my book-shelf while leaving the house.
Mediator:	How do you know this? How can you be sure?
Husband:	She has a habit of stealing money.
Wife:	Liar!
Mediator:	If you know that she has a habit of stealing money, you need to be cautious about that. Why did you keep so much money in an open place? [Assessing weakness of one party's claim]

In another in-court mediation, a wife claimed that her husband had not paid maintenance to her during a period of one and a half years when she had left her husband (though not divorced) and lived with her parents:

Wife:	He has not paid any maintenance and not even visited me a single day.
Mediator:	[to the husband] Why didn't you visit her and pay her maintenance? Don't you wish to continue your relationship with your wife? [Educating self about parties' interests]
Husband:	I did not know the address of her father's house.
Mediator:	[to the wife] Is that so?
Wife:	No, he was informed about my address while we were trying to resolve our dispute through community mediation earlier. My father has been living at the same address for the last four years, but he has not contacted me.

At this stage the mediator made his evaluation saying what the husband should do under such conditions:

Mediator:	[to the husband] You could visit the community mediation office and ask them to hand over the periodic maintenance payment

	to your wife on your behalf. Have you tried that? [Evaluation on the content of the dispute]
Husband:	I made a payment through the community mediation office once. Afterwards, I lost my job and so cannot continue.
Mediator:	[to the husband] You should have informed the community mediation office and also your wife about your incapability. [Evaluation] Did you do so?
Husband:	No, I did not.
Mediator:	That means you were not serious in your commitment. [Strong evaluation] [Assessing the weakness of husband's claim]

If we assess the mediator's role in the situation described above according to Riskin's (1996) grid, it can be said that in-court mediators play an evaluative role by making their evaluation on the content of disputes: they assess the weakness of claims made by husbands, both legally and morally, and predict court outcomes which may promote women's rights.

Assisted bargaining for outcomes under the shadow of law: As observed in the mediation sessions, when disputants have arguments with each other about any issue, judge-mediators are likely to inform the parties about the probable legal consequences that might follow if they go to litigation to resolve the issue. They also inform parties about their rights and duties relating to a dispute. While explaining such legal points, in all of the in-court mediation sessions that were observed, judge-mediators highlighted the strong legal position of a wife during mediation. However, where no specific remedy is mentioned in law, mediators made their evaluation to maximize party interest.

1. Maximizing child welfare

Promotion of party interest was apparent in some of the observed mediation sessions that related to the custody of children. In family courts, the provisions of the *Guardianship and Wards Act 1890* are used to determine child custody after divorce. According to section 5 of the *Guardianship and Wards Act 1890*, in Bangladesh major emphasis shall be given to the welfare of children when determining child custody. It was also observed in two in-court mediations that the consent of the minor appeared to be an important consideration in this regard.

For example, in one of the in-court mediation sessions, a father claimed the custody of his seven and a half year-old son on the grounds that, according to the Islamic law, a father is entitled to physical custody of his son.

Father: I have asked the *Imam* [religious priest] of our local mosque. My boy is more than seven. So, I will get custody.

Mediator: [to the boy attending mediation] Little fellow, will you be with your father?
[Educating self about parties' interests]

At that point, the boy attached himself even closer to his mother and held her even more tightly.

Mother: [to the father of the boy] Don't you know my boy is scared of you?

Mediator: As the child has been living with his mother since divorce, he seems to have more emotional attachment to his mother. Moreover, he is studying in a school located in a place near to his mother's residence. So, it may hamper the smooth development of the child if he is taken away from his present condition.
[Proposing broad (interest-based) agreement]

2. Attaining fair outcomes for women

In attaining fair outcomes for women, mediators used the more equitable "legal discourses" to challenge the legitimacy of a husband defended by patriarchal "social discourses" that would otherwise marginalise women's position in mediation. Since legislations and case-laws in Bangladesh presently protect women's rights,[29] evaluative mediators can upheld women rights and still maintain their impartial role in mediation by following pro-women legal discourses. As observed in the mediation sessions and later confirmed through interviews with mediators, the primary objective of four out of six judge-mediators was to reconcile the parties, especially when they had children. Mediators sometimes highlighted certain social points of view. For example, the social dignity of a child among his or her peers may be compromised when the child cannot answer who his or her father is or where he or she lives. However, mediators did not force reconciliations between the couples. If reconciliation was not possible, the next-best objective was to ensure fair outcomes for the women. Another important objective highlighted by a number of mediators was to ensure a quicker and less costly settlement of the dispute through mediation.

All the in-court mediators interviewed emphasised ensuring fair outcomes through mediation and helping the parties to determine their own outcomes. While assisting parties to get fair outcomes through mediation, mediators did not impose the outcome; rather, they helped the parties to understand their relative bargaining power by saying what a party can or cannot expect from the other according to law and if the case went to litigation.

[29] The shift in the attitude of the judiciary can be understood if the cases reported after the emergence of Bangladesh are considered. As observed by Justice S. M. Hussain: "It must be observed that the courts while adjudicating on family dispute and administering personal law shall take into account not only the factual and the legal position and questions involved in a particular case but also consider the social dynamics when the concept of law is changed in a changing society. Previously decades before where a wife's claim for a divorce could be resisted for well-established reasons it cannot be resisted for the self-same reasons because of the very basic fact that with the changing society women are coming of their own and their independence of mind and will must be respected while considering the legal and contractual obligation in marriage between man and woman as such." See *Hasina Ahmed vs. Syed Abul Fazal* (1980) 32 DLR 297.

Similarly, as was observed in all in-court mediation sessions in Bangladesh, mediators generally assessed the strengths and weaknesses of the parties' cases based on their legal rights, but they did not urge or push parties to agree to any specific settlement suggested by them. Instead, they took a broader perspective to serve party interest through mediation, taking law as the basis and assessing the outcome attainable through litigation. A quantitative analysis on the fairness of mediated outcomes is discussed in chapter six.

Agreement writing and closure of mediation: When agreement is reached through mediation, the mediator asks the lawyers from both sides to enter into his or her chambers and write down the terms and conditions of the mediated agreement reached. A date is then set to place the agreement before court. On that day, the court makes a decree on that agreement and makes it binding on the parties concerned. However, before such a decree is made, mediators go through the terms and conditions to ensure that they have been written accurately and as agreed by the parties before the court. Sometimes, I found that judge-mediators added safety clauses. For example, mediators sometimes asked husbands to make payments of dower or maintenance money through the court to make sure that any non-payment could be readily identified by the court.

4.5 Evaluative Mediation to Control Power Disparity in Mediation: Mediator's Powers and Possibilities

Mediation is an empowering process (Davis & Salem 1984, 18–19; Neumann, 1992, 231–32). Using Foucault's notion of the post-structural notion of power, this section demonstrates how a mediator can minimise the impact of gendered power disparity during mediation by challenging the dominant discourses — a source of male power in society, and by upholding gender equalising legal discourses to protect women's rights and empowerment (Cobb & Rifkin 1991, 62; Taylor 1997, 221; Astor 2002, 75–6). Different scholars have developed their own typologies and identified different factors that may affect the power of an individual. Mayer's (2000) typology explains how mediators affect power disparity between parties in mediation and is of special significance as it was developed specifically in the context of mediation and relates to the powers of a mediator (Mayer 2000, 55–60). More particularly, the primacy of Mayer's typology rests on his explicit inclusion of "structural power," which includes "the objective resources people bring to a conflict, the legal and political prerogatives, the formal authority they have and the real choices that exist." Mayer has identified different forms of power that are held by a mediator such as procedural power, formal authority, legal prerogatives, definitional power, etc. On the other hand, Mayer defines "personal power" of the parties as "determination, knowledge, wits, courage, and communication skills" (2000, 54).

In the following section, a post-structural notion of power is applied with Mayer's (2000) typology of power in mediation to demonstrate how a mediator may apply different forms of power to minimize the impact of gendered power disparity between parties in mediation. The sources of mediator power included in Mayer's typology assist them in creating a level playing field for males and females attending mediation and thereby maintain procedural equity. As demonstrated in the following section, mediators use their sources of power either to promote the participation of parties who are in a subjugated position or to control the participation of parties who otherwise have exerted excessive power in mediation and thereby jeopardized the participation of their counterpart.

4.5.1 Mayer's Typology on Mediator's Power: How It Operates to Minimise the Impact of Gendered Power Disparity in Mediation

In his article "The Dynamics of Conflict Resolution," Mayer (2000) develops a list of thirteen different types of power that may affect a party's ability to negotiate during mediation and also a mediator's ability to exert control over the process of negotiation. Although Mayer has not developed his typology with particular mention to evaluative mediation, all these avenues can be used by evaluative mediators as a means to express their evaluations to control power play and minimize power disparity between parties. During my observation of mediation sessions in Bangladesh, I found in-court and out-of-court mediators generally use the following nine sources of power to manage power disparity between parties and ensure the effective participation of women in mediation.[30]

[30] Besides the nine different types of power of mediators, Mayer (2000) discussed "resource power" that is not limited to financial resources, but rather extended to time, control over resources and reputation and resource and "sanction power" that may originate to a person from her or his ability to reward others, or the ability to inflict harm through imposing sanctions. Withholding of any reward is also treated

Formal authority: The most important power that a mediator possesses is formal authority. It is the authority given to a person by another person or organisation, or by an action of law (Mayer 2000, 55). A business organisation, for example, may authorise its CEO to hire or fire new employees. Likewise, law bestows formal authority on parents to look after their children. During mediation, mediators gain formal authority to intervene in the dispute resolution process between parties. This authority may arise out of statutory authority to perform their function or because both parties have authorised the mediator to intervene during mediation (Mayer 1987, 80; 2000, 55). As generally observed in all mediation sessions in Bangladesh, every in- and out-of-court mediator used their formal power to control the participation of the parties throughout mediation. Mediators do not just allow the parties in mediation to make their own decisions; rather, they intervene and interact between the parties to shape fair outcomes.

Procedural power: Procedural power is the power to control or influence the process of an event (Mayer 2000, 57). Because of their formal authority and knowledge of mediation theory and practice, mediators have the power to control the mediation process and ensure effective participation for both parties involved. For example, in the eighteen mediation sessions observed in Bangladesh, mediators generally invited women to share their story first. This simple procedural step could have a profound impact on emphasising the marginalised discourses of women in mediation, as a research study shows that parties given the opportunity to frame their story first had a much higher rate of success. This is because it is difficult for the subsequent speakers to come out of a negative position and establish their own position (Cobb and Rifkin 1991).

Definitional power: In mediation, definitional power means the ability to define the issues of a dispute and its potential outcome (Mayer 2000, 58). In cases of evaluative mediation, the mediator is able to define the issues

---

as a means of imposing sanctions and vice versa. "nuisance power" is the power to irritate, bother or harass another person but cannot fully restrict another person in exercising their rights. Parties may use the "personal power" i.e. power of personal characteristics like intelligence, communication skills, physical stamina and strength, concentration, perceptiveness, determination, empathy, and courage in mediation to attain a favourable outcome over others. See Mayer 2000, 54-56.

of a dispute in mediation and express his or her opinion on the potential outcome if it is to be dealt with at trial (Boulle 2005, 30). As was observed in all of the mediation sessions, mediators explain the probable outcome which parties may expect if a case is contested at trial.

Legal prerogative: Under the legal structure of a country, every person attending mediation has some legal rights over others. These legal rights can empower parties by giving them a sense of entitlement (Mayer 2000, 55). Conventionally, the shadow of law is considered to have a profound impact on distributional issues in divorce, such as the distribution of marital wealth and future income (Mnookin & Korhauser 1979, 959). For example, in a mediation session observed in court in the *Mymensingh* district, a husband demanded reconciliation while his wife claimed that he was not providing her with maintenance. She was therefore not willing to live with her husband. Facing this situation the mediator informed the husband of his legal obligations.

Mediator: Your wife claims that you are not providing maintenance to her. If you are not willing to maintain her, why don't you divorce her?

Husband: I am willing to live with her. So, I will not divorce her.

Wife: He is telling a lie. He forced me to leave his house. Now, I will not live with him. I will divorce him.

Husband: How can you divorce me? On what grounds? You cannot initiate divorce by yourself.

Mediator: [to the husband] Sometimes people think that wives cannot initiate divorce. But, in fact, according to law your wife can initiate divorce on the ground that you failed to provide proper maintenance to her.

Wife: I will divorce him and I want my dower money.

Husband: If she divorces me, how can she claim dower? She cannot claim it.

Mediator: Though sometimes it is thought that husbands do not need to pay unpaid dower if they (wives) initiate a divorce, dower is her inalienable right and has to be paid in all situations. According to law, you have to pay

> the unpaid dower even if your wife initiates the divorce.

In another in-court mediation, a wife was in a dilemma as to whether to apply for reconciliation or divorce. The husband expressed his preference for reconciliation, but the wife was undecided. She seemed anxious that the husband might prefer reconciliation to end the lawsuit and might not provide proper maintenance to her after reconciliation. Understanding the situation, the mediator informed the wife about her legal entitlement as follows:

> If you are anxious that your husband will be delinquent again after making reconciliation, for your extra security you have an option to demand the unpaid dower as a condition for reconciliation. That will not hamper your right to get regular maintenance anyway. Moreover, if your husband fails to provide regular maintenance, you can come to the court again and file execution suit against your husband.

Therefore, as described in the Riskin grid (1996), mediators provide an assessment of legal outcomes which can be attained through litigation. As mentioned by Mayer (2000, 55), power given to a person through his or her legal prerogatives will only be of use if he or she has access to the adversarial legal system that confers such prerogatives to the parties attending trial. For example, in three of the nine out-of-court mediation sessions observed, when husbands appeared to have behaved unfairly and held themselves in a rigid position, NGO mediators said:

> If you do not want to settle the case through mediation, we [NGO] will file suit on behalf of your wife to claim her right against you through litigation. At that time, you may have to pay even more.

After realising that a wife can access litigation with the help of NGOs, in two out of these three sessions the husband preferred mediated resolution. This is significant because the mediator not only reminded husbands of the law but also reminded them to provide support for their wives or to go to court if they did not negotiate fairly. Therefore, while legal rights can effectively increase the power of a woman, it may also reduce the relative power of her husband in mediation and *vice versa*. Moreover, according to all the twelve mediators interviewed, in both in- and out-of-court settings, they specifically mentioned that availability of pro-women law enhances the rights of women in mediation.

Power of association: Power may derive from a person's affiliation with another greater body or powerful organisation (Mayer 2000, 56). As observed by seven out of nine NGO mediators interviewed, women feel empowered when they are accompanied by their friends and family rather than coming to the mediation alone. In response to a question, an NGO mediator replied, "Women feel more empowered in mediation when they come in mediation with somebody. Association of friends and families strengthens their voice in mediation." However, this power cannot be observed in court-connected mediation as the family members, friends or relatives are generally not allowed to attend these mediation sessions.

Moral power: This relates to the belief and value system of the disputants that explains whether they have the moral right to do what they have done earlier, or what they are doing now (Kelly 1995, 93; Mayer 2000, 57). Moral power is an important source of personal power in negotiation. However, there is the possibility of conflict if one party perceives something as his or her moral right but the other party thinks the opposite. Such power is usually applied by the marginalised parties in a dispute (Mayer 2000, 57). For example, in one of the NGO mediation sessions observed in *Dhaka* district, a mediator asked a polygamous husband:

Mediator: [to the husband] How do you dare to marry again when you cannot maintain your first wife properly?

Husband: I can marry more than one as religion permits so.

Mediator: Religion permits you to take a second wife but it is permitted only when you can maintain them properly and equitably. You are also bound legally to obtain permission from your first wife before taking any second wife. Have you done so?

Husband: [Shakes his head to express "no"].

Mediator: [to the husband again] If your first wife sues you on this ground you have to face prosecution.

Husband: What if I pay maintenance to her?

Mediator: You better ask your wife and settle the issue between yourselves.

Though varying in degree, in all of the eighteen mediation sessions observed, mediators made statements regarding the content of the dispute to make each husband feel morally obliged to pay compensation to his wife for his wrong doings.

Information power: To have better information about a dispute is a source of great power to an individual (Mayer 2000, 55). Three different sources of information or knowledge identified by Fisher (1983, 154) are the knowledge about the opponent's personal concerns, values and habits; knowledge about the interests involved; and knowledge about facts. Information can also create expertise (Mayer 2000, 55). Mediators can enjoy greater power as they are better informed in law and other dispute resolution methods. In all of the eighteen mediation sessions observed, both in- and out-of-court in Bangladesh, mediators shared information with the parties both spontaneously and when asked to do so by the parties. In most of the cases, mediators provided information about the legal prerogatives of women when parties were unaware of their legal rights and responsibilities or when social dogma could lead husbands to deny women's legal rights. Similarly, while answering questions during interview, an NGO mediator at the *Dhaka* district emphasised the importance of providing information on legal rights and responsibilities to the parties. Such information helps to mitigate ignorance of the law and upholds women's rights in mediation. As she explained:

> Society has many misconceptions about women's right to dower. Sometimes their mindset is so strong that it is hard to make them believe that law says something different. That's why I pasted so many posters on women rights to dower on these walls. When anyone debates over the issue, I just refer them to the specific poster indicating a similar right for women. In many cases, it works.

Mediators also inform the parties about the lengthy and costly nature of litigation procedures that need to be followed if mediation fails. For example, in an in-court mediation at the *Narayanganj* district, a wife was undecided about whether she would settle through mediation and accept a partial amount of the total claim made or go to litigation to get a full decree. To help her make a decision, the judge-mediator informed her:

> If you go for trial there is a possibility that you will get more but for that you have to go through a lengthy litigation process that may last for the next two to three years. You also have to bear the cost for that. Moreover, if you get the decree, it is not certain that you are going to get the money instantly or even within a short period. If your husband remains

> delinquent, you will need to file another suit for execution that will need more money and time. So, you have to consider both sides before making any decision.

In another NGO mediation session, the mediator shared his expertise and knowledge to clarify the issue of a dispute. The mediator asked the wife whether the marriage was registered and she responded "yes," and submitted a copy of the registered marriage contract to the mediator. At that time, the uncle of the husband attending mediation spoke out saying "This is not a genuine marriage contract; in this document there is no fresh ink signature of either husband or wife." Then to inform the parties, the mediator explained:

> Listen, as I see it, it is a duplicate copy of the marriage contract that is issued by the registrar's office to be kept by the parties to the marriage and it would not be signed by the parties as the original one would be. The original one is preserved at the marriage registrar's office. So, if you wish, you may check it there.

It can be seen, therefore, that during mediation mediators can provide valuable information to make women aware of their legal prerogatives and the cost and complexities of litigation, and to redress common misconceptions in the society that may otherwise subjugate their position at mediation. All this information helps women to make informed decisions and secure their rights through mediation.

Perception of power: The power of a person also depends on how powerful they think they are relative to their counterparts (Mayer 2000, 58). Perception of power increases when a person comes to know his or her legal rights and is assured that he or she has sufficient resources to access legal remedies if required (Mayer 2000, 58). A poor and illiterate woman, for instance, may consider herself more powerful in mediation when a mediator informs her about her legal rights or provides her with the information about where and how to get legal aid. For example, in one in-court mediation observed at the *Narayanganj* district, when a husband urged the mediator to forgive a part of the unpaid dower because he did not have the ability to pay the entire amount, the mediator said:

> According to law, it is only your wife who has the right to forfeit any part of her unpaid dower, if she wishes to do so. Other than your wife, no one else has the authority to reduce the amount of her dower as it is her legal and religious right. Even the court does not have any power to forfeit or reduce any part of it unless she wishes so.

In all of the eighteen mediation sessions observed in in- and out-of court settings, especially when the issue of dower was being discussed, mediators shared the same view when husbands made similar pleas to mediators. Mediators are therefore able to change the perception of power held by the parties through providing information on legal prerogatives and the availability of legal aid. The power of an individual also depends on how opponents perceive the power of that individual (Mayer 2000, 58). For example, the relative power of a woman may be enhanced if her counterpart perceives that, with the help of legal aid, she can get recourse to trial.

Habitual power: Maintaining the status *quo* is easier than changing it (Mayer 2000, 57). Therefore, during mediation, the habitual power of husbands to dominate their wives in household decision-making may give them more power over their wives who are used to being silent and contribute only slightly in marital decision-making during their conjugal life (Kelly 1995, 90). Likewise, a perpetrator husband who uses coercive power to control the voice of his wife may also try to dominate her during mediation. In other words, it might be difficult for a mediator to break the silence of a battered woman and help her to articulate her demands, as this involves her breaking her long practice of silence in conjugal life (Astor 1994, 151).

As observed in all but two mediation sessions attended in Bangladesh, especially in out-of-court NGO mediations, mediators had to stop husbands and in-laws several times when they started to interfere with the woman's voice. For example, in one out-of-court NGO mediation session observed at *Dhaka* district, the mediator had to apply her procedural power several times to stop the sudden interference of the husband and in-laws while the wife was sharing her grievances. In addition, when the mother of the husband stood up and raised her voice, the mediator said, "Please be seated and remain silent. You will be given sufficient time to share your grievances."

In addition to the above-mentioned powers that mediators can deploy in mediation, another strategy of challenging social discourses is used as an extension of the procedural power of mediator. Mediators commonly exercise this strategy in all mediation sessions observed to ensure fair outcomes for women. As discussed in the next section, an evaluative role of mediator to control the power play, by challenging dominant social discourses and promoting legal discourses for the marginalised in mediation, could be one means by which women may be ensured fair outcomes despite the presence of gendered power disparity between the parties.

4.5.2 Challenging Discourses in Evaluative Mediation: Theoretical Underpinning of Practical Demands

As observed by Bagshaw (2002, 130), "stories and 'truths' are inevitably framed by dominant cultural discourses that specify what is normal and what can or cannot be talked about, by whom and in what contexts." This approach opens up the possibility that a mediator who knows local culture can contribute to shape a coherent story in mediation by considering the marginalised discourse of women that would not be heard otherwise. Mediators can also use the gender equalising legal discourses to challenge dominant discourses that would otherwise marginalise women's position in mediation. As an example of how a mediator might use his or her evaluation to minimise power disparity , in one out-of court NGO mediation observed in the *Dhaka* district, a husband made an unreasonable demand that his wife remain at home, even though he was not be able to provide her with necessities, including her regular maintenance. As the husband said:

Husband: [to the mediator] I am her husband; she has to comply with all my orders. I told her not to do work outside without my permission.

Wife: [to the mediator] I have to work because my husband remains absent from home for a long time and does not provide any maintenance. I do not have any other means to feed my children but to go outside for work.

Mediator: [to the husband] You cannot forbid your wife to work outside without providing for her maintenance. You are legally bound to maintain your wife and your children. If you do not provide her maintenance, you cannot expect that she will comply with your words. Moreover, your wife has also the right to work. You cannot solely decide on obstructing her to do work outside. Though people sometimes believe that women have to comply with all orders of husbands irrespective of their legitimacy or that they should not work without the consent of their husbands, legally you cannot restrict your wife's movement by preventing her right to work outside to maintain your family.

In one of the in-court mediation sessions, for example, it was observed that the mediator made an evaluation on the content of the dispute when a husband urged his wife to live with her in-laws without showing any reasonable grounds for his claim.

Mediator: [to the wife] What is your discontent with your husband?

Wife: He [my husband] told me not to come to *Dhaka* [the capital city where the husband resides] and instead live in the village with my in-laws. But, there are so many problems in rural areas. There is no pure water, no electricity.

Mediator: Where did you [the wife] grow up?

Wife: I grew up in *Dhaka* city but my husband says that after marriage, women should live with their in-laws. So should I?

Mediator: [to the husband] What is your problem if she lives in *Dhaka* city?

Husband: It is expected that a wife should live with her in-laws after marriage. My mother lives in the village alone.

Mediator: It would be OK if you lived with your wife in the village. But, you are working in the city and earning a handsome salary. Why don't you bring your mother to the city? As she [his wife] was born and brought up in the city, she might face many problems in rural areas where there are few amenities.

In this fashion, mediators challenge dominant discourses and promote the marginalised voice of women in mediation. They challenge the dominant discourses to manage the power play where it may subdue the expression of marginalised discourses in mediation (Bagshaw 2001, 217–18).

Without such intervention, there is a possibility that the discourse of a less empowered party will not be brought forward and that the dominant discourse will remain unchallenged. Following Foucault's (1980) theory of power discussed earlier (see chapter three), the existence of laws protecting women's rights in the country and the evaluative nature of mediation processes followed under a shadow of law (see chapter four) enhance the possibility that mediation will uphold the voice of women and assist them in getting fair outcomes through mediation, despite the existence of gender power disparity in the society. The extent to which such fair outcomes are actually attained by women in mediation is discussed in chapter six.

4.6 Evaluative Mediation and Self-Determination: Where Does the Solution Lie?

The most robust criticism of evaluative mediation is that it undermines the basic tenet of mediation, which is the principle of parties' self-determination (Feerick 1995; Kovach & Love 1996; Stulberg 1996–97; Alfini 1997). This is the fundamental principle upon which the definition of mediation is based. Kovach & Love (1998, 73) show their rigid mind-set towards parties' self-determination in the mediation process. They twist "evaluation" and "decision" together by making an assumption, which is perhaps misleading, that evaluation is inescapably linked to decision making for the parties. In a related vein, Alfini (1997, 933) also suggests that mediators should not evaluate as evaluation might interfere with self-determination. However, while understanding self-determination, it should not be confused with "evaluation/opinion" and "decision." Inevitably, evaluation is different from decision making. Nevertheless, it should be kept in mind that evaluation should not be practised in such a manner that it may overshadow the right of self-determination to disputing parties. Clearly, "evaluation becomes dangerous only when you start taking the decision-making process away from the parties" (Alfini 1997, 928)

In all of the mediation sessions observed in Bangladesh, in both in- and out-of-court NGO settings, mediators did not use a facilitative style of mediation. Rather, they helped parties, especially women, to express their opinions; to challenge the dominant discourses that husbands might use to subjugate the position of women in mediation; to educate parties about the probable outcome of the dispute if settled in litigation; and to warn them about the extra effort and money that could be required to settle the dispute through litigation. All these factors observed during mediation sessions in Bangladesh, when matched with Riskin's criteria (1996) set out above, demonstrate that mediators in Bangladesh generally use evaluative mediation, and the "shadow of law" has a strong impact on the mediation. The evaluative nature of mediation also opens up the possibility that mediation may provide fair outcomes for women, based on legal principles. Mediators help parties to evaluate proposals, or help parties to develop their proposals. However, evaluative mediators do not decide the outcomes of a dispute and do not dictate to parties what outcome they may demand.

4.7 Conclusion

As demonstrated in this chapter, mediators use legal discourses to protect women's rights in mediation. Since the law embodies equality, and as it is the touchstone for standards in mediation, the law is more likely to uphold women's rights and women's equality than recourse to community values that involve in-built discrimination against women. Therefore, at this point, we can at least propose that because the most reliable protections of women's rights exist in the law, the dominance of the values of law in mediation means that a practice of evaluative mediation is best able to protect women's legal rights and to provide fair outcomes for them. A detailed discussion on how and to what extent evaluative mediation conducted under the shadow of law can provide fair outcomes for women is to be found in chapter six. In order to examine the potential of evaluative mediation to provide fair outcomes, analysis of data collected from the respective court registries and NGO registries of Bangladesh has been analysed and illustrated in chapter six to support the argument that evaluative mediation has the potential to provide fairer outcomes for women than litigation. Before discussing the fairness of outcomes reached through evaluative mediation, the next chapter elaborates family violence, a factor which can significantly hinder women's effective participation in mediation and prevent their obtaining a fair outcome.

CHAPTER FIVE

FAMILY VIOLENCE: OVERCOMING THE HURDLES THROUGH EVALUATIVE MEDIATION

5.1 Introduction

Family violence is another impediment that exacerbates any existing gendered power disparity that women face in their family, and consequently may compel women to be acquiescent to their perpetrators. The spread of such violence is also pervasive in nature. Seventy percent of females murdered worldwide are killed by their male partners and around half of all women report that their first sexual intercourse was forced (Amnesty 2005). Irrespective of their economic position and historical and cultural diversity, family violence against women persists in both developed and developing countries of the world (Stubbs & Powell 1989, 2). For example, in a developed country like France, husbands perpetrate over half of the violent incidents against women (Jahan & Islam 1997, 64). In addition, in the United States, three to four million women are abused by their husbands every year (US Senate 1990, 12). Similarly, as cited by Brown et al. (2001, 2), according to a study conducted by the Australian Institute for Family Studies, "66 percent of separating couples point to partnership violence as a cause of marital breakdown, with 33 percent of the couples describing the violence as serious." This trend was reconfirmed by Personal Safety Australia (PSA) 2005. The PSA data indicate that 1,530,300 women in Australia have experienced physical assault from male perpetrators. Among these abused women, 780,300, or more than 51 percent, experienced assault from their current or ex-partners (ABS 2005, 40). During the period 1990 to 2002, 60 percent of total homicides were caused by intimate partners, and in 75 percent of cases women were the victims of the homicides (AIC 2003, 1).

To give examples from developing countries, 67 percent of women in the rural villages of Papua New Guinea and 45 percent of women in Ethiopia experience physical violence from their partners at some time in their current relationship. The rate varies to 31 percent in Nigeria and 30 percent in Barbados (WHO 2002, 90). Similar to many other developing countries, women in Bangladesh also face family violence, and it has emerged as a national problem deserving special attention (Sobhan 2005, 179; Chowdhury 2005, 60). As Monsoor (2008b, 17–18) observed:

> [Family] violence perpetuated in the home or family environment is [a] major social problem in Bangladesh. This violence is fairly common and widespread across the country and women of all economic strata are vulnerable to the domestic violence caused by the maltreatment and abuse of husbands, in-laws and other family members…There is not much scholarly literature on [family] violence and the official statistics do not give us a full picture of the incidence of violence against women.

The *NGO Committee on Beijing plus Five (NCBPF)*, Bangladesh, in one of its research reports, revealed that husband or in-laws of the victim (NCBPF 2001, 8) cause 63 percent of female homicides. 40 percent of physical assaults, and one third of the incidents of acid burns against women in Bangladesh, are also inflicted by their husbands or in-laws (NCBPF 2001, 12, 16). Since at present more and more family disputes in both developed and developing countries are settled through in- and out-of court mediations, there remains a concern that cases involving violence are referred increasingly to mediation. The effect of such violence on mediated outcomes, however, may vary depending on various factors discussed in more detail in this chapter.

Though not equally true for every woman, increasing referral of family violence cases to mediation remains a concern for feminist scholars because, as discussed in contemporary literature, violence against married women by their husbands and in-laws, combined with inadequate social responses to such acts, has intensely detrimental effects on their capacity to participate effectively in mediation (Gagnon 1992, paragraph 7; Astor 1994, 151; Johnson 1995, 287; Field 1996, 266). Society's reluctance to speak about family violence may also restrain women from reporting it to others (Astor 1995, 193). Even separated women may remain in a constant apprehension of further violence (Kaganas & Piper, 1994, 272; Astor 1994, 159–60). Therefore, in contemporary literature it is argued that violent consequences may make it impracticable for women to negotiate with their husbands and in-laws, or to express views or raise demands in mediation. Since in family mediations women have to negotiate with their husbands who are generally the perpetrators, it is widely argued that the effective negotiation capability of women may dwindle substantially as a result, which negatively affects their ability to get a fair outcome through mediation (Hart 1990; Gagnon 1992; Astor 1995; Mack 1995; Field 1996).

In this chapter, however, it is postulated that not every woman who experiences family violence is incapable of negotiating with her husband in mediation (Astor 2002, 353). Further, many of the scholars who argued against the mediation of family disputes involving violence are concerned with facilitative mediation in the context of Western democratic societies, which may not be fully applicable for the cultural context of many Eastern developing countries. Furthermore, as rightly observed by Neumann (1992), divorce is a time for change in spousal behaviour and women, in particular, become more receptive to outside intervention. Therefore, women who kept silent about family violence during their marital life may tell of their experiences when they attend mediation after deciding to get divorced. As observed by Astor (1995, 193):

> Separation and divorce threaten the idealised image of the family. They are events that result in the disintegration of the nuclear family and expose the conflicts, disputes and violence that occur in some families.

An analysis of responses, collected for this study through semi-structured interviews from a number of in- and out-of-court NGO mediators and observations of mediation sessions in Bangladesh (discussed later in this chapter), also confirm that women who decide to divorce do speak out during mediation sessions. In this chapter, it is argued that the following factors empower women to speak in mediation:

- changes in social attitudes towards family violence at the time of divorce
- social awareness and legal counselling of NGOs against family violence
- the protective influence of legislation
- long term separation of women from their partner before coming to mediation, which reduces the trauma of past violence, and
- the proactive role of mediators to support abused women.

Analysis of empirical data indicates that, under certain circumstances, the prevalence of family violence may not significantly hinder the effective participation of women in mediation. Though this participation in mediation can enhance the possibility of fair outcomes, whether or not women are actually getting them in mediation is discussed in the next chapter.

To examine the relationship between the existence of family violence and effectiveness of evaluative mediation, this chapter begins with defining family violence in different contexts of developed and developing countries, followed by a discussion of its impact on mediation. The chapter then explains the concern on family violence in terms of "control," "fear," and "silence" of women caused through violence and hinders effective mediation. Finally, it links the theoretical knowledge on family violence and mediation with the empirical evidence collected from Bangladesh to explain how and why a practice of evaluative mediation may overcome many limitations predicted in theory.

5.2 Defining Family Violence: Paradox in Practice

Academics and other national and international statutes have given varied definitions of family violence. According to the *Family Law Act 1975* (Cth.) (section 60D):

> Family violence means conduct, whether actual or threatened, by a person towards, or towards the property of, a member of the person's family that causes that or any other member of the person's family fear for, or to be apprehensive about, his or her personal well-being or safety.

While the *Family Law Act 1975* (*FLA*) indicates family violence as conduct that causes partners to reasonably fear about their personal wellbeing or safety, no explanation has been given to clarify the nature of such conduct. The nature of the conduct that might constitute family violence is, however, included in the definition given in the *Women Safety Survey 1996* (*WSS*), a survey conducted by the *Australian Bureau of Statistics (ABS)* to measure the degree of violence faced by Australian women in general, with particular mention of partner violence. Under the term "partner violence," one more element is added by the *WSS 1996* regarding the nature of violence. It defines violence as various types of physical and sexual harm either actually committed or threatened by the perpetrator (*ABS 1996*, 80–3). Though the *WSS 1996* categorically included physical and sexual harm as violence, it omitted psychological harm. The *International Violence against Women Survey 2005* (*IVAWS*) went a step further than *WSS 1996* by categorically including psychological harm inflicted on women as violence.

IVAWS 2005 has not given any separate definition of family violence; rather it has adopted the United Nations' definition of "violence against women" in their public and private life, following the *United Nations*

Declaration on the Elimination of Violence against Women. IVAWS 2005 defines "violence against women" as:

> Any act of gender-based violence that results in, or is likely to result in, physical, sexual or psychological harm or suffering to women including threats of such acts, coercion or arbitrary deprivations of liberty, whether occurring in public or private life (*IVAWS 2005*, 11).

A more extensive definition of family violence, which is particularly relevant in the context of Bangladesh, can be found in the *Family Violence (Prevention & Protection) Act 2010* in Bangladesh. Section 3 of the *Family Violence (Prevention & Protection) Act 2010* defines family violence as:

> The commission of any or more than one of the following acts by any member of the family, excluding a child or handicapped adult, against any other member of the family
>
> (a) Physical abuse:
> (i) assaulting including beating any member of the family for any reason whatsoever, whether the assault leads to any injury or not;
> (ii) damaging the physical beauty of a spouse by torture;
> (iii) indecently abusing, beating and maltreating the wife by the husband on being drunk;
> (iv) torturing the wife by the husband being influenced by others;
> (v) maltreatment, misbehaviour, torture or assault upon a domestic servant by any member of the family.
>
> (b) Sexual abuse:
> (i) compelling the wife to cohabit with anybody other than the husband;
> (ii) forcibly marrying a religiously prohibited woman or establishing illicit sexual connection with such woman voluntarily or otherwise;
> (iii) any kind of sexual abuse including sexual harassment of a member of the family.
>
> (c) Psychological abuse:
> (i) intimidation, harassment, denial of food or drink for adequate sustenance, denial of salary or expenses, threat of physical or psychological abuse by any member of the family to the other or others;
> (ii) inducing or compelling a spouse to attempt suicide through continued oppression by any member of the family;

> (iii) blaming a spouse of immorality without any rational basis;
> (iv) threatening to divorce a wife on demand of dowry[31] by the husband;
> (v) blaming or imputing insanity, or citing barrenness of a spouse with the intention to marry again;
> (vi) bringing false allegations upon the character of a female member by any member of the family;
> (vii) keeping a female member of the family disconnected with her father, mother, child, sibling and other relatives;
> (viii) threatening to get a male member of the family remarried by the other member or members of the family on the grounds of the female spouse giving repeated birth to female children;
> (ix) disallowing the children to see their father or mother during their separation, being divorced or otherwise;
> (x) torturing the parents or any other member of the family by the husband being instigated by the wife;
> (xi) confining or detaining the victim against the will of the victim;
> (xii) causing mischief or destruction or removal of the victim's property or personal belongings or documents and papers relating thereto.

The scope of this definition is even more comprehensive than the definition of family violence included in *WSS 1996* and *IVAWS 2005*. While WSS, IVAWS and many scholars have referred to family violence as the violence inflicted upon women by their husbands and other intimate partners (Stallone 1984; Hart 1990; Gagnon 1992, Behrens 1993; Blazejowska

[31] Dowry is sometimes confused with the concept of "dower." Legally speaking, both the concepts are opposite. While dower is the legal right of wives against their husbands which is paid to them at the time of marriage, dowry is the illegal demand by the husbands to their wives for payment of money or some valuables. In fact, one of the reasons, perhaps the single most important reason, for which many women in Bangladesh have to face physical and mental violence, is their inability to fulfil the dowry demands made by their husbands and in-laws (Chowdhury 2005, 153). Women are expected to remain mute and suffer innumerable agonies at the hands of their husbands and in-laws if they fail to provide handsome dowries (Monsoon 1999, 7). As a majority of women in Bangladesh remain in the lower income strata, they are unable to pay a dowry. Because of regular harassment and continual physical and mental violence associated with demands for dowries, women, in many cases, have resorted to suicide to free themselves from the suffering (Akanda & Shamim 1985, 9; UNDP 2002, 105; BNWLA 2005, 25).

1994; Laing 2003; Phillips 2006), by using the term "any member of the family," the *Family Violence (Prevention & Protection) Act 2010* in Bangladesh also includes family violence inflicted upon women by their in-laws, an event which is very common in Bangladesh, India, China and other countries of Asia and the Pacific Islander countries (Umar 1998, 158; Matsui 1999, 68; Dasgupta 2007, 4; Lockhart & Danis 2010, 109). For instance, the scope of in-law violence is common in Bangladesh because 75 percent of its people live in rural areas where it is expected that a married son will reside with his father and mother until death (Edlund & Rahman 2004, 3; BBS 2006, 5). The prevalence of in-law violence has also been observed by Hampton (2002, 97–98) among African-American women. Thus, women live in extended families with their in-laws, which raise their susceptibility to this type of violence.

Use of the gender-neutral terms "family violence" or "domestic violence" is sometimes criticised on the grounds that they do not reflect that women are the major victims of violence (Dobash et al. 1992; Behrens 1993; Johnson 1995). Thus, contemporary literature sometimes uses alternative terms like "wife battering" to mean violence perpetrated against women by their spouses (Astor 1990; Gagnon 1992; Kaganas & Piper 1994). Though gender sensitive, use of the terms like "wife battering" is not adopted for this book because it fails to include all aspects of the violence such as psychological and sexual violence inflicted upon wives. Further, in an earlier study, Sheehan & Smyth (2000, 107) observed that:

> Reliance on a definition of spousal violence based solely on physically violent actions or threats, however, fails to consider other forms of abusive behaviour, power differentials between parties, or the fear and intimidation that may have characterised the relationship between the parties.

Though gender sensitive, the term "wife battering" may undermine understanding the many types of violence women endure in their families. In their research study, Sheehan & Smyth show that the ratio of family violence inflicted upon males and females becomes asymmetric and is skewed towards women when all forms of sexual and psychological violence are considered. It excludes the incidences of child abuse that create psychological pressure on mothers and thus can be considered as psychological violence against them. Furthermore:

> The breadth of the definition of spousal violence obviously has implications for the estimated prevalence of such violence and the legal response to it: the broader the definition, the higher the prevalence, and the

> greater the potential impact of any related law reform (Sheehan & Smyth 2000, 108).

Therefore, in the context of the culture of in-law violence prevalent in many developing countries in the East, it is better to use the more comprehensive term “family violence.” This term is used throughout this text to mean all the different forms of physical, sexual and psychological violence that women may experience from their husbands or in-laws. Although scholars sometimes criticise the gender neutral term “family violence” as it conceals the fact that most of such violence is inflicted upon women by their husbands (Fehlberg & Behrens 2008), such an argument is not particularly applicable for the Eastern culture of family violence mentioned earlier. For instance, as discussed later in this chapter, a large part of family violence against women in Bangladesh is inflicted, or at least provoked, by in-laws.

5.3 Family violence: A Hidden Social Vice

Though it varies in nature and severity, family violence against women inside families exists as a global and deep-rooted social problem in developed and developing countries of the world (Ansari 2005, 199). Women in Bangladesh in particular face many types of family violence from their partners and in-laws. The violence may take the form of physical assault, sexual abuse, psychological or mental torture through forced social isolation, financial deprivation, or threats to inflict physical harm. In an empirical study conducted among 150 married women from three villages in Bangladesh, 90 women (66 percent) reported being physically assaulted (Begum 2005). One government report on married women in *Dhaka* city also depicts a 60 percent prevalence rate of battery or physical assault on women by their husbands (GOB 1999, cited in Begum 2005, 57). Though small in size, a study by the *International Women's Rights Action Watch (IWRAW)* on female hospital patients strengthens the validity of other research findings mentioned earlier. In a survey conducted on 79 women attending *Dhaka* Medical College Hospital, it was found that in 63 percent of cases women faced physical violence inside their home (IWRAW 2006, 11). As observed by Johnson (1995), non-random samples on women who came to law enforcement agencies, shelter homes and hospitals can better reveal the disproportionate rate of violence women face in their home compared with their male counterparts. Therefore, results of different empirical studies conducted on different rural and urban localities of Bangladesh using different methodologies confirm that over 60 percent of women in

Bangladesh face physical violence in their family. However, Begum (2005, 53) showed in one of her experimental studies that mental or psychological violence faced by women in Bangladesh is more prevalent than the physical violence that may be inflicted on them.

Women may also face sexual violence from their partners yet such violence is usually hidden from others because of the social stigma attached to it. For example, women in Bangladesh do not usually discuss the coerced sexual intercourse with their husbands that they must endure because of its personal nature. The occurrences of coerced intercourse may persist because today's society is still accepting of such actions (Hadi 2000). In their study, ICDDR, B found a 37 percent and 50 percent prevalence of sexual violence perpetrated by husbands in urban and rural areas respectively (ICDDR, B 2006). In an experimental survey in Bangladesh, over half of the women respondents were of the view that husbands have a right to coerce their wives to have sexual relations (Jahan 1994; Begum 2005). In Bangladesh, society considers sexual intercourse between husbands and wives as a private matter not to be interfered in by others (BNWLA 2005). Marital coercion, or coerced sexual intercourse by a husband, is not considered as an offence either in the *Penal Code 1860* (Act No. XLV) or in any other subsequent laws of Bangladesh, unless the coerced wife is aged below twelve years (Ameen 2005a). This implies social acceptance of marital coerced sexual intercourse in the country (BNWLA 2005).

Women living in extended families also face sexual harassment and sexual coercion from their male in-laws, especially when their husbands are absent from the house. Nevertheless, as society follows a victim-blaming strategy in the case of sexual harassment, women usually suppress these incidents to maintain the reputation of their family, avoid mistrust from their husbands and other in-laws, and to remove any other stringent social sanctions that may follow such incidents (BNWLA 2005). According to Khair (1998, 95):

> It is about exploitation of the gender advantage and institutional power that results in the loss of dignity and self-esteem of the victim. It provides "perpetrators the sordid opportunity to seek sexual gratification." All this leads to the under-reporting of family violence in the country and the consequent lack of reliable statistical data.

This personal nature of violence leads to the under-reporting of sexual family violence and the consequent lack of reliable statistical data.

However, one of the most comprehensive surveys of family violence in Bangladesh was conducted by the International Centre for Diarrhoeal Disease Research, Bangladesh (ICDDR, B 2006). Considering the responses of 3,130 randomly selected samples from 42 rural and 39 urban clusters, this study looked at the physical and sexual family violence inflicted on urban women compared with their rural counterparts. The study tried to identify the usual perpetrators of such violence and the extent to which women were reporting such violence to others (ICDDR, B 2006). In that study, ICDDR, B found 1878 women, or 60 percent of the respondents, were victims of physical or sexual violence at some point in their life. Jahan (1994) made a similar assessment to estimate the extent of violence.

In a study conducted by Nahar et al. (cited in Begum 2005), based on data collected from hospital patients, more than 60 percent of the women suffered from different psychological problems caused through mental torture from their husbands. Many of them were also victims of sexual coercion in their marital life. Social acceptance of coerced sexual intercourse was also observed in Mexico, India, and in different countries of Africa including Ghana, Zimbabwe and South Africa (Dasgupta 1998, 131; Joseph & Najmabadi 2003, 127; Jejeebhoy, Shah & Thapa 2005, 289). However, one common practice that remains prevalent in many Eastern developing countries is the internalisation of violence by women and a consequent under-reporting of family violence instances to others. Therefore, estimates of different forms of physical, sexual and psychological violence may vary across studies. Although estimates on the prevalence of sexual and psychological violence against women may vary in different studies, overall the existence of family violence has already become a concern for society (Monsoor 1999). For instance, considering the gravity of this problem, the Law Commission of Bangladesh expressed:

> [Family] violence in Bangladesh is not a rarity, but phenomenal in prevalence…Women are reported to be physically tortured, sexually assaulted, psychologically injured and mentally humiliated within their homes by their husbands or by other members of the family…The growing problem of [family] violence has been considered to be of such magnitude as to require the introduction of new legislation (LCB 2008, 5–7)

Despite the varied extent and forms of physical, sexual and psychological family violence around the globe, one of the common features of family violence is its interactive nature. The large percentage of violence perpetrated by husbands does not, however, mean that wives do not ever inflict violence against their husbands. For example, sometimes wives quite vigorously participate in verbal abuse of their husbands and in-laws. They even push or shove their husbands, especially when husbands start to perpetrate violence. In a study conducted by Jahan (1994, 71), 60 percent of female respondents mentioned that they had thrown items at their husbands at least once in the year before the survey. Nevertheless, women respondents in the survey confirmed that they resorted to such violent actions generally only as a means of self-defence and in most cases they managed to escape violence by running away from their husbands.

Women's use of such violence on their husbands is what Johnson (1995) calls "Male-controlling interactive violence." This is because women do not use violence to control their husbands; rather, they use it as a tool for self-defence and ultimately control is taken by the husbands as wives run to escape from the current threat (Jahan 1994, 71). On the contrary, in most cases husbands use violence as a means to punish their wives or to teach their wives a lesson. The violence perpetrated by husbands is thus aimed at controlling their wives (Jahan 1994, 69, 70). However, though wives sometimes take self-defence measures against their husbands, it becomes evident from the women's perception that husbands have a right to beat their wives (Begum 2005, 65). Although 77 percent of the women respondents in the survey mentioned earlier perceived that it is the right of their husband to inflict violence over them, none of them thought that it is either good, or normal, for them to batter their husband (Jahan 1994, 84; Begum 2005, 65). In contrast, more than 50 percent of the husbands believed that inflicting violence against their wives was normal (Jahan 1994, 83–4). This reflects a social attitude which legitimises family violence perpetrated by husbands at home in many developing countries in the East.

5.4 Mediation of Disputes Involving Family Violence: Some Concerns

Because of the prevalence of family violence in different societies and its negative impact on mediation, many feminist scholars oppose or have shown concerns about the use of mediation to resolve family disputes in cases involving violence. The concern of feminist scholars is about the effect of the violence on the negotiation capacity of women during mediation (Gagnon 1992, paragraph 7; Astor 1994, 151; Johnson 1995, 287; Field 1996, 266).

5.4.1 Family Violence with "Control": A Factor Hindering the Effective Participation of Women in Mediation

As already indicated, feminist scholars from different Western societies generally oppose the use of mediation in cases involving family violence (Graycar & Morgan 1992; Gagnon 1992; Astor 1994; Johnson 1995; Field 1996; Felhberg & Behrens 2008). It is argued that a history of family violence causes a strong power disparity between a perpetrator husband and his victimised wife that hinders wives from negotiating effectively in mediation. In the case of persistent family violence, the impact of such disparity may be so prevalent over target women that effective mediation becomes impossible (Gagnon 1992, paragraph 7; Astor 1994, 150; 1995, 179; 2002, 351; Field 1996, 266). As argued by many scholars, the objective of a perpetrator husband is to establish "control" over the activities and comments of his target, either by physical assault or by threats of violence (Astor 1995, 185; 2002, 350; Johnson 1995, 287). If a husband becomes successful in establishing such control, the wife may try to placate him by restraining herself from doing or saying anything that might provoke her husband into inflicting further violence. Control established by a husband over his wife has special significance on the effectiveness of mediation because women have to negotiate with their husbands, but a victimized woman, marked by control, may not dare to negotiate with her perpetrator husband. Therefore, it is claimed that family violence, in most of the cases, may restrict a target woman from negotiating effectively during mediation.

It is also argued that when perpetrators successfully establish control over their targets, it is almost impossible for the targets to escape such control and, therefore, to successfully negotiate with their perpetrators during mediation (Hart 1990, 319; Astor 2002, 351). The problem escalates when persistent assaults on targets lead them to follow some "self-censorship" of actions that could otherwise antagonise the perpetrators to initiate another assault. By habitually modifying their behaviours to placate the perpetrators, victims are unlikely to make any challenge to the proposals made by the perpetrators during mediation, even when the husband is not explicitly trying to intimidate his wife (Fischer et al. 1993, 129; Kaganas & Piper 1994, 72; Astor 1994a, 59–60). Though it might not always be the case, if such a condition arises, it would be difficult for a mediator to ensure fair outcomes through mediation because victimized women seem to voluntarily sacrifice their rights in mediation.

5.4.2 "Fear" in Mediation: A Further Impediment against Effective Negotiation

It is a fact that control established by perpetrator husbands over their wives hinders the effective negotiation capacity of women in mediation. Nonetheless, using any such dichotomous distinction of family violence based on the existence, or non-existence, of control, involves difficulties and "too easily enables disagreement" regarding the motive of perpetrators on inflicting violence (Felhberg & Behrens 2008, 197). Such disagreement overshadows the more important aspect of whether a victimized woman, despite the existence or non-existence of such control, is capable enough to attend mediation (Felhberg & Behrens 2008, 197). Scholars, who advocate an exclusion of violent disputes from mediation because of the control element, sometimes overlook the fact that a victimized woman may be too fearful to be able to attend mediation even when there is no actual control in their relationship: "It may be preferable, therefore, to focus on the victim's subjective experience of the conduct, and ask whether it creates harm [including fear]" (Felhberg & Behrens 2008, 197–98).

In her typology of violence, Johnson (1995, 18) states that males perpetrate "ongoing or episodic male violence" to intimidate women and thereby protect their "power, masculinity, and proprietary male rights. As women are intimidated and cowed physically and psychologically … they accommodate to the partner's demand to avoid confrontation." This type of persistent violence may terrorise women even long after their separation (Johnston 1995, 18). "Male-controlling interactive violence," on the other hand, is a kind of interactive violence that may be initiated by both men and women. Although a male tries to establish control by overpowering women, this is not marked by battery or any deployment of excessive physical coercion by the husband. Only that amount of force is employed which becomes necessary to gain the compliance of a resistant wife. This kind of violence is likely to cease after separation when spouses cannot provoke each other to get involved in violence (Johnson 1995).

On the other hand, the partner who is being left by the other usually inflicts "separation-engendered violence." Such violence escalates at the time of separation. These violent events are not marked by control; however, they may generate fear and distrust in the mind of a separating wife and *vice versa* (Johnston 1995). The fear that violence might continue after divorce may hinder the effective participation of women in mediation. Further, psychotic and paranoid reactions can also inflict violence. Though small in number, this kind of violence is inflicted by a partner who thinks that the other partner may harm them and so try to protect him or herself by inflicting violence first. This involves special danger when dealt with in mediation because:

> Those who seek to help these victims (family, friends, attorneys, or mediators) can also be at risk as the disturbed person's paranoid conspiracy theories are likely to expand to include them (Johnston 1995, 54).

In "female initiated violence," the male partners "tend to fend off the attack or restrain the woman from hurting them or herself" (Johnson 1995, 54). Therefore, not all types of family violence generate fear in the mind of women to restrain their effective negotiation capacity during mediation, and so all who are exposed to family violence should not be excluded from mediation.

5.4.3 Silence Regarding Past Violence: Do Women Always Remain Silent in Mediation?

Though the situation may be different in mediation in different contexts, the legitimacy of spousal violence in society, in many instances, restrains women from reporting violence to their neighbours or other outsiders. It is argued that women sometimes do not share the experience of their violence with others because of the social stigma attached to family violence. Therefore, during mediation, women may be too ashamed to discuss the violence inflicted on them by their partners (Astor 1994b, 15). Because of the victim-blaming nature of society, in many cases women suffer violence silently in order to maintain the reputation of their families (Jahan 1994, 22; UNDP 2002, 103). For instance, in Bangladesh, there is a wide perception that family violence is a private issue and so women should neither discuss it in open forums nor report it to others. In a survey of 1,691 women, 72 percent admitted they had endured severe battery by their husbands, while only 11 percent of them filed cases against the perpetrator (Begum 2005, 57). As exemplified in this section, social attitudes may also restrain others from becoming involved directly in the family violence issues. For example, two-thirds of the female respondents in the ICDDR, B (2006, 1) study never shared their experience of family violence with others. In addition, law enforcement agencies may be reluctant to involve themselves in family violence because it is an issue that they consider highly personal (Jahan 1994, 42). Couples who allow their neighbours to know about their marital disputes and battery are considered immodest (Jahan 1994, 23). However, as discussed in section 5.5.1 below, such responses may change at the time of divorce (Neumann 1992; Astor 1995). Further, an active support from a mediator may help women to overcome their hesitation and share the issue of violence in mediation (see section 5.5.5).

Western scholars have identified other reasons why women may keep "silent" about past family violence inflicted on them. As explained by Astor (1994b, 14), in Australia, sometimes women keep silent because if they expose the violence that they have encountered in their marital life, there is a possibility that they will be screened out from mediation and have to go through time consuming and costly trial processes. It is also relevant that women may be too poor to bear the expenses for litigation, and so they may prefer to resolve their disputes quickly and at minimum cost through mediation (Astor 1994a, 160; 1994b, 14). Thus, in Australia, abused women who want to resolve their dispute quickly through mediation may not have any other option but to conceal past violence, as according to the *FLA 1975* (Cth.) family disputes involving violence are referred back to formal trial (*Family Law Rules* O 25A, r5). Further, as discussed earlier, the presence of "control" and "fear" in women with regards to their husbands could be one reason that women suppress information about past family violence and remain silent in mediation. It is argued that target women may become frightened of experiencing further violence from their husbands if information about past violence is revealed to others (Kaganas & Piper 1994, 272; Astor 1994b, 14; Laing 2003, 7). Perpetrators may physically assault their targets after separation or threaten to do so in a quiet location, in case the abused women reveals past violence inflicted upon them, popularly known as "car park violence." In such instances, perpetrators may give instructions to the targets about their future conduct in mediation (Astor 1994, 159–60).

However, unlike Australia and many other countries where the period of separation may be more dangerous for women because of further violence during separation, the situation may be different in other developing countries like Bangladesh. The reason is that in those developing countries, for instance in Bangladesh, women usually return to their paternal home after divorce or to escape from violence inflicted by their husband and in-laws during their marital life (Hosain & Begum 1999; Monsoor 2008b, 90–110) As discussed earlier in chapter three, women in Bangladesh are not usually engaged in outside activities and so remain safe inside their paternal home during separation. Such a safe custody along with counselling from their parents and relatives during separation helps women find relief from the traumatic experience of past family violence (Langstaff & Christie 2000).

Furthermore, unlike Australia, family cases with violence are not screened out either from in-court or from out-of-court mediation in Bangladesh. Therefore, women's intention to avail themselves of low-cost mediation services from different in-court and out-of-court settings does not restrain them from expressing past violence in mediation. In addition to these factors, legal aid provided by the government and NGOs can also relieve women from their financial burden to file cases in family courts that may otherwise lead them to hasty solutions through mediation (Chowdhury 2011). Pertinently, there are many reasons, as discussed in the next section, for why women may become outspoken about family violence in mediation. To justify these reasons, the next section incorporates empirical results collected from the observation of mediation sessions and semi-structured interviews of mediators in Bangladesh. It also quotes the dialogue used by mediators and parties observed in mediation.

5.5 Effective Participation in Mediation of Women Involving Violence: Moving from Theory to Practice

Though contemporary literature argues that female victims of family violence are, in most of the cases, not capable of negotiating effectively in mediation, a different scenario has been observed through in- and out-of-court mediation sessions and semi-structured interviews of mediators taken in Bangladesh. In thirteen of the eighteen sessions observed, women voluntarily revealed past violence to mediators. For instance, the following example is taken from a family mediation observed in the family court of the *Dhaka* district.

Mediator: [to the wife] So, you complained that your husband beat you several times.

Wife: Yes, he wanted me to sell my inherited land and my jewellery for giving him as capital of business. But as I did not agree on it, he beat me.

Mediator: [to husband] So, you asked dowry, that is illegal.

Husband: I never asked dowry from her.

Mediator: [to husband] Dowry is not what you might get during your marriage or from the family of the bride, if you push your wife to provide any of her valuables including her jewellery without her consent that will also constitute dowry.

In two other instances, women admitted violence when asked by the mediators, as seen in the following in-court mediation at the *Narayanganj* district:

Mediator: What do you think about your husband's proposal to make reconciliation?

Wife: If I go back, he will beat me again, last time when I left my house, he beat me so seriously that I was about to die [trying to show the marks of bruises on her hand and face], how can you assure that he will not beat me again and my life will be safe?

Declining even a visitation right for her husband she continued, "if he comes to my house he will beat me again. He will beat my children too." Later the divorce was completed and it was agreed that the husband would meet his children in a third party's home and would lose his visitation rights if he tortured his children physically.

Therefore, the effect of family violence in Western liberal democratic countries—that hinders women's active participation in mediation and thereby limits their capacity to get fair outcomes through mediation—may not be applicable in different contexts, like Bangladesh. Evidence gathered from the observation of mediation sessions in Bangladesh is included to demonstrate that violence may not always affect women's capacity to negotiate during mediation. Based on literature, the following section further reveals some reasons that may have encouraged women to share their history of past violence and negotiate effectively in mediation.

5.5.1 Divorce: A Time for Change

As cultural knowledge determines "what is normal and what is able to be talked about, by whom, and in what context" (Bagshaw 2005, 207), women may not discuss family violence with others in a society that dismisses the topic as private and treats such discussions as inappropriate. Scholars, however, observe that the attitude of a society towards the revelation of family violence among married couples may change at the time of divorce. As observed by Neumann (1992, 234):

> During the divorce transition … the desire to please the husband is neither expected nor encouraged by others; indeed, society commands the wife to put aside her caretaking role and assume an adversarial role.

In an earlier study conducted by Chowdhury (2005, 52), in 85 percent of cases, neighbours in Bangladesh either help and encourage or remain indifferent about women's recourse to mediation and a discussion on their personal issues like past family violence in mediation. In only 15 percent of cases, woman's choice of mediation is condemned by the other members of their society. Such a changed attitude of the society towards family violence may help victim women to be more vocal against past family violence at the time of divorce.

One study shows that the rate of divorce initiated by women has increased in Bangladesh over the years (Monsoor 2008b, 18). Another study indicates that the prominent reasons for which women claim divorce against their husbands are dowry demand and cruel treatment (BBS 1996, 25). At present, "even the rural women are not prepared to tolerate any violence and such cases of wife battering may end up in divorce initiated by women" (Monsoor 2008b, 18). Although there is little scholarly literature on the response of women in Bangladesh towards family violence, it is rightly pointed out by Monsoor (2008b, 18), that "when a wife decides to seek a divorce, she often reports such violence." This means that divorce is a time for change which may result in a woman being outspoken about family violence that she had endured secretly to protect the idealised image of her family life (Astor 1995, 193).

5.5.2 Change of Social Knowledge against Violence

Though society remains less responsive towards family violence during the marital life of couples, help may be given to enable victimized women to take a bolder position against their perpetrator husbands at the time of divorce. As mentioned in the later part of this Chapter, NGOs operate different social and legal awareness programmes to develop knowledge of the attitude of society towards family violence and other issues of laws. For example, in the nineteen units of BLAST, information fairs are organised in the remote outlying areas to generate interest about spreading legal knowledge and justice and among grass-roots people. By entertaining them with musical programmes, they also raise awareness of their legal rights (BLAST 2005). Through their gender and social justice programmes, NGOs "seek to challenge and transform local knowledge and moral codes of conduct" (Siddiqi 2006a, 17). These supports, at both an individual and a social level, help to make changes in the knowledge of the society about family violence. Effective participation of the victims of family violence in mediation may also be possible through appropriate legal counselling and ensuring the safety of women in mediation (Field 2004). As revealed during interviews of out-of-court NGO mediators, NGOs provide counselling services to women and make them more conscious of their legal rights against family violence when they come to their offices, and they urge them to seek justice. Lawyers and mediators may be able to provide proper counselling and other legal support that helps to build confidence for victims of family violence and enables them to participate effectively in mediation. Research findings show that women have less anxiety about attending mediation when they are clearly informed about what they can expect from negotiation (Wade 1997).

5.5.3 Stringent Law to Restrict Further Family Violence

Women's awareness about the existence of stringent laws against family violence works as a source of courage during mediation. As shared by in-court mediators during interviews, in more than 85 percent of cases, along with family suits, women file a separate criminal suit against their husband with an allegation of inflicting violence during their marital life. Filing of such criminal suits in Bangladesh also places women in advantageous positions as such criminal cases may lead to non-bailable imprisonment for their perpetrator husbands. While mediating abusive couples, Marthaler (1989, 61) observed that "it is important to follow procedures that encourage and allow the legal consequences of abuse to follow their normal course." In many instances, "strict adherences to the view that past abuse has its consequence and future abuse will not be tolerated" can change the behaviour of couples regarding violence (Marthaler 1989, 61). While explaining how legal provisions are helpful to enable women to get better outcomes in mediation, one mediator in a *Dhaka* family court responded:

> To me, better law is the strength of women in mediation. Without legal support the mediator's evaluation may not bring any fruitful result in mediation. What we say is already said in law, what we try to attain for women is already granted as a legal entitlement for women.

Amongst the fifteen cases out of eighteen, where family violence was one of the issues, mediators state the severity of existing laws in the case of violence due to dowry—one of the most common grounds of husband and in-laws violence—for which perpetrator(s) might be punished with the death penalty (section 11(a) of the *Prevention of Oppression against Women and Children Act 2000*). In one mediation session observed in a *Mymensingh* family court, the mediator asked the wife:

Mediator:	In your complaint you wrote that your husband and mother-in-law beat you frequently.
Wife:	Yes, they wanted me to bring BDT 10,000 as dowry. My husband always threatens me to remarry, if I fail.
Mediator:	[to husband] Did you ask for dowry from your wife? Do you know dowry demand is illegal and severely punishable under law?
Husband:	I never asked dowry from her. She is just lying.
Wife:	Never believe him. He and his mother demanded dowry and tortured me, here you see there are many spots in my hand; all he and his mother did in demand of dowry.

The result of observations confirms that use of law gives strength to women during mediation. Amongst the fifteen cases observed where women revealed their history of family violence, in three cases women specifically mentioned law as a negotiating strategy:

Wife 1:	I will put him in jail by using the law.
Wife 2:	He thought he can do anything what he wants. No, now the law is with us … I will not tolerate this anymore.
Wife 3:	I will be happy if he gets the maximum punishment provided in law. I wish that he will be in prison for his whole life.

Therefore, it seems that the existence of stringent laws to protect women from family violence and access of such legal remedies makes them more courageous to raise their voice against their perpetrator husbands in mediation.

5.5.4 Long Separation before Attending Mediation

Another important factor that may help women to speak in mediation despite the presence of family violence in their marital life is their long separation before coming to formal courts or NGOs for mediation. As observed in both in- and out-of-court NGO mediation in Bangladesh, all women attending mediation mentioned that during their separation time, they were living in their paternal home. In many cases, women escape to their paternal home to get relief from family violence, and get recourse from court or NGOs when their husbands fail to take proper initiative to get them back or provide any maintenance. Such separation may continue from several months to three to four years or even more before women come to the family courts (Monsoor 2008b, 90–110). During separation, most of the women live with their parents or relatives (Hosain & Begum 1999). Therefore, counselling from family members could be another thing that helps women to get rid of the control and fear that results from the family violence inflicted earlier. Adequate care from their loved one is indispensable to get rid of the traumatic memory that women may experience during their marital life (Langstaff & Christie 2000).

The reason women remain separated for such a long period without going to lawsuit in Bangladesh is probably because of the gender role socialisation that teaches women to continue a lifetime relationship in marriage. As a matter of fact, the major reason women divorce their husband is non-payment of maintenance (BBS 1996, 25). Therefore, when women pass a long period without maintenance in their paternal house and there is no more hope that their husband can get them back by giving them proper maintenance, they decide to go for dissolution. After a period of separation, when it is evident to the wife that the husband has already married another woman without maintaining any communication or giving any maintenance to her, she is prepared to dissolve the marriage and claim her legal rights against the husband.

Target women may be able to negotiate effectively if the incidence of violence is “a long way in the past” and “the woman knows she is safe from further violence” (Astor 1994b, 19). Gribben (1992, 133) took a similar view as she considered that genuine negotiation can be made by a target woman if “separation and safety have produced a sufficient change in the old relationship” that existed when a wife used to live with her perpetrator husband (Gribben 1992, 133). The reason why separation may relieve women from the trauma of past family violence can be explained by Pavlov’s theory of “extinction”:

> Upon the identification of the same stressor (or similar) that caused a reaction for the previous situation, the body would instantly trigger an overstressed response. However, in most cases, the new event will not constitute a threat. For instance, a noise could be a stressor from a situation in which a person ended up being assaulted. The same noise, or something similar, could occur in other situations which are harmless. Unless that stressor is reinforced (results in danger over time), [o]ur brain will adapt to the stimulus and gradually reduce the stressful response. (AIPC 2009)

Mediation can take place if "separation and safety" produce a "sufficient change in the old relationship to make it possible for there to be a genuine negotiation" (Gribben 1992, 133). Therefore, as observed in Bangladesh, long separation and counselling from family members may enable the victimized women to find relief from the trauma of past family violence, speak about family violence and negotiate effectively in mediation.

5.5.5 Proactive Role of Mediators: An Avenue for Capturing the Possibilities

Both in- and out-of-court mediators were asked two specific questions relating to the participation of target women in mediation. They were asked about the percentage of cases in which women enduring family violence in their marital life may become afraid of attending mediation in the presence of their husbands, and if such a situation did arise, how they handled it. What was shared by eleven out of twelve in- and out-of-court NGO mediators interviewed is that in more than 80 percent of cases, women share their grievances and history of past violence freely in mediation. In an estimated 20 percent of cases women may initially be frightened to share information about family violence in mediation; proper counselling can overcome this problem. As informed by one out-of-court NGO mediator during the interview:

> When victimized women come to our office seeking justice, we sometimes bring them to a nearby police station to file a police complaint. Additionally, we provide some basic safeguards to target women, such as the phone number of police and a shelter home, or help them to attain a protection order against violence. All these help them to gain courage to participate effectively in mediation.

Table 5.1. Women speak about violence in mediation (interview)

Type of mediation	Percentage of women freely speak about past family violence	
	More than 80%	Less than 80%
In-court	5 (0.83%)	1 (0.17%)
Out-of-court	6 (100%)	0 (NIL)

Source: Interview of in-court and out-of-court NGO mediators in Bangladesh, 2009.

As depicted in Table 5.1, according to five out of six in-court mediators, more than 80 percent of those who attend mediation freely discuss the existence of violence in their marital life. In the case of out-of-court NGO mediation, all six mediators interviewed confirmed that in more than 80 percent of cases women discuss past family violence in mediation.

Even though in traditional Bangladeshi society, women are supposed not to share family violence with others, as discussed above, there is a possibility that this view of women may change at the time of divorce. Mediators interviewed also indicated several reasons why attitudes may change when women come to mediation. Firstly, to seek recourse from a court indicates that the agonies of their marital life must have become intolerable, and they feel they must end that relationship. When they decide to end the relationship, they may no longer want to suppress the secrets of their marital life. Secondly, they might even try to share as much as possible about the violence and other suppression they suffered over the years to establish the legitimacy of their claims during mediation.

In the case of out-of-court mediation performed by NGOs, women generally come alone or with one of their close companions when they make a complaint to an NGO to file a complaint for out-of-court mediation. Women feel more comfortable sharing their personal experiences about family violence either alone or with close personal allies. Moreover, many of the NGO mediation workers who hear women at their office also regularly take part in an awareness generation programme at the grass-roots level. Therefore, it would be likely for the woman to have already met the mediation worker who provides ongoing advice with the aim of bolstering their confidence in their rights in relation to family and social life. In response to a question, an out-of-court NGO mediator replied:

> Women discuss freely with us about their concerns including family violence. Because many of them are already known to us due to their presence in different social awareness programmes conducted by me and some of my colleagues. These women have utmost good faith that we are here to help them, and will not cause any harm even by sharing their grievances with other.

Therefore, sometimes women come to the office of NGOs as their first contact point after violence and share their grievances with NGO workers with whom they have some level of trust already, so there may be no need for rapport building. Some women even feel no hesitation in inviting mediators to look at the injuries inflicted by their husbands.

Unlike litigation, in-court family mediations are not conducted in open-court, but in the Chambers of family court judges. As shared by one family court judge-mediator, though the venue of in-court mediation has a more formal appearance, it may not create a barrier for women to share all of their personal feelings during in-court mediation. According to all in-court mediators interviewed, only in a very few cases may family violence cause serious problem to women's effective participation in mediation. The way in which mediators handle such situations is also revealed through the observation of mediation sessions in Bangladesh.

Table 5.2. Women speak about violence in mediation (observation)

Type of mediation	Revealed past violence	No violence revealed
In-court	6 (67%)	3 (33%)
Out-of-court	9 (100%)	Nil

Source: Observation of mediation sessions in Bangladesh (in-court and out-of-court), 2009.

Out of eighteen mediation sessions observed, in fifteen cases women freely shared their experience of past family violence, and were hesitant to do so in only three cases. Interestingly, all three events occurred in in-court mediation. In one in-court mediation session observed in the *Mymensingh* district, the woman was so scared of her husband that she remained silent even when the mediator asked her why she had come to mediation and what she demanded. Although the husband was saying that he was very willing to attend the mediation, and he would like to stay with his wife, it seemed that the wife felt so threatened that she would not make any comment. Following such silence, the judge-mediator conducted a brief private *caucus* to ask the woman whether she had been threatened by her husband not saying anything in mediation and whether she was willing to continue with mediation. But even then she remained silent and just said "do as you [mediator] think best to give me justice." Following this woman's silence, the in-court mediator referred the case to litigation due to ineffective participation of the parties.

In another in-court mediation at the *Dhaka* district, both the husband and wife were well educated and a part of the privileged class of the society. The wife refused to talk about any violence when asked by the mediator; rather, she urged the mediator to leave out those things which occurred in the past and to proceed with assisting her right to dower (BDT 100, 000) through mediation. As noted by the same mediator while giving an interview, the jurisdiction of his court covers mainly the more wealthy areas of the capital city *Dhaka*, along with a few poorer areas. What he observed over the years is that in most of the cases, more educated women from the higher income class are not interested in sharing details of events of family violence with him, and they prefer to settle the case by concentrating on the issues of the current dispute. On the other hand, less educated women who come from the lower income strata of society are more vocal in revealing details of family violence in mediation.

In another case observed in the *Narayanganj* district, the wife attending mediation cried continuously and was unable to participate in mediation. In that case, though the lawyers are not usually invited to attend mediation sessions, the mediator invited the lawyers from both sides and mediated the issues by facilitating the negotiations made by lawyers. Nevertheless, the woman was asked to give her consent before finalising issues. Unlike the frightened wife in the *Mymensingh* district, she expressed her opinion when asked by the mediator. During mediation, to relieve the anxiety of the wife, she was allowed to remain seated in the mediation room while the husband was kept waiting in an adjacent room. Though the inclusion of lawyers in mediation is sometimes criticised by in-court judge-mediators on the grounds of reduced party control and protracted delay in settlement, such inclusion is beneficial as it allows parties who are affected by power disparity and family violence "to express their views more fully in mediation" (Sternlight 1999, 320; Caputo 2007, 90).

More "importantly for victims of family violence, it can be argued that the legal profession has a history of accepting the responsibility for protecting the rights of traditionally disempowered members of society," e.g. for women in the context of Bangladesh (Field 2004, 89). Therefore, negotiation through lawyers would be a good strategy available to mediators by which they can protect the rights of those women in mediation, who are frightened enough to become incapable of negotiating effectively with their husbands. Such women, such as the one observed in the *Narayanganj* district, are capable of expressing their views when asked by the mediator. Therefore, such a strategy sometimes may allow victimized women the recourse of a low-cost mediation service that might not be otherwise available to them. On the other hand, for women like the one observed in the *Mymensingh* district who became silent perhaps because of severe and ongoing male violence, mediators choose to keep those cases out of mediation and deal with them through litigation.

Although these three indicative cases demonstrate the proactive role taken and the informed decisions made by the mediators when women may be afraid or reluctant to share past violence in mediation, both in- and out-of-court mediators use some general strategies that help victimized women to gain more confidence in mediation. As discussed in chapter four, these general strategies include informing women about their legal rights on divorce, asking directly about the existence of any past violence, and ensuring equal participation of women in mediation by asking direct questions about their demands. Mediators strictly control any dominating tendency or coercive behaviour from husbands. Further, they can also use a private *caucus* to provide necessary information sessions making the target women more aware about her legal and economic rights against the perpetrators who may not dare to share all their grievances before their husbands, and the use of counselling sessions to make the target more confident in negotiation (Gagnon 1992, 15). However, out-of-court NGO mediators usually do not need to arrange any separate *caucus* to reveal past violence because when women come to make a complaint individually or with their close companion, they often share their story of family violence even before submitting the formal complaint against their husbands. As observed by in-court mediators, compared with women from more educated and wealthy families, less educated women from lower income strata are more vocal about past family violence. Since Bangladesh is a poor developing country with a large majority of its women still living below the poverty line, we can reasonably expect that the trend set by less educated and poorer women dominates the scenario in Bangladesh. A similar scenario may emerge in other developing countries of the East.

5.6 Conclusion

The arguments of Western literature on the exclusion of violent couples from family mediation may be legitimate in Western cultures, but the socio-cultural context, the conditions of violence and the nature of mediation in many Eastern developing countries including Bangladesh are different. This means that Western knowledge on mediation may not be applicable in the different cultural contexts of the East. Women in the East are living in a society with different social norms to those of the women who are discussed in the Western literature. Following a long separation from their husband and living within the paternal house with the support of their own families, there is a possibility that even battered women may raise their voices in mediation. Further, effective counselling from mediators, lawyers, and NGO workers, along with some other factors, like stringent laws against family violence and generation awareness programmes from NGOs, may also enhance the confidence of target women and ensure their effective participation in mediation. Though in a traditional Eastern society like Bangladesh women remain shy in relation to discussing violence, because of the various factors discussed earlier, the position of women may change in mediation. This change can be understood easily if we consider the postmodern theory discussed in chapter three. As observed by Bagshaw (2001, 210–11) from a post modern perspective:

> Instead of fixed view of people as either villain or victim, or male or female, their subjective positions are varied as being fluid, contradictory, and dynamic … postmodernism decentres the self and promotes the notion of multiple selves. Instead of the concept of identity having fixed properties, attempts are made to conceive of it as fluid and shifting.

Thus, female victims of family violence may remain capable of raising their voices in mediation and so attend mediation by their own choice. In a related vein, Astor (1994b, 353) rightly observes that despite the existence of family violence, women should be able to attend mediation when they can make a free and informed choice to do so. Based on observation of mediation sessions and interviews with mediators, this chapter demonstrates that abused women may participate effectively in mediation. However, whether effective participation of women in mediation can ensure fair outcomes for them remains another concern and is discussed in chapter six.

CHAPTER SIX

FAIR OUTCOMES UNDER EVALUATIVE MEDIATION: AN EMPIRICAL EVALUATION AGAINST NORMATIVE *JURAL* STANDARDS

6.1 Introduction

It has already been demonstrated in chapter four that evaluative mediation can provide more "accessible" justice to vulnerable women. However, accessible justice through mediation does not necessarily ensure that mediated outcomes are fair. It has been said that "the caravan of judicial justice provides first class seats and that of mediation justice only economy class" (Boulle 1996, 55). Further, it has been argued by scholars in Western democratic countries that, because of many factors including family violence, gender role identity and power disparities, women may lack the ability to bargain effectively during mediation, and therefore may fail to attain fair outcomes or justice through mediation (Neumann 1992; Watson 1994; Kelly 1995; Mack 1995; Field 1996).

However, following the observations of other scholars (Davis & Salem 1984; Marthaler 1989), this chapter argues against the usual views expressed in Western literature that women with gendered power disparity and family violence may not be able to participate effectively in mediation and therefore fail to attain fair outcomes through mediation. However, as demonstrated in chapter one, mediation can ensure a quick resolution of disputes and a quick realisation of decree money in comparison with disputes settled through trial. Moreover, how a practice of evaluative mediation may ensure effective participation of women in mediation has been demonstrated in chapters four and five. Furthermore, in this chapter, it is demonstrated that evaluative mediation which is conducted under the shadow of law not only provides more accessible justice for women, a quick resolution of disputes, and a quick realisation of decree money, but also ensures fair outcomes for women in comparison with outcomes attained through trial.

To validate the claim that mediation is providing fair outcomes, Rawls' (1999) theory of justice is used to compare outcomes obtained through family mediation and those obtained through litigation, taking the outcomes of litigation as a benchmark for this purpose. As the outcomes attained through litigation follow the standards of law, they are used as standards for comparison between outcomes of mediation and litigation. This comparison of outcomes from mediation and litigation was made by using outcome data[32] on family cases and family mediations conducted at different court registries and NGO registries in Bangladesh.

As observed by Mnookin & Kornhauser (1979), though parties to mediation keep the legal standards in mind while making negotiated agreements, they may also tailor the standard outcomes according to their own needs and interests. Fulfilling such needs can also be considered as fair (Deutsch 1975, 1985; Mannix et al. 1995). Different philosophers and social scientists have discussed distributive justice from different perspectives (Thibaut & Walker 1975; Cohen 1986; Sabbagh 2001; Konow 2003). Taking the outcomes mentioned in law as a benchmark for distributive justice, making any such movement toward equality are justified as long as they do not worsen the situation of the least advantaged; movements away from equality are justified only if they benefit the least advantaged (Jones 1980, 284). Therefore, it may be desirable that mediated outcomes differ from the standard outcomes attained through litigation if they provide for the needs of the women and do not disadvantage them.

[32] Outcome data were collected from individual case files for in-court mediation and litigation and from individual complaint files for NGO mediation. These data included the amount of dower written in the marriage contract; the amount of paid dower, if any, in the marriage contract; the amount of unpaid dower; and the details of the decree passed (such as, whether the father or mother got custody of children; the amount of unpaid dower decreed; the amount of wife and child maintenance decreed, and any other details of the mediated agreement).

This chapter first highlights the notions of procedural justice and distributive justice, and then explains why distributive justice has been taken as the prime consideration for making such comparison between outcomes attained through mediation and litigation. Next, it depicts the justification for taking the litigation outcome as a standard of fairness that reflects both rule-bound and individualised law. When mediations are conducted under the shadow of law, mediated outcomes generally also reflect these legal standards. But in some cases, as predicted by Mnookin & Kornhauser (1979), the outcome chosen in mediation might vary from the standard outcome attained through litigation. The "difference principle" of Rawls' (1999) theory of justice is introduced to justify the differences in outcomes attained through mediation when compared with litigation. Using the notion of the difference principle, it is argued that such differences between the outcomes of mediation and litigation are for the greater benefit of women.

6.2 When is Justice Fair?

Scholars have a clear distinction when they come to the question of whether a dispute resolution system can ensure fair justice to its recipients. In many cases, scholars examine the fairness of a process or measure procedural fairness to comment on the overall fairness of justice (Landis & Goodstein 1986; Tyler 1988; Carney 1989). Other scholars emphasise distributive justice on the grounds that a fair process may not ensure fair outcomes, and participants of a dispute resolution process may not be happy with the outcome, even when they acknowledge positive aspects of the process (Cook & Hegtvedt 1983; Astor & Chinkin 2002). As explained later in this chapter, justice is defined as the state of affairs when a "person has been given what he is due or owed, and therefore has been given what he deserves or can legitimately claim" (Beauchamp 1980, 133). Following this argument, this part firstly discusses the notions of procedural and distributive justice and then the importance of distributive justice over procedural justice, or the importance of fair outcomes over a fair dispute resolution process.

6.2.1 Procedural Justice

As mentioned earlier, while determining the fairness of a legal system, many scholars have emphasised the procedural justice or fairness of the process through which a legal decision has been made. As observed by Tyler (1988, 105), four important criteria that make a dispute resolution process fair are "consistency," "accuracy," "bias suppression" and "representation." It is argued that a fair process leads to a fair outcome (Landis & Goodstein 1986; Tyler 1988; Carney 1989). Thibaut & Walker indicate two important factors—"process control" and "decision control"—against which we may measure the fairness of a justice system (Thibaut & Walker, cited in Tyler 1988, 104). While decision control means the ability of parties to influence the outcome of a dispute resolution process, process control refers to the amount of influence an individual has on the process through which a decision has been made or an outcome that the parties have settled upon (Claming & Giesen 2008). Scholars sometimes put more emphasis on participation (representation, as termed by Tyler) as the key to attaining fair outcomes, and raising the voices of participants in the dispute resolution process (Barr & Conley 1988, 137–8). Other scholars, however, state that parties may not be satisfied with the outcome attained, even when they admit that the dispute resolution process is fair (Cook & Hegtvedt 1983; Astor & Chinkin 2002).

6.2.2 Distributive Justice

Distributive justice can be described as a distributive "function to divide given collections of benefits and burdens to known individuals, when there is such a collection to be divided" (Beauchamp 1980, 134). The principles of distributive justice are usually evaluated under three competing criteria—equality, equity and need[33] (Buttram, Folger & Sheppard 1995). While under egalitarian theory, everyone should get an equal share from a common pool of goods or services distributed among all. According to equity theory, a distribution is made according to the effort a person made when compared with another. The socialist theory, on the other hand, emphasises the need of an individual. It neither requires a distribution to be equal for all, nor considers the contribution made by each person when compared with others (Beauchamp 1980). As discussed later in this chapter, outcomes attained through litigation can ensure all these three criteria of justice simultaneously. Therefore, in this chapter the three terms: "equality," "equity" and "need" are not treated separately, rather all three criteria of justice have been used simultaneously by using the more

[33] Two other criteria used are: (1) according to societal contribution and (2) according to merit (Beauchamp 1980, 134). See more on Nicholas Rescher, *Distributive Justice*, New York, The Bobbs-Merrill Co., Inc., 1966.

generic term "fairness" and have considered the outcome attained through litigation as a standard of fairness.

6.2.3 Procedural vs. Distributive Justice

As "process is not all" and the fairness of process may not ensure the fairness of outcome (Menkel-Meadow 1991, 220), procedural justice has not been considered as a standard of fairness in this text. Thus, by the term "justice," this chapter means distributive justice rather than procedural justice. As mentioned earlier, while measuring distributive justice, the average outcome attained through litigation is used as a benchmark for a fair outcome. The following section discusses why the outcome attained through litigation rather than other benchmarks of fair outcome is considered as more appropriate benchmark for this purpose. Furthermore, Rawls' (1999) theory of justice is used to demonstrate why the outcome attained through litigation can be considered as fair.

6.3 Measuring Distributive Justice: Law vs. Other Measures of Fair Outcome

One method of measuring distributive justice is to ask parties about their satisfaction with the outcomes of a dispute resolution process. After interviewing criminal defendants, Casper (1977–78) concluded that the perception of parties about their satisfaction with outcomes does not depend on any abstract notion of what is just, rather on the reality i.e. what others are usually getting in similar cases (Casper 1977–78; Tyler 1984; Casper, cited in Landis & Goodstein 1986). So, to measure distributive justice, Casper (1977–78) emphasises the relative outcome, i.e. the outcome attained by one individual when compared with others in similar cases. In the current context of this book, however, to evaluate the fairness of outcomes attained by women through mediation, such a relative measure of fairness depending on client satisfaction may not serve our purpose. As explained in chapter three "women generally expect fewer entitlements and are less experienced at asserting their own entitlements" (Mack 1995, 132). Moreover, women formulate reward expectations based on what other women rather than men in similar situations obtain. Since most women receive lower societal rewards than men, comparison to other women perpetuates "women's low reward expectation" (Bryan 1992, 476–77). Because of their gender, less belief in their own efforts, less awareness about their legal rights and lower reward expectation from the society, women who are asked about their satisfaction with the outcome of mediation may form a response based on what they think they *should* get rather than what other people would get in a similar situation (Bryan 1992, 576). Further, it may be expected that women will be more cooperative in bargaining and negotiation than their male counterparts (Watson 1994, 118). As observed by Taylor (2002, 259), in Asian economies women may "prefer harmony in interaction to open conflict or self-assertion." Therefore, if we rely on client satisfaction for evaluating outcome, the positive remarks made by women clients may not reflect the fairness of outcome even when they, especially the less empowered women, are satisfied. Additionally, many scholars suggest that community standards might not be an appropriate benchmark for measuring fair outcomes because, as described in chapter three, community standards are still discriminatory against women in many developing countries of the world. It is therefore better to compare the fairness of mediated outcomes with another normative standard, i.e. the law. In the following section it is discussed why, in the context of many poor developing countries, legal standards are not only legitimate, but also can be considered to be a more appropriate standard for women, in comparison with other available standards of fairness, such as party satisfaction or community standards.

6.3.1 Law as a Normative Standard to Evaluate Distributive Justice

Standards set out in law are sometimes considered fair outcomes for a dispute resolution process as law could be a combination of all three criteria of distributive justice—equality, equity and needs (Barendrecht et al. 2006). There may be errors in judgment or settlement agreements, but their expected average outcome is considered to be fair (Rawls 1999; Barendrecht et al. 2006). Moreover, law "is a system which knowingly struggles against inequalities" (Astor & Chinkin 2002). Therefore, when citizens respect and accept the probity of those who make laws and those who apply them, because of its struggle against inequalities, the law provides a benchmark outcome that is generally accepted as legitimate. Legitimacy of legal standards is important if we want to take legal standards as a benchmark for mediated outcome because all parties must accept a negotiated settlement as legitimate. Since family laws in many developing countries have knowingly struggled against gender inequalities, they can be considered as a legitimate standard for measuring the fairness of outcomes attained by women through mediation. Using the notions of Rawls' theory of distributive justice, the following part discusses how the family laws involving abstract rules and individuation can be considered as fair.

6.3.2 Rawls' Theory of Distributive Justice

In this Chapter, Rawls' (1999) theory of justice is used to examine distributive fairness. The criteria of justice set by Rawls can be applied to practices, particular actions, or persons. Though in his 1958 paper, Rawls confined his analysis of the theory of justice to the practices of society, the same theory of justice can also be used at the individual level. "The term 'person' is to be construed variously depending on the circumstances. On some occasions, it will mean human individuals, but in others it may refer to nations, provinces, business firms, churches, teams, and so on" (Rawls 1999:193–4). According to Rawls (1971):

First principle: Each person is to have an equal right to the most extensive total system of equal basic liberties compatible with a similar system of liberty for all (1971, 250).

Second principle: Social and economic inequalities are to be arranged so that they are both:

- to the greatest benefit of the least advantaged, and
- attached to offices and positions open to all under conditions of fair equality of opportunity (1971, 302–3).

The two principles of Rawls are concerned with the allocation of basic liberties and primary goods. The first principle is concerned with the distribution of basic liberties,[34] while the second is concerned with the distribution of primary goods that create social and economic disparity.

In his theory, the first principle considered by Rawls is related mainly to the rights we usually consider as fundamental and human rights under different constitutions and conventions. Rawls considers the distribution of

[34] By the term basic liberties, Rawls (1971, 61), means:

- freedom of participation in the political process (the right to vote, the right to run for office etc.)
- freedom of speech (including freedom of the press)
- freedom of conscience (including religious freedom)
- freedom of the person (as defined by the concept of the rule of law)
- freedom from arbitrary arrest and seizure, and
- the right to hold personal property.

a second set of goods, i.e. social and economic, from a different perspective. He accepted a "difference principle" to distribute these goods among its recipients based on their position as "least advantaged" in the society.

The difference principle of Rawls' theory of justice advocates a distribution of economic and social goods following the social theory of need. Unequal treatment among persons is justified if such treatments enhance the utility of the most disadvantaged section of a society:

> The Difference Principle requires that the basic structure be arranged in such a way that any inequalities in prospects of obtaining the primary goods of wealth, income, power and authority must work to the greatest benefit of those persons who are the least advantaged with respect to these primary goods (Buchanan 1980, 10).

For example, the Constitution of Bangladesh admits positive discrimination in law towards the "backward" section of the society[35] and also recognises equality of its citizens.[36] Similar assertions have been made in the Constitutions of many other developed countries of the East including India, Thailand and Colombia (Baines & Rubio-Marin 2005, 87; Nutiyal, Bourai & Semwal 2009, 52; Catherine & Evelys 2009, 15). While clarifying the principle of "equality before law" and principle of "positive discrimination," in the case of *Anwar Hossain Chowdhumy vs. Bangladesh* (1989) 41 DLR 43, Justice Sahabuddin observed:

> Equality before law is not to be interpreted in its absolute sense to hold that all persons are equal in all respects disregarding different conditions and circumstances in which they are placed or special qualities and characteristics which some of them may possess but which are lacking in others.

---

[35] Article 28(4) of the Constitution of the Peoples' Republic of Bangladesh provides that "Nothing in this article shall prevent the State from making special provision in favour of women or children or for the advancement or for any backward section of citizen."

[36] Article 27 further ensures equality before law to all its citizens. Article 31 of the constitution also provides that, "To enjoy the protection of the law, and to be treated in accordance with the law, and only in accordance with the law, is the inalienable right of every citizen …. "

Therefore, the principle of equality before law has to be illustrated not in its absolute sense (Brownlie 1972, 58; Sharma 1993, 14; Agarwal 1996, 21), but rather in its relative sense, depending on the persons "who are not by nature, attainment or circumstances in the same position, as the varying needs of different classes of persons often require separate treatment" (Shankar 2008). Thus, following the Constitution, different laws and government policies of many developing countries recognize special treatment for women and disadvantaged sections of the society.

For instance, in Bangladesh, a 10 percent quota is reserved for women in public service recruitment (World Bank 2007). One of the laws, for instance, that admits positive discrimination is the *Legal Aid Act 2000,* which makes only poor people eligible to get government legal aid. Likewise, according to the provisions of the *Guardianship and Wards Act 1890*, primary emphasis is given to children's welfare when determining child custody (section 17), because during divorce negotiation, children become the most vulnerable third parties who might not have voice in the settlement attained after divorce. Furthermore, as a disadvantaged section of the society, the rights of ethnic tribal groups are especially protected. For instance, 5 percent of seats in all university level institutions and a special quota in governmental job recruitment are reserved for them. Such positive discriminations are recognised because it enhances the welfare of the least advantaged section of the society.

Though Rawls' theory of justice involves two principles, the second principle, i.e. the difference principle, is mainly used in this chapter to justify the fairness of outcome of mediation in comparison with outcome attained through litigation. This is because family mediation is not concerned with the distribution of fundamental rights as mentioned in the first principle, rather with the distribution of dower, child custody etc. that are related to the distribution of wealth, authority and power as analysed in Rawls' "difference principle" of justice. The following section discusses how to measure distributive justice and how the concept of distributive fairness in Rawls' theory can be integrated in such measurement.

6.3.3 Rawls' Difference Principle to Legitimize Abstract Rule vs. Individuation in Law

As observed by Sunstein (2006), a court may provide justice on the basis of two different types of principles: abstract rules and individuation. Abstract rules specify legal standards unambiguously and are equally applicable for all. According to Rawls' first principle of justice, law can be considered as an abstract rule when it takes place in "a hypothetical situation in which people are behind a 'veil of ignorance' of their places in society, i.e., their social status, wealth, abilities, strength, etc." (Konow 2003, 1195). For example, the Constitution of India declares that "all citizens are equal before law and are entitled to equal protection of law" (Article 27). This principle of justice should attempt to give guidance to justice through abstract rules laid down in advance of actual applications and is equally applicable in similar situations. But such abstract rules may not provide justice to the poor and vulnerable who have "special needs." Therefore, we may not use abstract rules[37] as benchmarks of fairness as such laws advocate equal distribution among all without considering the special needs of the poor and disadvantaged in a society. However, a quality justice system should protect the interests of the vulnerable (Astor & Chinkin 2002). Therefore, in practice, the portions of the substantive laws that are rule-bound or abstract in nature are complemented by individuation[38] the interpretation of which depends on the circumstance and the individuals concerned in a dispute.

---

[37] "Rule-bound judgments focus on the arbitrariness and error that come from the exercise of unbounded discretion; those who favour individualized judgments focus on the arbitrariness and error that come from rigid applications of rules … Public authorities should avoid 'balancing tests' or close attention to individual circumstances. They should attempt instead to give guidance to citizens through clear, specific, abstract rules laid down in advance of actual applications." See Cass R. Sunstein, "Two Conceptions of Procedural Fairness," *Social Research* 73 (2) (2006): 619–620.

[38] It "emphasizes the value of individualized treatment and highly attentive to the facts of the particular circumstances. On this view, public authorities should stay close to the details of the controversy before them and avoid rigid rules altogether." See Cass R. Sunstein, "Two Conceptions of Procedural Fairness," *Social Research* 73 (2) (2006): 619.

For example, prior to the enactment of the *Guardian and Wards Act 1890*, the custody of children was guided under the Muslim personal law where it is said that a boy should live with his mother until he is seven years old and a girl should stay with her mother until puberty, and this rule was equally applicable in every situation. Subsequently however, this personal law has not been strictly maintained, and the law now gives emphasis to individuation under the principle incorporated in the *Guardian and Wards Act 1890*. At present, the custody of children depends on the principle of "welfare of the child" of the *Guardian and Wards Act 1890* (section 17). According to this principle, before deciding on the custodian of a child, courts have to decide in individual cases whether the welfare of the children will be maximised if custody is granted to the father or mother. To give another example, according to the *Muslim Family Laws Ordinance 1961* (MFLO) in Bangladesh, a husband should provide adequate maintenance to his wife and children. What will be the "adequate maintenance" for a wife depends on her socio-economic condition; it is personalised in nature. Therefore, individualised judgments, depend on the context of the cases involved (Sunstein 2006). As laws are not always specific, judges have the discretion to enhance the benefit to women, usually the more disadvantaged in the society, through the application of law. But the individual situation in different cases may vary widely. Therefore, the next concern is how to find a reliable benchmark for outcomes attained under individuation.

As we know, a judgment made by a highest court in a case can be taken as a precedent in other similar cases. "As these small rules accumulate, they often develop into a system of rules£ over time (Sunstein 2006, 622). For example, though not explicitly mentioned in law, analysis of empirical data collected from both family mediation and family court trial in Bangladesh indicates that in almost all cases, child custody is given to mothers. It has probably become a tradition which is not usually altered by judges except on exceptional grounds. Therefore, in practice, a sharp line cannot be drawn between the practices of these two different types of principles—rules vs. individuation. As Sunstein (2006, 621) observed:

> The line between the two conceptions is not always sharp. There is a continuum here, not a dichotomy. A procedure may be relatively rule-like; it may call for only a limited exercise of discretion … or a procedure may appear open-ended, but everyone might know that at the point of application, authorities cannot do whatever they wish.

In a mixed system, rule-free decisions are forbidden, but "rule-based decisions are banned as well … It works within the tolerable line between unacceptably mandatory rules and unacceptably broad discretions" (Sunstein 2006, 624).

Because of the blend of abstract rules and individuation of the legal standards, texts of abstract rules cannot be taken directly as normative standards to measure fairness in mediated outcomes. The objective values of individuation are not explicitly mentioned in legislation; rather, they evolve over time through practice. Therefore, the quality of mediated outcomes could be measured by comparing the decisions made under mediation and a '"legally sound decision that a fully informed and objective court would reach" under similar cases on litigation (The Study Group 2006, 15). As different criteria of fairness, namely equality, equity and need, are all considered while making decisions under litigation, we do not need to think about these standards of fairness differently. Rather, the outcome of litigation can be used as a composite index of these three criteria of fairness.

6.3.4 Application of Individuation in Mediated Outcomes

As pointed out in Mnookin & Kornhauser (1979), parties to mediation use the shadow of legal norms in negotiating disputes among themselves. According to them:

> To divorcing spouses and their children, family law is inescapably relevant. The legal system affects when a divorce may occur, how a divorce must be procured, and what the consequences of divorce will be. (Mnookin & Kornhauser 1979, 951)

Therefore, we can expect that mediated outcomes follow the shadow of legal principles. Critics, however, sometimes argue that under facilitative mediation, parties make their own decisions based on their interests and the mediator, being neutral, only facilitates parties to attain the decision through negotiation (Stitt 2004). Therefore, no matter how beneficial for women, a facilitative mediator may not be able to ensure that legal rules are applied while assisting parties to settle the outcome through mediation. However, the criticisms referred to above are of facilitative mediation where mediators take a strictly neutral role. As discussed in chapters one, two and four, mediators in many developing countries in the East including China, Thailand and Bangladesh conduct mediation in an evaluative mode with an extended view of neutrality and use legal principles as a standard of fairness while making their evaluation on the content of a dispute. The explicit use of legal norms by mediators is common in evaluative mediation (Riskin 1996; Boulle 2005).

Therefore, it can be expected that in the case of evaluative family mediation currently being practised in Bangladesh, mediators' evaluations are greatly influenced by the fairness standards set by family laws and those standards are reflected in the outcome of mediations. While conducting mediation, mediators can use both rules and individuation to enhance the welfare of disadvantaged women through mediation. As observed in chapter four, family mediators in Bangladesh conduct evaluative mediation under the shadow of law and inform parties about their rule-bound legal rights However, as explained in the next section, while making such evaluations, mediators sometimes may diverge from the expected outcome of litigation to enhance the welfare of the women through mediation.

6.3.5 Divergence of Outcome Attained through Evaluative Mediation and Litigation: "Difference Principle" as a Means to Rationalise the Gap

The difference principle under Rawls' (1999) theory of justice can be used to justify the difference between outcomes attained through mediation and litigation. As mentioned earlier, under Rawls' theory of justice, a difference principle admits deviation from a rule when such deviations are made to the advantage of the least favoured. In the context of Bangladesh, the difference principle is seen in action when women accept only a part of the unpaid dower money (though it is their legal prerogatives to get full realisation of unpaid dower money after divorce) in return for an immediate, lump-sum payment made by their husbands. There are substantial savings when a couple can resolve distributional consequences of divorce without resorting to courtroom adjudication. The financial cost of litigation, both private and public, is also minimised (Mnookin & Kornhauser 1979).

Fig 6.1. Cost differential on different paths of dispute resolution

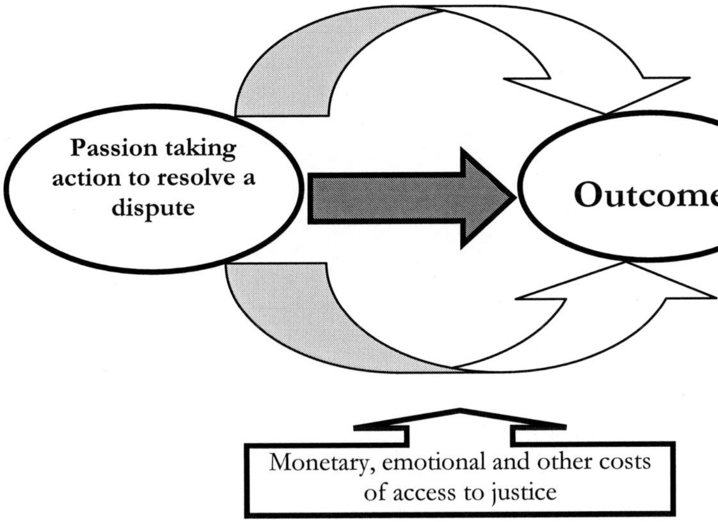

Source: Adapted from Barendracht et al. 2006, 7.

As shown by Barendracht et al. (2006), people may not always prefer to take the straightforward route to seek justice by, for example, filing a lawsuit in court. They may prefer an alternate way considering the time, cost, and emotional toll they have to bear. Therefore, as mentioned earlier, although every Muslim woman, for instance in Bangladesh, has a legal right to get the full amount of unpaid dower after divorce, sometimes receiving a discounted amount through mediation can be considered as a fair outcome under Rawls' difference principle when this discount is made for the enhanced welfare of the least advantaged women. As discussed by Mnookin & Kornhauser (1979), there are several reasons, such as risk of default, cost of enforcement on default and present value of money, for which parties to mediation may agree to accept a lower outcome than that which can be attained through formal court decrees. As discussed in chapter one, scarce availability of legal aid and a very low rate of realisation of contested decrees make realisation of post-divorce entitlements (e.g. realisation of unpaid dower etc.) uncertain for poor women through litigation. As shown later in this chapter, from the analysis of data collected from court registries, there is only a 17.7 percent possibility that women get "full" realisation of unpaid dower through litigation, compared with 58 percent (around 3.5 times of the rate attained through litigation) of full realisation through mediation. The next section of this chapter discusses this issue further.

As discussed in chapter one, the rate of realisation through litigation is very low. Therefore, while expecting realisation through litigation, women also have to take a risk that they will have to bear extra costs for a further execution suit. Moreover, by investing the unpaid lump-sum dower money realised quickly through mediation into other income earning activities,[39] poor women in Bangladesh can attain a source of income to meet their subsistence after divorce (BLAST 2007). Putting the lump-sum money into a bank account also attracts some interest. By comparison, if women choose to litigate they might only receive a very small return. Therefore, though discounted, such an immediate lump-sum amount could be more beneficial for women. While making a comparison of outcomes, we cannot ignore the context of women's life in a society like Bangladesh. We have to evaluate an outcome under the social structure that regulates the result. As Rawls wisely commented (1971, 61), "A distribution cannot be judged in isolation from the system of which it is the outcome." Given women's socio-economic situation in a poor developing country like Bangladesh, the cost and time-consuming litigation process, and scarce availability of legal aid in the country, there is a possibility that mediators and the parties will also consider factors like the risk of default, cost of enforcement on default and the present value of money etc. while evaluating an outcome through mediation. As observed through the mediation sessions attended in Bangladesh, in both in- and out-of-court NGO mediations, mediators highlight the issues of lengthy litigation periods, higher costs involved in litigation and the probable need for a further execution suit to realise the decree money. They urge parties to exploit the advantage of low-cost, quick resolution of disputes that can be attained through mediation.

The following section discusses how mediated outcomes deviate from outcomes attained through litigation. Firstly, the financial aspects: the realised portion of unpaid dower and the amount of monthly maintenance provided for women and children are discussed. Secondly, the non-financial aspects: the settlement of child custody and restitution of

---

[39] *Grameen* Bank and other NGOs in Bangladesh are operating many small-scale income earning activities in which women can invest to earn their livelihood.

conjugal life in mediation as well as litigation are considered. This section also highlights whether the non-financial aspect—child custody—has any impact on the settlement of financial issues in mediation.

6.4 Comparative Outcomes Attained through Evaluative Mediation and Litigation: An Empirical Evaluation on Financial and Non-Financial Outcomes

This section provides a comparison of how different financial and non-financial issues are resolved through mediation compared with litigation, and how non-financial issues like child custody and restitution of conjugal life may affect the financial outcomes that women receive through mediation. As already discussed, during mediation clients may make agreements that deviate from the rules stated in law. For example, as demonstrated in Table 6.1, unlike litigation, women in mediation may make mediation agreements that involve taking less than their full amount of unpaid dower. Whether such deviations in mediated outcome can benefit women is our next concern in this chapter. Criteria given by Mnookin & Kornhauser (1979) are used to evaluate the fairness of mediated outcomes compared with litigation outcomes.

6.4.1 Realisation of Dower Money

Dower can be explained as a safeguard for Muslim women against post divorce economic vulnerability (Chowdhury 2011). Repaying unpaid dower to a wife after divorce is not only a religious obligation for Muslim husbands but also a legal responsibility for them under section 10 of the MFLO. Therefore, in the case of litigation, judges in family courts always make full provision for the repayment of unpaid dower to women after divorce. Table 6.1 suggests that, in the case of litigation, every woman gets a decree for full realisation of unpaid dower. However, on average, only 17.7 percent of these women got full realisation of their decree money in 2006. Therefore, only 17.7 percent of decree money for unpaid dower is realised through litigation, and only a negligible amount of such money was realised before an execution suit. A study by former Chief Justice Hasan (2002) showed a similar trend.

Table 6.1. Realisation of unpaid dower through litigation

	Decree for full (100%) realisation on trial	Decree for Partial realisation on mediation *		
		65%	80%	95%
Percentage of women getting such decree	100%	None	None	None
Percentage of unpaid dower realised on an average	17.7%	N/A	N/A	N/A

* In case of litigation, every woman got a decree for 100 percent realisation of their unpaid dower. Therefore, none received a decree for partial realisation of dower. The 65 percent, 80 percent and 95 percent rates were calculated as an average of 60–70 percent, 70–90 percent and 90–100 percent rate of realisation respectively.
Source: Data from court registries in *Dhaka*, *Narayanganj* and *Mymensingh* districts, Bangladesh.

As shown in Table 6.2, in the case of in-court mediation, 69.7 percent of women got a mediation decree for 100 percent realisation of their unpaid dower money. However, there is a possibility that women may get a decree to receive a part of the unpaid dower money payable by their husbands under the marriage contract. In the three different districts covered by this study, for the remaining 30.3 percent of women, the decree amount varied from 65 percent to 95 percent of their unpaid dower money. A detailed calculation in Table 6.2 shows that on an average, women realised 78.7 percent of their unpaid dower money through in-court mediation.

The calculations in Table 6.2 indicate that on average, women in in-court mediation realised 78.7 percent of their unpaid dower money. On the other hand, in the case of litigation, though all women got a decree for 100 percent realisation of their dower money, the average rate of realisation for litigation is only 17.7 percent. Therefore, women in in-court mediation can realise their unpaid dower at around four and a half times the rate of unpaid dower realised under litigation. One reason why men are not interested in repaying under litigation could be the increased level of hostility between the parties in litigation. Another reason may be that in mediation, parties make a mediation agreement authenticated by the court as a decree and they cannot appeal against a mediated decree. Therefore, defendant husbands may feel a greater obligation to repay. However, in the case of litigation, defendant husbands do not make a mutual agreement and can appeal to a higher court against the contested decree passed by a family court. Therefore, defendant husbands may not repay until plaintiffs file a further execution suit. However, as agreed earlier, due to their poor economic condition and scarce availability of legal aid, women may not be able to proceed with execution suits and so fail to realise their entitlement under litigation.

Table 6.2. Realisation of unpaid dower through in-court mediation

	Decree for full (100%) realisation on mediation	Decree on partial realisation of dower up to		
		65 %	80 %	95 %
Percentage of women getting such a decree	69.7	4.3	10.7	15.3
Percentage of unpaid dower realised on an average	82.3	82.3	82.3	82.3
Percentage of unpaid dower realised for this group	57.4	2.3	7.0	12.0

Note: Full decree means women got a decree for the total amount of their unpaid dower.
Source: Data from court registries in *Dhaka*, *Narayanganj* and *Mymensingh* districts, Bangladesh.

Table 6.3 indicates that 72.1 percent realisation of unpaid dower through out-of-court NGO mediation, though slightly behind, is comparable with the realisation through in-court mediation of 78.7 percent. Careful observation, however, reveals that the rate of realisation of unpaid dower through in-court mediation is higher than the similar rate in out-of-court NGO mediation for two reasons. Firstly, the average rate of realisation through in-court mediation (82.3 percent) is higher than the average rate of realisation through out-of-court NGO mediation (78.2 percent). Further, the percentage of women getting a decree for 80 percent or more of their unpaid dower is higher for in-court mediation (12 percent) in comparison with out-of-court NGO mediation (7.7 percent). Nevertheless, in terms of probable realisation of unpaid dower, women who use in- or out-of-court NGO mediation fare better than if they choose litigation, which offers only a 17.7 percent probability that the full amount of unpaid dower could be realised.

Table 6.3. Realisation of unpaid dower through out-of-court NGO mediation

	Decree for full (100%) realisation on mediation	Partial decree on mediation for realisation up to			Total
		65 %	80 %	95 %	
Percentage of women getting such a decree	61.7	11.1	16.9	10.3	
Percentage of unpaid dower realised on an average	78.2	78.2	78.2	78.2	
Percentage of unpaid dower realised for this group	48.2	5.6	10.6	7.7	72.1

Source: Data from court registries and BLAST registries in *Dhaka*, *Narayanganj* and *Mymensingh* districts, Bangladesh.

It is not only that women have a very low chance of getting full realisation of the total unpaid dower through litigation when compared with mediation. To get realisation through litigation rather than mediation, women also have to pay high-cost lawyer's fees and other related expenditures (Barendrecht et al. 2006, 14). As discussed in chapter one, while only 5 percent of in-court mediation cases require a lawyer's fee exceeding BDT 5000, in more than 75 percent of the litigation cases lawyers' fees exceed BDT 5000 and could even exceed BDT 10,000. This cost differential between litigation and mediation should be considered while considering the fairness of mediated outcomes in comparison with outcomes from litigation. While doing so, we should not look only at how much women can realise through mediation and litigation, but also how much all parties can save.

The cost differential for lawyers' fees is a significant amount for most women when compared with their unpaid dower. Analysis of data collected from marriage contracts kept in different court and NGO registries indicates that in more than 80 percent of cases, the amount of unpaid dower was BDT 50,000 or less. Therefore, to ensure recovery through litigation, more than 80 percent of women might have to sacrifice 10 percent or more of their unpaid dower as an extra fee for lawyers. This ratio increases when clients need to run a further execution suit. Cases resolved through out-of-court NGO mediation do not require parties to bear any legal cost. Therefore, women might have to sacrifice comparatively more of their unpaid dower if they choose litigation in favour of out-of-court NGO mediation. The possibility of realisation through litigation in comparison with mediation becomes even more marginal when we consider other costs of litigation, such as more days of court attendance, higher cost of transportation and lodging, lost wages etc. (Barendrecht et al. 2006, 14).

6.4.2 Child and Wife Maintenance

According to Islamic law, a father has to pay periodic child maintenance to the custodian of the children (usually mother) after divorce until the maturity of a boy and until the marriage of a girl. Further, a wife is eligible to get maintenance for a three months period after divorce. Past maintenance for wives and children may also be applied for, if the parents separated before divorce. The amount of post and past maintenance for the wife under in-court mediation is usually paid as a lump sum payment or as instalments for the amount of unpaid dower. In the case of litigation, post-divorce child maintenance is determined as a periodic payment. Therefore, due to the lower rate of realisation in litigation, periodic child maintenance may stop after a few instalments. However, in the case of mediation, child maintenance is usually calculated as a lump sum or in a limited number of instalments. These payments are also usually paid along with the unpaid dower. As shown in Table 6.4, the recovery rate for past and post maintenance of wife and children is much better under mediation when compared with litigation.

After comparing financial matters attained through litigation and those of mediation, the following sections discuss some non-financial benefits and consequences of mediated outcomes over litigation.

Table 6.4. Recovery of child and wife maintenance in mediation and litigation

	Wife Past maintenance	Wife Post maintenance	Child Past maintenance	Child Post maintenance
Litigation	12%	9%	20%	13%
In-court mediation	65%	65%	65%	65%
Out-of-court mediation	45%	78%	50%	62%

Source: Data from court and BLAST registries in the *Dhaka*, *Narayanganj* and *Mymensingh* districts, Bangladesh.

6.4.3 Child Custody

Issues of children for women in mediation are more than economic (Haynes 1983, 90) as children usually have a more emotional attachment to their mother. Though it is presumed by Mnookin & Kornhouser (1979) that women may need to sacrifice a part of their post-divorce financial rights in order to get custody of children, no strong presence of such a presumption was found during the observation of mediation sessions in Bangladesh. The court grants child custody to a guardian in consideration of the children's welfare. In reply to a question during an interview, it was found that in all of the twelve in- and out-of-court NGO mediation sessions that, in consideration of the children's welfare, custody was granted to mothers. Statistics prepared from the data on mediation collected from court and NGO registries in three districts of Bangladesh indicated that, in cases of litigation in in-court mediation and out-of-court NGO mediation, custody of the children was granted to the mother in 85 percent to 90 percent of cases.

Table 6.5. Custody received by wives (mothers) over husbands (fathers) through litigation and mediation

	Dhaka	*Narayanganj*	*Mymensingh*
Litigation	88%	81%	83%
Mediation (in-court)	85%	86%	85%
Mediation (out-of-court)	92%	89%	90%

Source: Data from court and NGO registries of the *Dhaka*, *Narayanganj* and *Mymensingh* districts, Bangladesh.

Sometimes it is argued that husbands may bargain for child custody as a strategy to curtail the financial claim of their wives in mediation (Moonkin & Kornhauser 1979). However, fifteen out of eighteen mediation sessions observed in Bangladesh involved the issue of child custody. Out of these fifteen cases where child custody was an issue, in only one case of in-court mediation did the father seek physical custody of his children and bargain with the mother in this regard. Therefore, in more than ninety per cent (fourteen out of fifteen) of the cases, fathers were not inclined to ask for custody of their children. While responding to a question, nine out of the twelve in- and out-of-court NGO mediators interviewed reported that while mediating the issue of child custody they keenly observe the willingness of father and mother to get custody of their children. Mediators, both from in- and out-of-court NGO settings, agreed that in 80 percent to 90 percent of cases, fathers do not argue strongly for getting physical custody of their children. One in-court mediator replied:

> This is probably because; in many cases fathers got remarried and are not interested in getting physical custody of children from their former wives.

However, it was more common that fathers sought visitation rights. Among the fifteen mediation sessions observed where child custody was an issue, in thirteen cases fathers sought visitation rights in relation to their children. As mentioned earlier, in only one case the father sought physical custody of his children. In the remaining two cases, fathers did not even asked for visitation rights. Therefore, it can be assumed that in the context of family mediation in Bangladesh, it is not a frequent issue for wives to

sacrifice their other legal rights to retain custody of their children.
Though in most of the family cases, wives have to negotiate with their husbands to get a decree on different family matters, sometimes, after the death of husbands, wives have to negotiate with other in-laws, such as uncles and fathers-in-law to receive guardianship of their children. As is revealed by the analysis of data collected from different courts and NGO registries, when contested with other in-laws, widows (mothers) get custody of their children in two thirds of the cases. This trend persists in every district both in the case of litigation and in- and out-of-court NGO mediation. As shown in Table 6.6, the rate that widows (mothers) retain custody is higher in mediation (both in- and out-of-court NGO settings) in comparison with litigation.

Table 6.6. Custody received by widows (mothers) over other in-laws through litigation and mediation

	Dhaka		*Narayanganj*		*Mymensingh*	
Custody received by	In-laws	Mother	In-laws	Mother	In-laws	Mother
Litigation	32%	68%	25%	75%	37%	63%
Mediation (in-court)	25%	75%	24%	76%	35%	65%
Mediation (out-of-court)	20%	80%	22%	78%	24%	76%

Source: Data from court and NGO registries, Bangladesh.

Analysis of data presented in Table 6.3 indicates that the ratio at which mothers get custody of their children does not vary much between in-court mediation and out-of-court NGO mediation in any of the three districts covered in this study.

6.4.4 Voluntary Reconciliation of Parties in Mediation

Islamic law ensures the right to personal freedom (Chowdhury 2005, 163). Therefore, in Bangladesh, under the *Family Courts Ordinance 1985*, husbands and wives were previously eligible to ask the courts to pass a decree to restore their conjugal life if one member of a couple intentionally maintained separation from the other. It has been argued that although this remedy theoretically allowed for both husband and wife, its Anglo-Indian development has strengthened the already strong position of a Muslim husband when compared with Muslim wives (Monsoor 1999). It seems that husbands usually claim for restitution. The High Court Division of the Supreme Court pronounced that involuntary restitution against the will of the other party through litigation is opposed to fundamental human rights and therefore unconstitutional. This ensures that no husband can now file an independent case to restore conjugal rights and get his wife back if the wife does not intend to return (*Nelly Zaman vs. Giasuddin Khan* [1982] 34 DLR 221). If any such independent case is filed for restitution, the family courts rejects it. However, when family cases are filed with other issues, e.g. dissolution of marriage, or maintenance and dower of wife and/or child custody, mediators may attempt to make a voluntary reconciliation between spouses in mediation. Therefore, if both parties agree, sometimes reconciliation is possible in mediation. As observed in the mediation sessions, however, mediators never compel the parties to reinstate their conjugal life.

Reconciliation made under mediation is not unlawful because while attending mediation, parties may "voluntarily" agree to reinstate their conjugal life. In the case of litigation also, while disputing other matrimonial issues, parties may apply to the court to withdraw their case on the grounds that they have already made reconciliation to continue their conjugal life. Reconciliation under mediation has more strength to protect women's matrimonial rights because it is made under a decree passed by a court. Therefore, if a husband becomes delinquent after making reconciliation through mediation, a wife can sue him on the grounds of explicit breach of a court order. But in the case of litigation, if a case is withdrawn on the grounds of reconciliation outside the court, such withdrawal does not have any further legal effect if a husband becomes delinquent after reconciliation.

Data on reconciliation of conjugal rights through in-court mediation, out-of-court NGO mediation and litigation, as collected from court and NGO registries in Bangladesh, is shown in Tables 6.7 and 6.8. The percentage of reconciliation has been calculated from the total number of samples chosen in different rural, urban and suburban districts to see how the rate of reconciliation might vary among urban and rural areas in Bangladesh. For example, the rate of reconciliation was the higher for both in- and out-of-court NGO mediation in the rural district *Mymensingh*.

Table 6.7. Rate of reconciliation of parties (in-court mediation)

Reconciliation of cases	*Dhaka*	*Narayanganj*	*Mymensingh*
Total number of sample cases	118	29	27
Number of cases of reconciliation	36	4	15
Percentage of sample cases of reconciliation	31%	14%	56%

Source: Data collected from court registries in Bangladesh.

As depicted in Table 6.7, in 31 percent, 14 percent and 56 percent of all sample cases in the *Dhaka*, *Narayanganj* and *Mymensingh* districts, the parties agreed to return to live together. Comparison of the rate attained in the *Narayanganj* and *Mymensingh* districts supports our hypothesis that the rate of reconciliation is higher in rural areas compared to their urban counterparts. The rate of reconciliation was highest in the *Mymensingh* district, which is the rural area chosen for this study. The rate of reconciliation in the *Dhaka* district, which represents the urban area in the sampling, was around half of that rate for rural the *Mymensingh* district. The rate of reconciliation is lowest in the *Narayanganj* district where only a small number of total resolutions were made through mediation.

Table 6.8. Rate of reconciliation of parties (out-of-court mediation)

Restitution of cases	*Dhaka*	*Narayanganj*	*Mymensingh*
Total number of sample cases	90	30	30
Number of cases of reconciliation	32	12	18
% of sample cases of reconciliation	36 %	40%	60%

Source: Data collected from NGO registries

As indicated in the earlier discussion, reconciliation made through in-court mediation with specific written terms and conditions upholds women's rights better than the withdrawal of cases under litigation where reconciliation is made without any protection of their rights. Discussion of the qualitative aspects of reconciliation through mediation is as follows:

(a) Reconciliations are voluntary

It could be argued that cunning husbands may use mediation to persuade their wives to return to them and thus withdraw cases which would otherwise impose an unwelcomed financial burden on them. Another concern is that women may feel pressure to accept reconciliation when a mediator makes evaluative statements regarding the content of a dispute. However, observations and interviews with mediators indicate that no compulsion is made through mediation for reconciliation. Rather, if both parties agreed voluntarily to reconcile, mediators acted to preserve the women's rights while accepting such reconciliation. In five out of eighteen mediation cases observed, the couples came to the family court after they completed their divorce through the local authority, as mentioned in MFLO. Therefore, for these five there was no question of reconciliation as they had already completed their divorce. Amongst thirteen other cases where divorce had not been completed, in six cases women rejected the offer of reconciliation from the very beginning. Among the remaining seven cases, restitution was made in three cases—one in-court and two out-of-court. The last two women had initially considered restitution but later preferred dissolution of marriage and recovery of their matrimonial rights.

Though out-of-court NGO mediation shows a higher rate of reconciliation, and the rate of such reconciliation is higher in rural areas, the reconciliations made through NGO mediation are effective in creating lasting solutions among couples. A survey conducted by an NGO on post-mediation revealed that among 232 randomly selected previously reconciled couples, 207 (89 percent) were found to be living a peaceful conjugal life: "The good effect of mediation is expanding day by day and thus people are turning out to be capable of resolving their disputes through mediation" (BLAST 2007, 31). It was also observed during the observation of out-of-court NGO mediation sessions that poor women are not forced to return to their husband. Rather, mediators asked for the consent of women for possible reconciliation and in none of the cases observed did mediators pressure women to make reconciliation by using evaluative language. Mediators focused on the content of the dispute and tried to reconcile parties by providing some advice that could be acceptable to both. For example, in the *Dhaka* district, the following was observed in an NGO mediation attended by a couple with one child:

Mediator: [to wife] You have every right not to reinstate your conjugal life. Since you have children, you may consider reconciliation as proposed by your husband with some pre-cautionary clause. It's completely upon your decision. If you do not agree, your husband will be liable to pay your unpaid dower and maintenance and does not have any right to force you on this issue.

Wife: I do not want to go back. But what about my girl?

Mediator: According to law, your girl may reside with you until her marriage.

Husband: But I will get my son.

Mediator: You cannot certainly claim so. It depends on his willingness to go with you and also on his welfare.

Even when out-of-court NGO mediation fails, women may prefer to go to court using the legal aid services provided by NGOs. For example, among the total complaints received by BLAST, an NGO in Bangladesh, in 2006, 21.7 percent were resolved through mediation. Only a few of these cases were resolved through reconciliation. BLAST offers legal aid to every case that cannot be resolved through mediation. For 25.5 percent of the total complaints received, BLAST filed a lawsuit on behalf of their female clients. The rate of case filing is even higher in rural areas where the rate of reconciliation is high. For example, in the *Mymensingh* district, BLAST filed cases against 30.4 percent of the total complaints received. This rate exceeds the 24.9 percent of case filing in the *Dhaka* district.

(b) Conditional reconciliation of conjugal life

In case of conditional reconciliation, a woman may demand from her husband the payment of a portion of the dower money instantly, before reconciliation. According the Islamic law prevailing in Bangladesh, such demands can be made by a wife anytime during the marital relationship or afterwards. It can be termed as "prompt dower." The other part of the dower, i.e. the "deferred dower" can be claimed only after the termination of the marital relationship, either through divorce or otherwise. From data collected through this study, it is revealed that mediation agreements on reconciliation were made with a condition that husbands pay 50 percent of the unpaid dower money as prompt dower to their wives. It was also observed during mediation sessions that when husbands show their interest in reconciliation, in- and out-of-court NGO mediators generally followed a strategy that tests the genuineness of a husband's claim for reconciliation. They ask the husband whether he is willing to reconcile by paying the total unpaid dower to his wife or a part of it. As shared by one in-court mediator during interview, such a strategy works when a husband wants reconciliation. Moreover, an advance payment of dower enhances women's right to access their legal prerogatives. In a mediation agreement for reconciliation, a husband may agree to pay the prompt dower before reconciliation. For example, see the following from one in-court mediation observed in *Dhaka* court:

Mediator: [to the wife] Would you like to go back to your husband as he wishes? If you do not want to, your husband cannot force you to stay with him. Alternatively, you may demand a full payment of your dower and maintenance before making such reconciliation.

Wife: I tried for long to stay with him, but he does not provide a single penny for my maintenance. I would like to get a part of my dower as security before making any reconciliation with him.

Mediator: [to the husband] If you want to continue conjugal life with your wife, you have to pay a part of her dower money before reconciliation. Do you agree with her proposal?

Husband: I would like to stay with my wife. Though it will be hard for me to pay a part of her dower, I will pay it before taking her back with me.

Moreover, a mediation agreement on reconciliation is prepared where the husband consents to provide proper maintenance to the wife and children. Mediators also assure wives that if their husband fails to provide such maintenance, wives may come to the court again to make complaint against their delinquent husband. In such a case, the court issues summons and may arrest and prosecute a husband if he remains delinquent.

However, in some cases, reconciliation was made for a trial six-month period and with a provision to re-evaluate the desire of the wife to continue the relationship at the end of that period. Such a practice can safeguard a woman's likelihood of getting fair justice through mediation, and is followed when an agreement of reconciliation is signed in the presence of a mediator. However, in many cases, especially in the family courts outside urban areas, parties jointly submit a mediation agreement to the court and apply for the withdrawal of a case. In most cases, such mediation agreements are negotiated outside the court in the presence of friends, relatives or local elites. However, lawyers rarely make settlement out-of-court when a case is ongoing through in-court mediation. In response to a question, all of the in-court mediators interviewed during this study denied the possibility of any out-of-court NGO settlement when a case is ongoing through in-court mediation.

One problem of reconciliation that is made outside the court is the non-inclusion of specific terms and conditions. Sometimes, it is loosely stated that both parties agree to withdraw the case and to reinstate their conjugal life on the ground that they will continue to lead a peaceful family life. Though such reconciliation could have a detrimental effect on the welfare of women, according to all except one of the in-court mediators interviewed in this study, the rate of reconciliation varies from only 3 percent to 5 percent of total cases through in-court mediation. According to one in-court mediator, the rate of such reconciliation could be as high as 10 percent of total cases resolved through in-court mediation. Therefore, family courts may be more cautious about negotiated agreements prepared out-of-court and, through judicial screening, may add the clauses of such agreements discussed earlier to enhance the fairness of outcomes in mediation and safeguard women against any malicious reconciliation arrangement made out-of-court.

6.5 Fairness of Outcomes Attained through Evaluative Mediation: A Summary Evaluation

Considering the evaluation of outcomes attained through mediation, it can be demonstrated that the only area in which litigation delivers a better outcome for women is if a 100 percent decree against unpaid dower money is made in every case. However, these 100 percent decrees may not benefit women when it is considered that in only 17.7 percent of cases women are able to get a full realisation of these decrees. Though women usually sacrifice a part of their financial claim in mediation, this sacrifice may be seen to benefit women overall if it is considered that quick realisation of decree money can fulfil women's immediate financial needs after divorce. Earlier it is mentioned that, on average, women could realise 78.7 percent and 72.1 percent of total unpaid dower through in-court mediation and out-of-court NGO mediation respectively. Therefore, for in-court mediation and out-of-court NGO mediation, they sacrifice 21.3 percent and 27.9 percent of their unpaid dower to secure the quick realisation attained through mediation. Further, when women decide to resolve their dispute through mediation, they have to pay lower fees to their lawyers and this saving is equivalent to 10 percent of their unpaid dower for in-court mediation. In the case of out-of-court NGO mediation, this cost saving is even more as this mediation does not require the payment of lawyers' fees.

Furthermore, to realise their decree money under litigation, in most cases women have to file a further execution suit. This involves at least a few more years of delay in realisation. During this period, women can get 5 to 6.5 percent interest if they save the lump sum money attained through mediation in a savings account (Sonali Bank 2010). Investment in small ventures attracts even higher rates of return. They can get interest or earn profit by investing the realised amount in small income generating activities.[40] As further observed by Justice Hasan (2008, 14):

---

[40] In a random survey between 238 mediation beneficiaries, 217 (91 percent) utilised the realised fund for their socio-economic development. Some of those income-generating activities include (a) purchase of a Rickshaw-van, (b) deposits in Bank, (c) opening shops, (d) purchase of a lease. See more on BLAST Annual Report 2005–06, BLAST, Dhaka 2007.

> The female parties are benefited immensely by immediate realisation of the claim and recovery of lump-sum money through mediation[41] which might have otherwise taken years in a trial. It not only helps to alleviate their poverty but also encourages them to invest the money for financial security or to get trained for a career. Thus many of them enjoy financial independence for the first time.

Similarly, in a study it was observed that out of 38 beneficiaries who received their entitlement through mediation, 33 beneficiaries used the money to be self-dependent[42]. (BLAST 2006). Moreover, as demonstrated in earlier studies, the rate of realisation through litigation (even after an execution suit) is much worse than can be attained through in-court mediation (Hasan 2005, 133). Since the average rate of realisation under litigation is only 17.7 percent even after execution suit, there is an 82.3 percent risk that women may not get their unpaid dower realised through litigation. Women can minimise this risk by accepting a lump sum payment through in-court mediation (Barendrecht et al. 2006). Therefore, the minimisation of net risk when women switch from litigation to in-court mediation is 64.6 percent.

All these financial and non-financial costs justify the point that, considering the socio-economic context of Bangladesh, the welfare of women is enhanced through lump sum and immediate payment in mediation. Therefore, as indicated by Mnookin & Kornhouser (1979), to ensure quicker realisation, and to avoid future risk of non-payment, women may prefer to receive only a part of their unpaid dower through mediation. In response to a question relating to their role, mediators reported their various perspectives on the outcomes of mediation, all of which ultimately upheld the rights of women in mediation.

---

[41] From 1985 to 2000, the total money realised in connection with family court cases of the three courts [in the Dhaka district] is BDT 6,199,795 whereas the total realisation through mediation since the introduction of mediation in the same courts from June 2000 up to May 16, 2001, i.e. in twelve months, is BDT 5,094,501. See Hasan 2008, 14.

[42] Four beneficiaries set up small poultry farms or purchased livestock, fourteen beneficiaries purchased land, six paid off their debts, six others deposited money in the bank and three beneficiaries bought ornaments. Most of them were found to be independent and taking part in household decision-making.

Mediator 1: [In-court mediator, *Dhaka* district] I always try to promote a settlement so that women get as much as possible from their unpaid dower. When women may prefer to sacrifice a part of their dower for quick realisation, I impose a clause that non-payment of an instalment will impose a 50 percent penalty charge on next payment.

Mediator 2: [Out-of-court NGO mediator in the *Mymensingh* district] To provide women a due share in mediation, it is very important that the terms of the contract are very clear, especially when realisation is made through instalments. I always make the points concrete and double check whether women have an informed consent on that.

Mediator 3: [In-court mediator, *Narayanganj* district] What I try first is to make the point clear that to get dower and maintenance from their husband is an inalienable right for women both in religion and law. In my long practice of mediation, I found it an effective strategy to empower women in negotiation.

Therefore, when such evaluative efforts are made by mediators, it is highly likely that a fair outcome may be equally achievable for other developing countries in the East that share similar cultural practices as those observed in Bangladesh.

6.6 Conclusion

The comparison to outcomes attained through litigation and mediation suggests that though in the case of mediation women commonly settle a dispute with less money than when compared with litigation, if the context of a very low rate of recovery in litigation cases is considered, mediated outcomes still seem to be more beneficial for women. Although women have to sacrifice a portion of their unpaid dower money or child maintenance, in most of the cases women get a much quicker recovery of the decree amount along with a lump sum payment in many cases. If the outcome of mediation and litigation in the context of the framework provided by Mnookin & Kornhauser (1979) is considered, it seems that the large disparities between outcome attained through litigation and mediation arises mainly because of their markedly different rate of realisation, enhancing women's access to justice through quicker realisation of decree money and a higher financial security in their post-divorce life.

Although in many of the mediation cases women did not get regular maintenance for their children, they still got better financial outcomes compared with cases tried in court. This is because in litigation cases, women get a decree for child maintenance but it becomes very hard for women to realise the maintenance amount regularly if the husband becomes delinquent. Therefore, the sacrifice of child maintenance made by women in many cases in exchange for a lump sum payment under mediation adds positively to their welfare after divorce. Unlike litigation, mediation admits reconciliation yet women are not compelled to reconcile. As was observed in the mediation sessions in Bangladesh, reconciliations are always made with the "full consent" of the women. Moreover, in more than 80 percent of mediation cases, wives get full realisation of their unpaid dower money before making such a reconciliation, whereas in the case of litigation, such realisation can be made only after divorce. Therefore, the results of this study can reasonably conclude that family mediation in Bangladesh, both in- and out-of-court, provides fair justice to women than when compared to the outcome they could attain through litigation, and provides more financial security to women whether divorced or reinstated in their conjugal life.

CHAPTER SEVEN

CONCLUSION: TOWARDS AN *AEQUUS* SOCIAL DISCOURSE

7.1 Synopsis of the Findings

Discussion on the evaluative mediation made so far in this text candidly revealed that practices of evaluative mediation, conducted under the shadow of law, in many instances have the potential to put effective control on gendered power disparity and attain a fair outcome for less empowered parties, especially women, in mediation. A more interventionist role of mediators can minimise the impact of power disparity during mediation by challenging dominant discourses (i.e. pro-male social biases) and upholding legal discourses in mediation (Cobb & Rifkin 1991, 62; Taylor 1997, 221; Astor 2002, 75–6). Thus, gender equalizing and progressive changes in law have a positive impact by transforming the social knowledge and acting as a contributing factor to enhance access to justice through evaluative mediation informed by law. However, it is sometimes argued that changes in law cannot bring about effective change in society, and that legal changes cannot progress without social change. It is possible that such generalisation may not always be true. In fact, changes in law might only work smoothly to bring changes in society and redress social disparity when legal principles collide with widely accepted social norms that promote disparity (Graycar & Morgan 1990). Thus, even if social norms accept gender disparity, women can be empowered through gender equalising progressive legal changes in the society. A change in social attitude is not always a pre-condition for such empowerment. As observed by Foucault (1980, 132–33), the construction of truth is not the:

> "Ensemble of truths which are to be discovered and accepted" but rather "the ensemble of rules according to which the true and the false are separated" … It's not a matter of emancipating truth from every system of power … [e.g. power generated through social discourses] but of

> detaching the power of truth from the forms of hegemony, social, economic, and cultural, within which it operates at the present time.

Since legislation and case law are sources of rules that can define what is right or wrong, law can be used as a remedy to gendered power disparity even if such disparity remains in social discourses. This is because "the problem is not changing people's consciousnesses—or what's in their heads—but the political, economic, institutional regime of the production of truth" (Foucault 1980, 133). Therefore, gender-equalising legal changes can empower women by giving them a sense of entitlement (Mayer 2000, 55) even when considerable gendered power disparity exists in the society. In other words, the knowledge of a society towards right or wrong may change through law prior to a change in social attitude.

For instance, in many developing countries including Bangladesh, while society's attitude towards gender equality is progressing (ADB 2004, 1), gendered power disparity and family violence still remain in the society (Jahan 1994; Haq 1995; Monsoor 1999; Sobhan 2005; Khair 2008). However, legal practices in many developing countries are constantly redressing such inequality, and legal changes protecting women's rights are more forward-looking than attitudinal and social changes in the society (Chowdhury 2011). Normative evaluative approach is one such tool used to redress inequality in mediation, though not in the society at large. It is worth noting here that mediation is not able to correct basic social ills (Mayer 1987, 84); it is highly unlikely that a mediator will be able to change the sex role ideology, self-esteem or learned helplessness of a woman during mediation (Bryan 1992, 501). This means that a mediator cannot change the legal entitlement of a wife, which may affect her negotiation skill. Despite such limitations, an evaluative mediator has the potential to destabilize dominant discourse and create a marginalized one and thereby can control the power play of dominant discourse and can enhance access to fair justice for the vulnerable and marginalized groups in society. Considering the prospect of evaluative mediation in many developing Eastern countries, this chapter summarises the major findings so that such results could contribute to and encourage other developing countries, in the same context, to promote or replicate evaluative mediation as a mechanism for justice.

7.1.1 Evaluative Mediation Enhancing Access to Justice

At the beginning of this text, it was demonstrated that women's access to justice in many developing countries of the East, including Bangladesh,

India, Pakistan and Sri Lanka, is limited by the huge backlog of cases and high-cost of litigation (Kamal 2002, 2–3; The Asia Foundation 2002a, 7; Cheema 2005, 171; International Monetary Fund 2010, 158; Freedom House 2010, 577; Rios-Figueroa 2011, 313). The scarcity of legal aid (LGCBP 2004, 3), low cognizance of illiterate people about complex judicial process, and inadequate capacity of the judicial system to serve large populations have made the formal trial process even more off limits and obscure for poor and illiterate justice seekers in society (Singh 2002, 155; Joseph & Najmabadi 2003, 373; Calleros 2009, 170; Hualing 2010, 172; Chowdhury 2011, 2–5). Some scholars contend that a backlog of cases in courts and the consequent delay "has reached a point where it has become a factor of injustice, a violation of human rights," while others consider that the system of litigation becomes "too costly, too painful, too destructive, too inefficient for a truly civilised people" (Burger 1984, 2471; Alam 2000). Following this scenario, Evaluative mediation has been considered as a safeguard of access to justice for vulnerable citizens who may not be able to access justice through the courts.

Mediation has been praised by scholars for providing the low-cost and quick resolution of disputes (Folberg 2004, 20; Stockdale & Ropp 2007, 37; Crosby, Stockdale & Ropp 2007, 37; Gold 2009, 224; Lee & Hwee 2009, 15). It is also observed that the consensual decision made through mediation results in a higher rate of abidance in comparison with trial and the quick realisation of entitlements settled through mediation agreements (Picard 2002, 32; Sember 2009, 80; Chowdhury 2011, 218–22). Since the process of mediation is simpler and more easily comprehendible in comparison with trial, parties who attended mediation remain more satisfied with the process (Picard 2002, 32; Beck, Sales & Emery 2004, 457; Gold 2009, 224). Out-of-court or community mediation services are even more accessible and sometimes delivered free of charge (Chowdhury 2011). As discussed in chapter two, parties may remain more satisfied about the mediation process when the process matches with the pre-conceived cultural expectations of the attending parties.

7.1.2 Long Standing Cultural Root of Evaluative Mediation in the East

As discussed in chapter one, many countries in the East, including India, China, and Thailand, have a rich history and culture of practicing evaluative mediation. While an indigenous practice of evaluative mediation in the Indian sub-continent is considered as old as the villages themselves, in Thailand more than seven hundred years earlier, King Ramkamhang practised evaluative mediation for his people (Siddiqui 2005, 29; Yuprasert 2005, 199). A similar practice of evaluative mediation has been observed by scholars in other countries in the East (Cohen 1966; Chen 1996; Limparangsri & Yuprasert 2005; Siddiqi 2006a). Though the introduction of court-connected mediation remains a new phenomenon in many countries of the region, the practice of a traditional form of evaluative mediation exists in Eastern countries from ancient times, while the practice of facilitative mediation is a recent introduction in the West (Chen 2002, 2).

As elaborated in chapter two, a practice of evaluative mediation, rather than facilitative mediation, is more desirable in high-powered distant Eastern societies where disputants expect mediators to intervene in the content of their dispute and rely more on this quasi-authoritative intervention than on their own negotiation capacity and participation in decision making to attain a desirable outcome (Adamopoulos & Kashima 1999, 184; Kramer 2003, 342; Lee & Hwee 2009, 124). Though individual value systems of people living in different cultures are not identical, broad cultural values among them remain the same, on average (Rafel 2003, 56; Peterson 2004, 23; Spencer-Oatey 2004, 55; Wood 2011, 148). Furthermore, though cultural values on the surface may changes over time, the root cultural values may remain the same over centuries (Peterson 2004, 28). Therefore, the practice of evaluative mediation in many Eastern countries can be considered as a result of their culture of traditional dispute resolution and acceptance under their cultural norm.

Moreover, as disputants from Eastern cultures may have expectations that mediators would help them in the decision making process, evaluative mediators in the East may help parties to accelerate their decision making process by providing assessments, predictions, or direction, [which] removes some of the decision-making burden from the parties (Riskin 1996, 44). Similar to Riskin (1996), the importance of evaluative mediation has been emphasized by many other scholars (Bickerman 1996; Stark 1996; Lowry 2004). However, there is considerable debate and disagreement among Western scholars on whether a mediator may provide such evaluation without violating their neutrality (Love 1995, 104; Stulberg 1996–97, 990; Alfini 1997, 929). Therefore, the notion of neutrality or the nature of intervention made by mediators in evaluative mediation revolves around the centre of the dispute between supporters of facilitative and evaluative mediation.

7.1.3 Evaluative Mediators Rely on Impartiality Rather than "Strict" Neutrality

As illustrated in chapter two, many Western scholars have opposed the view of evaluative mediation or mediators' intervention in the content of disputes. According to scholars adherent to Western style facilitative mediation, a mediator shall only facilitate the process and not intervene in its content or outcome (Love 1995, 104; Stulberg 1996–97, 990; Alfini 1997, 929). Further, while making their intervention into the mediation process, mediators need to treat each side even-handedly (Astor 2007, 222; Boulle 2011, 77). However, the effectiveness of third party intervention in mediation depends on whether the nature of such intervention conforms with the disputants' prior expectation based on their cultural values (Adamopoulos & Kashima 1999, 184; Pel 2008, 58; Robbins 2009, 100). Therefore, since disputants in the East do not have a cultural expectation that mediators should remain neutral, neutral mediators who only facilitate the dispute resolution process and do not provide any of their evaluation on the content may not satisfy the disputants' needs. The role of a strictly neutral mediator may also leave mediation ineffective to provide fair justice when substantial power disparity exists between parties (Wing 2008; Bercovitch 2008).

To find conformity between theory and a demand from practice, an extended view of neutrality or a more robust approach is sometimes defined as a process where a mediator may intervene in the context of a dispute following a principle of equidistance (Astor 2000, 75–6; Taylor 2002, 172–73; Spencer & Brogan 2006, 93). It is argued that even when mediators may favour one party in one point and favour the other in another point to protect their interest, the "summative outcome" of such interventions shall be symmetric towards the parties so that mediators maintain their impartial position. However, treating two unequal sides equally results in inequality (Astor 1994, 153). Therefore, in this context, the impartiality of mediators is not defined from the perspective of the ethics of equality, rather from the perspective of the ethics of equity and fairness. An evaluative mediator may need to make more intervention to provide an equal standing of marginalized discourse in mediation. An evaluative mediator may not make equal intervention to each party but still maintain their impartial position if they define impartiality not on the basis of equality, rather on the basis of fairness. An evaluative mediator can protect the interest of a marginalized party in mediation, until it becomes unfair to the other.

As discussed in chapter six, evaluative mediators may consider legal entitlements and other associated costs to set their standard of fairness in mediation. Though evaluative mediators shall not determine the outcome of mediation, they can still intervene in the process and content of the dispute to help parties attain fair outcome. As observed by Lowry (2004, 84) even facilitative mediators make some internal evaluation to get progress in mediation. However, there is a legitimate concern that while making their intervention into the content of a process, an evaluative mediator may not bring their own perspective in such a way or to such extent that parties lose their ability to self-determine the outcome of mediation.

7.1.4 Evaluative Mediation Acts under the Shadow of Law

As illustrated in chapters four and six, mediators exercising a normative-evaluative approach may ensure fair outcomes for women. The reason that mediation appears to be protective of women's rights is not just that mediators are being directive or using an evaluative style, it is that they are insisting that the norms and values used in mediation are derived from the law and give women their legal rights. It is demonstrated in chapter four that the use of law to protect women's rights in mediation plays a dominant role to ensure fair outcomes for women. Observation of mediation sessions following the Riskin grid (1996) indicates that mediators educate parties about their legal rights and advise them about expected court outcomes. Mediators also used evaluative statements about the content of disputes based on legal principles, though leaving parties to make their own decisions on the outcome of mediation. The normative-evaluative approach used under the shadow of law is particularly beneficial when substantial power imbalances exist between the mediating parties. Taylor (2002, 172–73) termed these normative evaluative approaches as an "expanded view of neutrality" (different from a strict view of neutrality), and Astor (2000, 75–6) termed it a "robust approach" (different from the "minimalist approach") of mediation. Under the extended view of neutrality or the robust approach, a mediator takes a more active and interventionist role to settle the dispute.

7.1.5 Empowerment and Party Self-Determination Remain the Keys for Effective Evaluative Mediation

Evaluative mediation is an empowering process which may help parties to understand their best alternative to negotiated outcome and engage in more informed bargaining with their counterpart (Riskin 1996, 44). Parties may feel empowered when an evaluative mediator informs them about their legal entitlement (Mayer 2000). Mediators may have their own perspective. However, while making their evaluation to empower parties they need to practice self-reflexivity or remain open to listening and analysing party perspectives and should not impose their own perspective on the attending parties in mediation (Astor 2007). Moreover, while considering parties' opposing perspectives, evaluative mediators need to view from below or examine the marginalized discourse first (Cobb & Rifkin 1991, 56). This will assist evaluative mediators in their effort to ensure fair justice without being trapped by the dominant discourse that is usually taken as true and normal in a society (Bagshaw 2001; Astor 2007). Therefore, in pro-male societies where social discourses usually place men in privileged positions in comparison with women, evaluative mediators need to consider the narratives from women participants first.

Evaluative mediators need not follow equidistance but may set fairness as a standard to maintain their impartiality in mediation. Nevertheless, as evaluative mediators do not make decision for the parties, rather empower parties to bargain for a fair outcome, they need to decide about the extent of their evaluation so that parties can still be in control when deciding the outcome. As discussed in chapter two, this objective can be attained by applying evaluation until parties are able to analyse the perspectives raised by the mediators, and accept or reject them to maximize their interest. Empirical evidence collected from Bangladesh through observation of mediation sessions and from interviews with mediators also confirmed that it is the parties who ultimately make decisions on the outcome of their mediation. For instance, as illustrated in chapter six, evaluative mediators may abandon mediation and refer a dispute to trial if victims of family violence remain silent and are unable to make their own decision through mediation. Nevertheless, one of the core advantages of evaluative mediation lies in the power to challenge dominant discourses and uphold marginalized discourse to attain a fair outcome which may not be possible through neutral facilitative mediation in practice.

7.1.6 Challenging Dominant Discourse and Controlling Power Play through Evaluative Mediation

A mediator may intervene on the content of a dispute by adopting an extended view of neutrality or a robust approach, depending on the context of the dispute and if such interventions are made with the informed consent of the parties involved in mediation. This view is also supported by Stintzing (1994, 58) who argues that the important principle of the legal system is to protect the right of the weak and so any kind of alternative dispute resolution system that supplements or complements the formal legal system should also uphold this principle. Therefore, the interventionist role of the mediator to protect the right of less empowered women for controlling the impact of power disparity during mediation does not contradict with basic legal principles and so should be promoted.

Although there is disagreement about whether such a strong evaluative role should be taken by mediators, the decision about which type of mediation is appropriate is contextual. Using Foucault's (1980) post-structural notion of power, it was demonstrated in chapter three that a mediator can minimise the impact of power disparity during mediation by challenging the dominant discourses (i.e. pro-male social biases) and upholding legal discourses to protect women's rights under a normative-evaluative or robust approach of mediation (Cobb & Rifkin 1991, 62; Taylor 1997, 221; Astor 2002, 75–6). According to the mediators interviewed in the empirical study presented in this text, in 90 percent of cases, women attending mediation can express their views freely during mediation once evaluative mediators control the power play by challenging dominant discourses and empowering women by educating them about their legal prerogatives and rights against their husbands (see chapter five). However, concerns still remain on the effectiveness of evaluative mediation in resolving family disputes involving a prior history of violence.

7.1.7 A Culture of Long Separation and Post-Divorce Support from Others Might Lead to Success of Evaluative Mediation over Family Violence

The extent that past family violence affects women in mediation is an important issue discussed in the literature. As is the case for gendered power disparity, many scholars from Western liberal democratic countries have expressed strong reservations about the conduct of mediation with women who have a past history of family violence (Hart 1990, 326; Gagnon 1992, 272; Astor 1994a, 147, Astor 1994b, 3; Mack 1995, 125; Field 1996, 266). However, as mentioned earlier (see chapter five), women having a history of family violence may get fair justice through evaluative mediation. To explain this apparent dilemma, what was found based on the mediation sessions observed by Chowdhury (2011) was that mediators work to raise the voice of women during mediation by highlighting their legal rights and stringent legal provisions against family violence. It helps women to understand their legal prerogatives and express their views in mediation. During semi-structured interviews, mediators further claimed that women who are victims of family violence do not remain silent in mediation.

As was discussed in chapter five, target women may also be able to negotiate more effectively when they remain separated from their husband for a long time before attending mediation. The time spent apart may help them to recover from the past trauma of family violence and not worry about future violence (Gribben 1992, 133; Astor 1994b, 19). For instance, as illustrated in chapter five, in Bangladesh, more than 72 percent of women who attend in-court mediation remained separated from their husbands and mostly lived with their parents for an average of more than two years. The tenure of separation might exceed three or four years (Monsoor 2008b, 90–109). This delay is not necessarily due to an inefficient legal process and the courts, but is partly a matter of choice. The reason women remain separated for such a long period without seeking to claim their legal rights is because of the gender role socialisation which teaches women in many Eastern countries to continue a lifetime relationship in marriage. When women are separated from their husband for a long time without maintenance in their paternal house, and there is no hope that he is going to make the effort to repair the relationship by giving them proper maintenance, they finally decide to apply for dissolution (Chowdhury 2011). After a long time, if it is proved to the wife that the husband has already married another woman, without maintaining any communication and giving any maintenance to her, the wife might become desperate for dissolution and claim her legal rights against the husband. A long separation and a fear-free life among their parents and relatives also help women to come out of the control established by husbands through past violence. All these factors help them to negotiate effectively in mediation, despite a history of family violence.

7.1.8 Evaluative Mediation Providing Fair Outcomes in Comparison with Litigation

Mediation ensures quicker realisation of post-separation entitlement, and attains a better rate of realisation of post-separation entitlements in comparison with litigation. Results from earlier studies indicated that people are more inclined to pay the decree amount when they mutually agree on the amount settled. As observed by Hasan (2008, 132), a former Chief Justice of Bangladesh and one of the pioneers of in-court mediation in Bangladesh:

> For default [of instalment payment], a new case can be brought against the defaulting party, but it is our experience that rarely parties to a mediation get involved in further litigation for breach of term in mediation settlement. The compromise attitude continues to persist long after mediation settlement.

As mediation is a forum where parties can attain such mutual consent to resolve their disputes, the rate of full realisation of post-separation entitlement is much higher in mediation than litigation (Astor & Chinkin 2002). As demonstrated in chapter six, women can expect full realisation of their unpaid dower money through litigation in only 17.7 percent of cases compared with a full realisation in 78.7 percent of cases resolved through in-court mediation. The 72.1 percent realisation of unpaid dower money through out-of-court mediation is roughly comparable with the rate attained through in-court mediation.

The "difference principle" of Rawls (1971) was introduced in chapter six to rationalise the use of objective legal prerogatives for women as a standard of fairness or a benchmark that can be used to test the fairness of outcomes attained through mediation. However, women may sacrifice a part of their post-separation entitlement to attain quicker realisation through mediation. The framework given by Mnookin & Kornhauser (1979) has been incorporated to validate the reason for which women in mediation may sacrifice a part of the legal prerogative which they might attain through litigation, without reducing the value of the outcome. The result demonstrates that women may sacrifice a part of their unpaid dower in mediation, in consideration of the uncertainty of future receipts and legal costs to run a further execution suit versus potential returns from early investment of the money. Therefore, women may sacrifice a part of their legal entitlement in mediation, but compared with litigation, the net gain from in- and out-of-court mediation is much higher after taking into account the cost of savings and return on investment from the early realisation of post-separation entitlements through mediation.

In addition to their realisation of post-divorce financial entitlements, women are also realising better non-financial gains. As discussed in chapter six, in some non-financial issues such as child custody, mediated outcomes can be seen to be fair in comparison with outcomes that women may attain through litigation. For example, out of the fifteen mediation sessions observed in which child custody was an issue, in only one in-court mediation case was the father awarded custody of the children. In all other cases, women kept custody of their children. Interviews with family court judge-mediators and NGO mediators also confirmed that in most of the cases, mothers are awarded custody of their children. Therefore, empirical observation confirmed that evaluative mediation practiced in Bangladesh not only fulfils the cultural expectation of its disputants but also has a promise to ensure fair justice for the disadvantaged and vulnerable groups of the society.

7.2 Further Avenues for Evaluative Mediation

Though evaluative mediation remains an effective tool to provide justice to the poor and vulnerable groups of society, especially to women, the following recommendations would make this new avenue to justice even more available to socially disadvantaged people.

7.2.1 The "Extended Neutrality" Should be Handled Cautiously

The term "neutrality" is a much contested issue and there is no concrete yardstick by which we can rank what neutrality is or the extent by which neutrality should attach to its strict or expanded form. In fact, the desirability of using different forms depends mainly on the context of the dispute (Taylor 1997, 219). The concept of neutrality also varies depending on the cultural background of mediators and disputants. A mediator who is from a Western orientation is more likely to adhere with strict neutrality attained through a purely facilitative model, whereas a mediator with a background of Eastern culture may try to establish extended neutrality by using a normative-evaluative model (Taylor 1997, 220). Thus, while conducting an effective mediation, the context of the dispute and the cultural background of the mediator and disputants should be taken into account.

The shift of concentration from strict neutrality of mediators to extended neutrality and from neutrality to party control is, of course, a positive movement that can enhance the access to justice for mediation. However, while shifting such concentration, mediators should pay proper attention to the context of a dispute and the informed decisions made by the parties to accept more positive intervention by a mediator. Mediators should also require much training on understanding the context of a dispute and also know how to deal with people from different social and cultural backgrounds. Under the notion of extended neutrality, mediators can use the normative-evaluative approach to make normative comments about what parties should or should not do. While adopting the notion of extended neutrality, mediators need to remember that conforming to a dominant culture and not providing appropriate attention to the discourse of a party from a marginalized culture risks a power imbalance. To establish some standard for normative evaluation, mediators sometimes concentrate on a law-based approach (Mnookin & Kornhauser 1979).

7.2.2 The Practice of In-Court Evaluative Mediation Should be Advanced

As explained in chapters one and six, in-court mediation can provide quicker access to fairer outcomes for women in comparison with litigation. Resolving cases through in-court mediation can save the clients' money in terms of lawyers' fees, court fees, cost of transportation, accommodation to attend court, and the cost of lost wages. As demonstrated in chapter six, in-court mediation can provide a fair outcome in terms of women's net receipts. However, despite quicker resolution and realisation, the rate of settlement through in-court mediation is still low and remains in a primary stage for many Eastern developing countries. Therefore, governments should take the initiative to popularise wider use of in-court mediation in formal courts.

7.2.3 Proper Documentation of Mediated Agreements Should be Maintained by Providers

As discussed in chapter six, sometimes mediation agreements on reconciliation or withdrawal of cases include unspecific terms, such as "the husband will pay adequate maintenance as per his capability" or "the husband and wife will live peacefully" etc. In the case of reconciliation (both in- and out-of-court), it is imperative not to allow parties to make any mediation agreement based on such unspecific terms. Parties may mutually agree to continue their conjugal life, however the details and conditions of such reconciliation should be specifically written in the mediated agreement. It is then easier for women to make definite claims later on the basis of the written mediated agreement if the husband becomes delinquent in future. Moreover, if women agree to the condition of reconciliation, mediators may also encourage them to claim their unpaid dower at that time and to take a commitment from their husband that they will make regular maintenance. These provisions safeguard wives' future protection for post-separation entitlements if husbands do not comply with the mediated reconciliation agreement.

7.2.4 In-Court and Out-of-Court Mediation Linkage Should be Promoted

One limitation of out-of-court NGO mediation is that when any of the parties fail to abide by the mediation agreement and NGOs file a lawsuit to dispose of the matter through a formal court, the outcome of the time and money spent to conduct out-of-court NGO mediation becomes zero. This is because family courts initiate fresh in-court mediation without considering any outcome attained or evidence generated earlier through out-of-court NGO mediation. However, consideration should be given to the development of a mechanism to give legal validity to out-of-court NGO mediation agreements through a linkage with a formal court as done when disposing of the petty civil and criminal offences which are resolved by different local government bodies in Bangladesh. Thus, redundancy or repetition of the same process (i.e. mediation once in the out-of–court NGO and then within the court) can be avoided. This could provide women with access to justice at a more affordable cost and in a shorter time.

Furthermore, as discussed in chapter two, family disputes can be resolved in a much quicker time and at a lower cost through out-of-court mediation, in comparison with in-court mediation. Therefore, while exploring the opportunity of mediation, the government should also promote the use of out-of-court mediation services through NGOs. This would reduce the case load burden on formal courts and could provide justice to women in an even more accessible fashion with a fair outcome. Since NGOs provide legal aid in a much more efficient way than government, the government's legal aid fund could be channelled through NGOs. Moreover, better access to legal aid would also strengthen the effectiveness of NGO mediation through the potential for enforceability thorough a court of law.

7.2.5 Social Awareness Should be Generated to Change the Power Structure in the Society

As women can make their legal claims in mediation based on their marriage contract, and because parents arrange most of the marriages in

Bangladesh, appropriate social awareness programmes should be launched to educate parents to register the marriages of their daughters (see chapter six). Careful scrutiny of the terms of those marriage contracts (e.g. the amount of dower, paid and unpaid portion of dower, power of divorce, provision of maintenance etc.) should also be made while making such a contract. NGOs providing out-of-court services could play a major role in generating such awareness.

7.2.6 Legal Aid Services Should be Increased for the Efficiency of Evaluative Mediation

As discussed in chapter one, NGOs provide quicker, low-cost mediation services to their clients when compared with the in-court mediation services. An average time-to-resolution for out-of-court NGO mediation is only two months, or less than one fifth of the average time-to-resolution required for in-court mediation (see chapter one). Besides time and cost of resolution, provision for legal aid is often described as the "tooth" of mediation efforts, meaning that when one of the parties to a resolution violates the agreement reached or refuses to perform his part of the compromise, the other party has the option of resorting to a formal judicial remedy with legal aid support, if required (Sattar 2007, 31). As demonstrated by Chowdhury (2011), NGOs provide legal aid following a much easier process and a higher rate of success in courts, while a lion's share of the government legal aid fund remains idle in the legal aid committees of respective districts (see chapter one). It indicates that a better provisioning of legal aid to cases not settled through mediation increase the success rate of mediation. Better provisioning of legal aid creates a presumption in the mind of a stronger counterpart in mediation that the vulnerable party may get recourse to legal provisions at court, if amicable settlements are not made through mediation.

7.2.7 Gender Equalising Law Should be Moved on to Protect Women's Rights through Evaluative Mediation

As discussed in chapter four, the legitimacy of out-of-court NGO mediation may derive from the application of law in mediation. As reported by the out-of-court NGO mediators during interviews, in most cases a husband may not initially respond to a NGO invitation to attend mediation. Once NGO mediators issue a final invitation mentioning that they will instigate a lawsuit if a husband continues to remain absent from mediation, husbands attend mediation. Therefore, the better the application of laws for protecting women's rights in the country, the more it can protect women's rights through out-of-court mediation. Further, as discussed in Chapter 4, both in-court and out-of-court mediators may uphold women's rights by applying legal norms in mediation. When evaluative mediations are conducted under the shadow of law, mediations can also provide better outcomes to women because of the existence of laws that well protect the rights of women. Stringent laws against violence may also reduce the possibility of post-separation violence and can act as a bargaining chip for women in mediation (Marthalar 1989; Chowdhury 2011). Therefore, laws protecting women's rights and protecting women against violence need to be promoted.

7.3 Concluding Remarks

Mediation literature reflects a quandary and the struggles against the facilitative-evaluative dichotomy. Multi-cultural diversities also affect the content of mediation literature: "The needs of a heterogeneous, multicultural society will give rise to more diversity in the shape of mediation" (Lichtenstein 2000, 29). Accordingly, one point that needs to be borne in mind by prospective readers of this text who may come from Western democratic countries is that the cultural and religious base of family law and the nature of the society in the East, particularly in Bangladesh, are different from those of Western liberal democratic societies. For example (though in a restricted manner), evaluation on personal matters by community members may be permissible in the East but not welcomed in Western democratic societies informed by individualism.

Therefore, readers who have orientation with Western democratic society and a wide practice of facilitative mediation, might be justified in their respective contexts and the theory of their arguments might be convincing, however there is room to question the validity of transferring such theories in contexts of diverged cultural and philosophical paradigms. Any unthinking transfer of knowledge could lead to "cultural imperialism" which would not result in a positive change for any society.

Perhaps the most important lesson for the readers of this content is that any mode of mediation is not uniform; rather it is contextual. What is suitable for Western culture might not be perfect in Eastern society. Thus, facilitative mediation which is termed by Western scholars a "pure mediation" might not be suitable in Eastern culture. Apart from cultural variations, since mediation "theory itself is in flux" and its "practice in mediation are constantly changing" (Rothfield 2001, 247; Cohen 1995, 25), we cannot take a single mode of mediation (i.e. facilitative mediation) as an universal one and taking it as relevant to all contexts. It should be kept in mind that by itself, a mere decision to introduce or increase the availability of mediation services, following the Western patterned facilitative model, will not be the guarantee *per se* for ensuring women's access to fair outcomes in many developing countries. Analysis of empirical data shows that if mediators used legal principles, pursued an evaluative mode of mediation, and enabled women to have recourse to litigation using legal aid if mediation fails, a fair outcome for women is achievable. Thus, evaluative mediation has much potential, which is contrary to facilitative mediation, in accelerating access to fair justice for marginalized sections of societies, especially women. However, this text provides some important indications regarding the evaluative practice of family mediation particularly in Bangladesh under the shadow of law which contribute to the existing debate that the conduct of family mediation in the presence of gendered power disparity and family violence may attain fair outcomes for women. If the lessons are heeded, the experience of attaining higher resolution of disputes through mediation may also lead to a fair outcome for women. Thus, it is possible that the current trend of popularising evaluative mediation as an alternative means of justice will ultimately create a robust pedestal for women's access to fair justice in Bangladesh. Practically speaking, it will not be ingenuous to acknowledge at this point that many of its findings which are particularly applicable in Bangladesh might have importance in many other developing countries in the East with a similar contextual underpinning.

APPENDIX I
CHINA

The People's Mediation Law of the People's Republic of China[1]

Order of the President of the People's Republic of China (No.34)

The People's Mediation Law of the People's Republic of China, which was adopted at the 16th meeting of the Standing Committee of the 11th National People's Congress of the People's Republic of China on August 28, 2010, is hereby promulgated, and shall come into force on January 1, 2011.

President of the People's Republic of China: Hu Jintao

August 28, 2010

People's Mediation Law of the People's Republic of China

(Adopted at the 16th meeting of the Standing Committee of the 11th National People's Congress of the People's Republic of China on August 28, 2010)

Contents

Chapter I General Provisions

Chapter II People's Mediation Commissions

Chapter III People's Mediators

Chapter IV Mediation Proceedings

Chapter V Mediation Agreement

Chapter VI Supplementary Provisions

Chapter I: General Provisions

Article 1: To improve the people's mediation system, regulate the people's mediation activities, timely solve disputes among the people and maintain social harmony and stability, this Law is formulated pursuant to the

---

[1] Source:<http://www.procedurallaw.cn/english/law/201010/t20101030_460391.htm>l

Constitution.

Article 2: The term "people's mediation" as mentioned in this Law refers to a process that a people's mediation commission persuades the parties concerned to a dispute into reaching a mediation agreement on the basis of equal negotiation and free will and thus solves the dispute between them.

Article 3: People's mediation commissions shall observe the following principles for the mediation of disputes among the people:

1. Mediating on the basis of free will and equality of the parties concerned;
2. Abiding by laws, regulations and policies of the state; and
3. Respecting the rights of the parties concerned, and refraining from stopping the parties concerned from protecting their rights through arbitration, administrative means or judicial means in the name of mediation.

Article 4: People's mediation commissions may not charge fees for the mediation of disputes among the people.

Article 5: The administrative department of justice under the State Council shall be responsible for guiding the people's mediation work of the whole nation, while the administrative departments of justice of the local people's governments at or above the county level shall be responsible for guiding the people's mediation work within their respective administrative regions.
The grassroots people's courts shall provide guidance to the people's mediation commissions in their mediation of disputes among the people.

Article 6: The state encourages and supports the people's mediation work. The local people's governments at or above the county level shall appropriately guarantee the funds needed for the people's mediation work, and commend and reward people's mediation commissions and people's mediators that make outstanding contributions according to the relevant state provisions.

Chapter II: People's Mediation Commissions

Article 7: People's mediation commissions are mass-based organizations legally formed to settle disputes among the people.

Article 8: Villagers' committees and neighbourhood committees shall form the people's mediation commissions. Enterprises and public institutions have the discretion to form or not form the people's mediation commissions based on their own needs.

A people's mediation commission is composed of 3 up to 9 members. It shall have one director and, if necessary, two or more deputy directors. A people's mediation commission shall have female members and, as in an area of multiethnic population, have members from ethnic minorities.

Article 9: The members of the people's mediation commission of a villagers' committee or neighbourhood committee shall be selected at the villagers' meeting, the villagers' representative meeting or the residents' meeting; while those of the people's mediation commission of an enterprise or a public institution shall be selected by the employees' assembly, the employees' representative meeting or the labour union.

The term of office of the members of the people's mediation commissions is three years, and any of them can be re-elected as a member thereof upon the expiration of the term.

Article 10: The administrative department of justice of a county people's government shall collect statistics about the formation of the people's mediation commissions in this administrative region and inform the local grassroots people's courts of the composition of the people's mediation commissions, the members thereof and any changes therein.

Article 11: People's mediation commissions shall establish systems and rules for the mediation work, hear opinions from the people, and subject their mediation work to the supervision of the people.

Article 12: Villagers' committees, neighbourhood committees, enterprises and public institutions shall provide working conditions and necessary funds for the people's mediation commissions to carry out the mediation work.

Chapter III: People's Mediators

Article 13: People's mediators shall be members of and persons hired by the people's mediation commissions.

Article 14: People's mediators must be adult citizens who are impartial, decent and dedicated to the people's mediation work, and have a certain level of education, policy understanding and legal knowledge.

The administrative departments of justice of the county people's governments shall provide vocational trainings for the people's mediators on a regular basis.

Article 15: Where a people's mediator commits any of the following acts in the mediation work, the people's mediation commission which he belongs to shall criticize and educate him and order him to correct; if the circumstances are serious, the entity which recommends or appoints him shall dismiss him from the position or employment:

1. Showing favouritism to a party concerned;
2. Insulting a party concerned;
3. Asking for or accepting money or goods, or seeking for other illicit benefits; or
4. Divulging the individual privacy or trade secret of a party concerned.

Article 16: People's mediators shall be properly subsidized for loss of working time. Where a people's mediator gets injured or disabled in the process of doing the mediation work, the local people's government shall provide necessary assistance for his medical care and livelihood. Where a people's mediator dies for the mediation work, the spouse and children thereof shall get compensation and preferential treatment according to the relevant state provisions.

Chapter IV: Mediation Proceedings

Article 17: The parties concerned to a dispute may apply to a people's mediation commission for mediation, and a people's mediation commission may also voluntarily offer to mediate. However, no mediation may be made if one party has expressly refused to settle the dispute by mediation.

Article 18: For a dispute solvable by mediation, the grassroots people's court or the public security organ concerned may, before accepting the case, notify the parties concerned that they can apply to a people's mediation commission for mediating the dispute.

Article 19: Based on the needs for mediating a dispute, a people's mediation commission may designate one or more people's mediators, or the parties concerned may select one or more people's mediators.

Article 20: Based on the needs for mediating a dispute, a people's mediator may, upon the consent of the parties concerned, invite the relatives, neighbors or colleagues of the parties concerned, persons with specialized knowledge or experiences and persons from the relevant social organizations to participate in the mediation process.

People's mediation commissions encourage impartial, decent persons who are dedicated to the mediation work and are approved of by the people to participate in the mediation work.

Article 21: In the process of mediating disputes among the people, people's mediators shall stick to principles, make legal reasoning and do justice to the parties concerned.
The disputes among the people shall be mediated in a timely manner and on the spot so as to prevent the intensification of disputes.

Article 22: People's mediators may adopt various means to mediate disputes among the people in light of the actual circumstances of disputes, hear the statements of the parties concerned, explain the relevant laws, regulations and state policies, patiently persuade the parties concerned, propose solutions on the basis of equal negotiations and mutual understanding between the parties concerned, and help them reach a mediation agreement on free will.

Article 23: In the people's mediation of a dispute, the parties concerned are entitled to:

1. Select or accept the people's mediators;
2. Accept or refuse the mediation, or require the termination thereof;
3. Require that the mediation be made publicly or privately; and
4. Freely express their wills and reach a mediation agreement on free will.

Article 24: In the people's mediation of a dispute, the parties concerned are obliged to:

1. Truthfully state the facts of the dispute;
2. Abide by the order of the mediation scene and respect the people's mediators; and
3. Respect the other party's exercise of rights.

Article 25: The people's mediators shall take pertinent precautions if a dispute is likely to get intensified in the process of mediation and timely report to the local public security organ or other competent department if a dispute is likely to become a public security case or criminal case.

Article 26: If the mediation efforts fail, the people's mediators shall terminate the mediation process and, pursuant to the relevant laws and regulations, notify the parties concerned that they may protect their rights by arbitration, administrative means or judicial means.

Article 27: People's mediators shall note down the mediation process. People's mediation commissions shall set up files for the mediation work and place the mediation registration documents, mediation records and mediation agreements on file.

Chapter V: Mediation Agreement

Article 28: A written mediation agreement can be made once an agreement is reached between the parties concerned upon mediation by a people's mediation commission. If the parties believe it unnecessary to make a written mediation agreement, an oral agreement can be made, in which case the people's mediators shall note down the contents of the oral agreement.

Article 29: A written mediation agreement may contain:

1. The basic information about the parties concerned;
2. The major facts of the dispute, the disputed matter, and the liabilities of all parties concerned; and
3. The contents of the mediation agreement reached by the parties concerned, and the mode and term for fulfilling the agreement.

A written mediation agreement shall become effective from the date when the parties concerned affix their signatures, seals or fingerprints and the people's mediators affix their signatures and the seal of the people's mediation commission on it. Each of the parties concerned shall hold one copy and the people's mediation commission shall also keep one.

Article 30: An oral mediation agreement shall become effective from the date when the parties concerned reach the agreement.

Article 31: A mediation agreement reached upon mediation by a people's mediation commission is binding to all parties concerned, and the parties concerned shall fulfil it as agreed.
The people's mediation commission shall oversee the fulfilment of the mediation agreement and urge the parties concerned to honour their obligations as agreed.

Article 32: Where, after a mediation agreement is reached upon mediation by a people's mediation commission, the parties concerned have a dispute regarding the fulfilment or contents of the mediation agreement, they may bring a lawsuit to the people's court.

Article 33: After a mediation agreement is reached upon mediation by a people's mediation commission, when necessary, the parties concerned may jointly apply to the people's court for judicial confirmation within 30 days after the mediation agreement becomes effective, and the people's court shall examine the agreement and confirm its effect in a timely manner.

After the people's court confirms the effect of the mediation agreement, if one party concerned refuses to perform or fails to fully perform it, the other party may apply to the people's court for enforcement.

If the people's court confirms that the mediation agreement is invalid, the parties concerned may alter the original agreement or reach a new agreement through people's mediation, or bring a lawsuit to the people's court.

Chapter VI: Supplementary Provisions

Article 34: If it is necessary, villages, towns, sub-districts, social organizations and other organizations may form people's mediation commissions under the guidance of this Law to mediate disputes among the people.

Article 35: This Law shall come into force on January 1, 2011.

APPENDIX II
INDIA

ADR IN CIVIL DISPUTES

(A) *The Code of Civil Procedure (Amendment) Act, 1999*[1]
(No 46 of 1999)

Chapter II - Amendment of Sections

7. Insertion of new section 89 —

In the principal Act, after section 88, the following section shall be inserted, namely:—

Section 89. Settlement of disputes outside the Court-

(1) Where it appears to the court that there exist elements of a settlement which may be acceptable to the parties, the court shall formulate the terms of settlement and give them to the parties for their observations and after receiving the observation of the parties, the court may reformulate the terms of a possible settlement and refer the same for-

(a) arbitration;

(b) conciliation

(c) judicial settlement including settlement through Lok Adalat; or

(d) mediation.

---

[1] Source: <http://www.docstoc.com/docs/99607313/CODE-OF-CIVIL-PROCEDURE-AMENDMENT-ACT>

(2) Where a dispute had been referred-

(a) for arbitration or conciliation, the provisions of the Arbitration and Conciliation Act, 1996 shall apply as if the proceedings for arbitration or conciliation were referred for settlement under the provisions of that Act.

(b) to Lok Adalat, the court shall refer the same to the Lok Adalat in accordance with the provisions of sub-section (1) of section 20 of the Legal Services Authority Act, 1987 and all other provisions of that Act shall apply in respect of the dispute so referred to the Lok Adalat;

(c) for judicial settlement, the court shall refer the same to a suitable institution or person and such institution or person shall be deemed to be a Lok Adalat and all the provisions of the Legal Services Authority Act, 1987 shall apply as if the dispute were referred to a Lok Adalat under the provisions of that Act;

(d) for mediation, the court shall effect a compromise between the parties and shall follow such procedure as may be prescribed.]

(B) Mediation and Conciliation Project Committee's Draft Guidelines on Mediation[2]

Guidelines to the Mediation Process

The Chief Justice of India has constituted a Mediation and Conciliation Project Committee (MCPC) at the national level to lay down guidelines to make the Mediation Process as an effective tool for alternate dispute resolution mechanism. The Draft Code of the Canons of Ethics for mediators suggested by the committee provides:-

- Mediator enables communication, promotes understanding, focuses the parties on their interests, and seeks a creative solution to facilitate the parties to a dispute in reaching a mutually satisfactory agreement.
- At the commencement of mediation, it is a good practice for a Mediator to explain the process to the parties to a dispute and advise them

---

[2] Source: *Devendra Kumar Tiwari*, Adopted from Allahabad High Court Mediation and Conciliation Centre, India, available at <http://hcbaalld.com/Mediation.pdf>.

of their need of focus on their real interests and concerns. The parties ought to be advised that the process is entirely confidential and a settlement will be reached only if they voluntary agree to it.

- Mediation is a structured process but is conducted in an informal manner. A Mediator does not impose his judgement upon the parties to a dispute nor does he advise them on which proposal should be accepted or rejected. He only ensures to the extent possible, that the parties to a dispute have taken an informed decision while entering into a binding agreement and are fully aware of the consequences of the decision that they have taken.

- Impartiality is the fundamental basis for conducting any mediation. It is a good practice for the parties to a dispute to be made aware that the Mediator has no interest in respect of any of them or in respect of the subject matter of the dispute.

- In the event of a Mediator learns that he has any interest in either of the parties or the subject matter of dispute, it is his duty to so inform the parties in their presence and in case any one of them desires or suggests that the Mediator refuse from the Mediation, he must do so.

- During the mediation process, the Mediator must ensure that any action or communication by him does not raise any doubt in the mind of any of the parties that he has greater concern for one of them at the expense of the other.

- A Mediator must be well-versed in the law relating the subject matter of dispute and must be competent to remove any doubts that the parties may have with regard to technical legal issues that may arise during the course of mediation.

- Conflict of interest is a dealing that might create an impression of possible bias. It is a fundamental rule that justice must not only be don't but it must seem to be done.

Similarly it is a fundamental rule that not only must the mediation proceedings be impartial, free from prejudice and bias, but must also seem to be impartial, free from prejudice and bias. Mediation cannot result in a settlement if the parties lack confidence in the integrity of a Mediator.

The Mediator has a responsibility to disclose all actual and potential conflicts that are reasonably known to him or her and could reasonable be seen as raising a question about impartiality.

- A Mediator should not disclose any matter that a party requires to be kept confidential unless;

a) A Mediator is specifically given permission to do so by the parties at the mediation with an interest in the preservation of the confidence; or

b) A Mediator is required by law to do so.

It is good practice for a Mediator to inform the parties that all communications to him or her privileged and cannot be disclosed by him or her to anybody, unless specifically permitted to do so by the party disclosing the privileged information.

- A Mediator shall ensure;

a) That no third party is adversely affected by the voluntary settlement entered into between the disputants, without third party being involved in the mediation.

b) That where he or she is a judicial officer, he or she is not acting as a Mediator in respect of a dispute pending in his or her court.

c) That where he or she is an advocate he does not appear for any of the parties in respect of the dispute that he had mediated, either successfully or unsuccessfully.

It is good practice for a Mediator not record any reason why the mediation has been terminated or to convey to anybody (including a court if the mediation is conducted under the auspices of the court) the reason for termination of the mediation.

Mediation session

The mediation session has been summarized by *Sri Braja Bihari Dasa* as under:

1. Preparation
a) Arrange the room chairs and tables (seating arrangements), lighting, temperature, extra room for separate meetings, flip chart.
b) Review case notes, memorize people's names.

2. Opening Statement
a) Welcome and words of encouragement.
b) Purpose of mediation and mediator's role.
c) Logistics (time of session/bathroom, etc.)
d) What will happen

e) Confidentially
f) Separate meetings (caucus)
g) Willingness to go ahead

3. Uninterrupted Time
a) Set a courteous, unhurried tone
b) Explain listening and speaking
c) Each person with have a turn to speak
d) Listen to what each person has to say
e) Select someone to start
f) Protect each person's speaking time
g) check that the person has finished

4. The Exchange
a) Keep control of the session
b) Include each person
c) Ask relevant questions
a) Listen for interests and issues
b) Refrain from finding solutions yet
c) Watch for moments of understanding of reconciliation (golden moment)
d) Summarize their interests and concerns

5. Separate meetings/caucus
a) Assure them of confidentially
b) I wanted to talk to you about … (stay focused)
c) Be understanding but impartial
d) Check what you are permitted to say
e) When we go back to the table you will … (make an offer/behave better)

6. Setting the agenda
a) Summarize what has been accomplished so far
b) List the issues they need to negotiate
c) Agree on an agenda
d) If useful, agree on guidelines for subsequent discussions and decision making.

7. Building the agreement
a) Work through each issue in turn:

a. Generate options and ideas
b. Evaluate and refine alternatives
c. Test for agreement and explore consequences
d. Write down tentative agreements
e. Keep discussion on track

8. Writing the arrangement

a) Review each point of agreement:

    a. Workable
    b. Wording OK
    c. Acceptable?

b) Write out the final copy, read it aloud

c) Have everyone present sign and give each party a copy

9. Closing statement

    a) Acknowledge what they have accomplished
    b) Make payment/donation arrangements
    c) Review next step/follow up (more meetings?)
    d) Wish them well.

APPENDIX III
BANGLADESH

MEDIATION IN CIVIL COURTS

(A) *The Code of Civil Procedure (Amendment) Act 2003 (Act IV of 2003)*[1] *and The Code of Civil Procedure (Amendment) Act 2006* (Act VIII of 2006)[2]

Mediation

89A.(1) Except in a suit under the *Artha Rin Adalat Ain* [Money Lending Court Act], 1990 (Act No. 4 of 1990), after filing of written statement, if all the contesting parties are in attendance in the Court in person or by their respective pleaders, the Court may, by adjourning the hearing, mediate in order to settle the dispute or disputes in the suit, or refer the dispute or disputes in the suit to the engaged pleaders of the parties, or to the party or parties, where no pleader or pleaders have been engaged, or to a mediator from the panel as may be prepared by the District Judge under sub-section (10), for undertaking efforts for settlement through mediation:

Provided that, if all the contesting parties in the suit through application or pleadings state to the Court that they are willing to try to settle the dispute or disputes in the suit through mediation, the Court shall so mediate, or make reference under this section.

(2) When the reference under sub-section (1) is made through the pleaders, the pleaders shall, by their mutual agreement in consultation with their respective clients, appoint another pleader, not engaged by the parties in the suit, or a retired judge, or a mediator from the panel as may be prepared by the District Judge under sub-section (10), or any other person whom they may seem to be suitable, to act as a mediator for settlement:

---

[1]<http://bdlaws.minlaw.gov.bd/sections_detail.php?id=86&sections_id=15219>
[2]<http://bdlaws.minlaw.gov.bd/sections_detail.php?id=86&sections_id=25101>

Provided that, nothing in this sub-section shall be deemed to prohibit appointment of more than one person to act as mediator:

Provided further that, a person holding an office of profit in the service of the Republic shall not be eligible for appointment as mediator.

(3) While referring a dispute or disputes in the suit for mediation under sub-section (1), the Court shall not dictate or determine the fees of the pleaders and the mediator, and procedure to be followed by the mediator and the parties; and it shall be for the pleaders, their respective clients and the mediator to mutually agree on and determine the fees and the procedure to be followed for the purpose of settlement through mediation; and when the Court shall mediate, it shall determine the procedure to be followed, and shall not charge any fee for mediation.

(4) Within ten days from the date of reference under sub-section (1), the parties shall inform the Court in writing as to whether they have agreed to try to settle the dispute or disputes in the suit by mediation and whom they have appointed as mediator, failing which the reference under sub-section (1) will stand cancelled and the suit shall be proceeded with for hearing by the Court; and should the parties inform the Court about their agreement to try to settle the dispute or disputes in the suit through mediation and appointment of mediator as aforesaid, the mediation shall be concluded within 60 (sixty) days from the day on which the Court is so informed, unless the Court of its own motion or upon a joint prayer of the parties, extends the time for a further period of not exceeding 30 (thirty) days.

(5) The mediator shall, without violating the confidentiality of the parties to the mediation proceedings, submit through the pleaders, to the court a report of result of the mediation proceedings; and if the result is of compromise of the dispute or disputes in the suit, the terms of such compromise shall be reduced into writing in the form of an agreement, bearing signatures or left thumb impressions of the parties as executants, and signatures of the pleaders and the mediator as witnesses; and the Court shall, thereupon, pass an order or a decree in accordance with relevant provisions of Order XXIII of the Code.

(6) When the Court itself mediates, it shall make a report and passed order in a manner similar to that as stated in sub-section (5).

(7) When the mediation fails to produce any compromise, the Court shall, subject to the provision of sub-section (9), proceed with hearing of the suit from the stage at which the suit stood before the decision to mediate or reference for mediation under sub-section (1), and in accordance with

provisions of the Code in a manner as if there had been no decision to mediate or reference for mediation as aforesaid.

(8) The proceedings of mediation under this section shall be confidential and any communication made, evidence adduced, admission, statement or comment made and conversation held between the parties, their pleaders, representatives and the mediator, shall be deemed privileged and shall not be referred to and admissible in evidence in any subsequent hearing of the same suit or any other proceeding.

(9) When a mediation initiative led by the Court itself fails to resolve the dispute or disputes in the suit, the same court shall not hear the suit, if the Court continues to be presided by the same judge who led the mediation initiative; and in that instance, the suit shall be heard by another court of competent jurisdiction.

(10) For the purposes of this section, the District Judge shall, in consultation with the President of the District Bar Association, prepare a panel of mediators (to be updated from time to time) consisting of pleaders, retired judges, persons known to be trained in the art of dispute resolution, and such other person or persons, except persons holding office of profit in the service of the Republic, as may be deemed appropriate for the purpose, and shall inform all the Civil Courts under his administrative jurisdiction about the panel:

Provided that, a mediator under this sub-section, shall not act as a mediator between the parties, if he had ever been engaged by either of the parties as a pleader in any suit in any Court.

(11) Notwithstanding anything contained in the Court-fees Act, 1870 (Act No. VII of 1870), where a dispute or disputes in a suit are settled on compromise under this section, the Court shall issue a certificate directing refund of the court fees paid by the parties in respect of the plaint or written statement; and the parties shall be entitled to such refund within 60 (sixty) days of the issuance of the certificate.

(12) No appeal or revision shall lie against any order or decree passed by the Court in pursuance of settlement between the parties under this section.

(13) Nothing in this section shall be deemed to otherwise limit the option of the parties regarding withdrawal, adjustment and compromise of the suit under Order XXIII of the Code.

Explanation-(1): "Mediation" under this section shall mean flexible, informal, non-binding, confidential, non-adversarial and consensual dispute resolution process in which the mediator shall facilitate compromise of disputes in the suit between the parties without directing or dictating the terms of such compromise.

(2): "Compromise" under this section shall include also compromise in part of the disputes in the suit.

Mediation in Appeal

89C.(1) An Appellate Court may mediate in an appeal or refer the appeal for mediation in order to settle the dispute or disputes in that appeal, if the appeal is an appeal from original decree under Order XLI, and is between the same parties who contested in the original suit or the parties who have been substituted for the original contesting parties.

(2) In mediation under sub-section (1), the Appellate Court shall, as far as possible, follow the provisions of mediation as contained in section 89A with necessary changes (mutatis mutandis) as may be expedient.]

MEDIATION IN FAMILY COURTS

(B) *Family Courts Ordinance 1985*[3] (Ordinance XVIII of 1985)

Short title, extent and commencement

1. (1) This Ordinance may be called the Family Courts Ordinance, 1985.
(2) It extends to the whole of Bangladesh except the districts of *Rangamati* Hill Tract, *Bandarban* Hill Tract and *Khagrachari* Hill Tract.
(3) It shall come into force on such date as the Government may, by notification in the official Gazette, appoint.

Definitions

2. (1) In this Ordinance, unless there is anything repugnant in the subject or context,-
(a) "Code" means the Code of Civil Procedure, 1908 (V of 1908);
(b) "Family Court" means a Family Court established under this Ordinance;

[3] Source: <http://bdlaws.minlaw.gov.bd/>

(c) "prescribed" means prescribed by rules made under this Ordinance.

(2) Words and expressions used in this Ordinance, but not defined, shall have the meanings respectively assigned to them in the Code.

Ordinance to override other laws

3. The provisions of this Ordinance shall have effect notwithstanding anything contained in any other law for the time being in force.

Establishment of Family Courts

4. (1) There shall be as many Family Courts as there are Courts of Assistant Judges].

(2) All Courts of Assistant Judges shall be Family Courts for the purposes of this Ordinance.

(3) All Assistant Judges shall be the Judges of Family Courts.

Jurisdiction of Family Courts

5. Subject to the provisions of the Muslim Family Laws Ordinance, 1961 (VIII of 1961), a Family Court shall have exclusive jurisdiction to entertain, try and dispose of any suit relating to, or arising out of, all or any of the following matters, namely:-

(a) dissolution of marriage;
(b) restitution of conjugal rights;
(c) dower;
(d) maintenance;
(e) guardianship and custody of children.

Institution of suit

6. (1) Every suit under this Ordinance shall be instituted by the presentation of a plaint to the Family Court within the local limits of whose jurisdiction-

(a) the cause of action has wholly or partly arisen; or
(b) the parties reside or last resided together:

Provided that in suits for dissolution of marriage, dower or maintenance, the Court within the local limits of whose jurisdiction the wife ordinarily resides shall also have jurisdiction.

(2) Where a plaint is presented to a Court not having jurisdiction,-

(a) the plaint shall be returned to be presented to the Court to which it should have been presented;

(b) the Court returning the plaint shall endorse thereon the date of its presentation to it and its return, the name of the party presenting it and a brief statement of the reasons therefore.

(3) The plaint shall contain all material facts relating to the dispute and shall contain a schedule giving the names and addresses of the witnesses intended to be produced in support of the plaint:

Provided that the plaintiff may, with the permission of the Court, call any witness at any later stage, if the Court considers such evidence expedient in the interest of justice.
(4) The plaint shall also contain the following particulars, namely:-
(a) the name of the Court in which the suit is brought;
(b) the name, description and place of residence of the plaintiff;
(c) the name, description and place of residence of the defendant;
(d) where the plaintiff or the defendant is a minor or a person of unsound mind, a statement to that effect;
(e) the facts constituting the cause of action and the place where, and the date when, it arose;
(f) the facts showing that the Court has jurisdiction;
(g) the relief which the plaintiff claims.
(5) Where a plaintiff relies upon a document in his possession or power as evidence in support of his claim, he shall produce it in the Court when the plaint is presented and shall at the same time deliver the document or a true or photo-stat copy thereof to be filed with the plaint and shall also enter such documents in a list to be added or annexed to the plaint.
(6) Where the plaintiff relies upon a document not in his possession or power as evidence in support of his claim, he shall enter such document in a list to be added or annexed to the plaint and state in whose possession or power it is.
(7) The plaint shall be accompanied by twice as many true copies thereof, including the schedule, and the lists of documents referred to in sub-sections (5) and (6) as there are defendants in the suit for service upon such defendants.
(8) The plaint shall be rejected on the following grounds:-

(a) where it is not accompanied by true copies of plaint including the schedule and the lists of documents required under sub-section (7);
(b) where the cost of service of summons and postal charges for notice required to be paid under section 7(5) are not paid;
(c) where the fees required to be paid at the time of presentation of the plaint under section 22 are not paid.
(9) A document which ought to be produced in Court by the plaintiff where the plaint is presented, or to be entered in the list to be added or annexed to the plaint, and which is not produced or entered accordingly, shall not, without the leave of the Court, be received in evidence on his behalf at the

hearing of the suit:
Provided that the Court shall not grant such leave save in exceptional circumstances.]

Issue of summons and notice

7. (1) When a plaint is presented to a Family Court, it shall-
(a) fix a date ordinarily of not more than thirty days for the appearance of the defendant;
(b) issue summons to the defendant to appear and answer the claim on the date specified therein;
(c) send to the defendant, by registered post with acknowledgement due, a notice of the suit.
(2) Every summons issued and notice sent under sub-section (1) shall be accompanied by a copy of the plaint and copies of the list of documents referred to in sections 6(5) and 6(6)].
(3) A summons issued under sub-section (1)(b) shall be served in the manner provided in rules 9, 10, 11, 16, 17, 18, 19, 19A, [20], 21, 23, 24, 26, 27, 28 and 29 of Order V of the Code; and a summons so served shall be deemed to be due service thereof on the defendant.
(4) A notice sent under sub-section (1)(c) shall be deemed to be duly served on the defendant when the acknowledgement purporting to be signed by the defendant is received by the Court or the postal article containing the notice is received back by the Court with an endorsement purporting to have been made by a postal employee to the effect that the defendant had refused to take delivery of the postal article containing the notice when tendered to him:
Provided that where the notice was properly addressed, prepaid and duly sent by registered post with acknowledgement due, it may be deemed to be duly served on the defendant after the expiry of thirty days from the date of posting of the notice notwithstanding the fact that the acknowledgement having been lost or mislead or for any other reason has not been received by the Court within that period.
(5) The cost of service of summons issued under sub-section (1)(b), which shall be equal to the cost of service of similar summons under the Code, and the postal charges for notice sent under sub-section (1)(c) shall be paid by the plaintiff at the time of presentation of the plaint.

Written statement

8. (1) On the date fixed for the appearance of the defendant, the plaintiff and the defendant shall appear before the Family Court and the defendant shall present a written statement of his defence:

Provided that the Court may, on the prayer of the defendant and for good cause shown, fix another date not beyond twenty-one days for the presentation of the written statement of his defence.

(2) The written statement shall contain a schedule giving the names and addresses of the witnesses intended to be produced in support of the defence:

Provided that the defendant may, with the permission of the Court, call any witness at any later stage, if the Court considers such evidence expedient in the interest of justice.

(3) Where the defendant relies upon a document in his possession or power as evidence in support of his defence, he shall produce it in the Court when the written statement is presented and shall at the same time deliver the document or a true or photo-stat copy thereof to be filed with the written statement and shall also enter such documents in a list to be added or annexed to the written statement].

(4) Where the defendant relies upon a document not in his possession or power as evidence in support of his written statement, he shall enter such document in a list to be added or annexed to the written statement and state in whose possession or power it is.

(5) The written statement shall be accompanied by twice as many true copies thereof, including the schedule, and the lists of documents referred to in sub-sections (3) and (4), as there are plaintiffs in the suit.

(6) Copies of the written statement, including the schedule, the documents and the list of documents referred to in sub-section (5) shall be given to the plaintiff, his agent or advocate present in the Court.

(7) A document which ought to be produced in Court by the defendant when the written statement is presented, or to be entered in the list to be added or annexed to the written statement, and which is not produced or entered accordingly shall not, without the leave of the Court, be received in evidence on his behalf at the hearing of the suit:

Provided that the Court shall not grant such leave save in exceptional circumstances.]

Consequence of non-appearance of the parties

9. (1) Where on the day fixed for the appearance of the defendant, neither party appears when the suit is called on for hearing, the Court may dismiss the suit.

(2) Where the plaintiff appears and the defendant does not appear when the suit is called on for hearing, then-

(a) if it is proved that the summons or notice was duly served on the defendant, the Court may proceed ex parte;

(b) if it is not proved that the summons or notice was duly served on the defendant, the Court shall direct a fresh summons and notice to be issued and served on the defendant;

(c) if it is proved that the summons or notice was served on the defendant, but not in sufficient time to enable him to appear and answer on the day fixed for his appearance, the Court shall postpone the hearing of the suit to a future day not exceeding twenty-one days] to be fixed by the Court, and shall give notice of such day to the defendant.

(3) Where a Court has adjourned hearing of the suit ex parte, and the defendant, at or before such hearing, appears and assigns good cause for his previous non-appearance, he may, on such terms as the Court thinks fit, be heard in answer to the suit as if he had appeared on the day fixed for his appearance.

(4) Where the defendant appears and the plaintiff does not appear when the suit is called on for hearing, the Court shall dismiss the suit, unless the defendant admits the claim or part thereof, in which case the Court shall pass a decree against the defendant upon such admission, and, where part only of the claim has been admitted, shall dismiss the suit so far as it relates to the remainder.

(5) Where a suit is dismissed under sub-section (1) or wholly or partly dismissed under sub-section (4), the plaintiff may, within thirty days of the making of the order of dismissal, apply to the Court by which the order was made for an order to set the dismissal aside, and if he satisfies the Court that there was sufficient cause for his non-appearance when the suit was called on for hearing, the Court shall make an order setting aside the dismissal, and shall appoint a day for proceeding with the suit:
Provided that the Court may set the dismissal of a suit under sub-section (4) aside on such terms as to costs or otherwise as it thinks fit:

Provided further that no order setting the dismissal of a suit under sub-section (4) aside shall be made unless notice of the application has been served on the defendant.

(6) Where a decree is passed ex parte against a defendant,

he may, within thirty days of the passing of the decree, apply to the Court by which the decree was passed for an order to set it aside, and if he satisfies the Court that there was sufficient cause for his non-appearance when the suit was called on for hearing, the Court shall make an order setting aside the decree as against him on such terms as to costs or otherwise as it thinks fit, and shall appoint a day for proceeding with the suit:

Provided that where the decree is of such a nature that it cannot be set aside as against such defendant only, it may be set aside against all or any of the other defendants also:

Provided further that no order shall be made under this sub-section unless notice of the application has been served on the plaintiff.

(7) The provisions of section 5 of the Limitation Act, 1908 (IX of 1908), shall apply to an application under sub-section (6).

Pre-trial proceeding

10. (1) When the written statement is filed, the Family Court shall fix a date ordinarily of not more than thirty days for a pre-trial hearing of the suit.

(2) On the date fixed for pre-trial hearing, the Court shall examine the plaint, the written statement [* * *] and documents filed by the parties and shall also, if it so deems fit, hear the parties.

(3) At the pre-trial hearing, the Court shall ascertain the points at issue between the parties and attempt to effect a compromise or reconciliation between the parties, if this be possible.

(4) If no compromise or reconciliation is possible, the Court shall frame the issues in the suit and fix a date ordinarily of not more that thirty days] for recording evidence.

Trial in camera

11. (1) A Family Court may, if it so deems fit, hold the whole or any part of the proceedings under this Ordinance in camera.

(2) Where both the parties to the suit request the Court to hold the proceedings in camera, the Court shall do so.

Recording of evidence

12. (1) On the date fixed for recording of the evidence, the Family Court shall examine the witnesses produced by the parties in such order as it deems fit.

(2) The Court shall not issue any summons for the appearance of a witness for any party, unless, within three days of the framing of issues, the party intimates the Court that it desires the witness to be summoned through the Court and the Court is satisfied that it is not possible or practicable for the party to produce the witness.

(3) The witnesses shall give evidence in their own words and may be cross-examined and re-examined.
(4) The Court may forbid any question which it regards as indecent, scandalous or frivolous or which appears to it to be intended to insult or annoy or be needlessly offensive in form.
(5) The Court may, if it so deems fit, put any question to any witness for the purpose of elucidation of any point which it considers material in the case.
(6) The Court may permit the evidence of any witness to be given by means of affidavit:
Provided that the Court may, if it so deems fit, call such witness for the purpose of examination.
(7) The evidence of each witness shall be taken down in writing, in the language of the Court, by the presiding Judge of the Court and shall be signed by such Judge.
(8) Where the evidence of a witness is given in any language other than the language of the Court, the presiding Judge may take it down in that language, if possible, and an authenticated translation of such evidence in the language of the Court shall form a part of record.
(9) When the evidence of a witness is taken down, it shall be read over to him and shall, if necessary, be corrected.
(10) If the witness does not accept the correctness of any part of the evidence, the presiding Judge may, instead of correcting the evidence, make a memorandum of the objection made by the witness, and shall add such remarks as he thinks necessary.
(11) If the evidence is taken down in a language different from that in which it has been given and the witness does not understand that language, the evidence shall be interpreted to him in the language in which it was given or in a language which he understands.

Conclusion of trial

13. (1) After the close of evidence of all parties, the Family Court shall make another effort to effect a compromise or reconciliation between the parties.
(2) If such compromise or reconciliation is not possible, the Court shall pronounce judgment and, on such judgment [either at once or on some future day not beyond seven days of which due notice shall be given to the parties or their agents or advocates], a decree shall follow.

Compromise decree

14. Where a dispute is settled by compromise or conciliation, the Court shall pass a decree or give decision in the suit in terms of the compromise or conciliation agreed to between the parties.

Writing of judgment

15. (1) Every judgment or order of a Family Court shall be written by the presiding Judge or from the dictation of such Judge in the language of the Court and shall be dated and signed by the Judge in open Court at the time of pronouncing it.
(2) All judgments and orders which are appealable shall contain the point for determination, the decision thereon and the reasons therefore.

Enforcement of decrees

16. (1) A Family Court shall pass a decree in such form and manner, and shall enter its particulars in such register of decrees as may be prescribed.
(2) If any money is paid, or any property is delivered, in the presence of the Court in satisfaction of the decree, it shall enter the fact of such payment or delivery in the aforesaid register.
(3) Where the decree relates to the payment of money and the decretal amount is not paid within the time specified by the Court, the decree shall, on the prayer of the decree-holder to be made within a period of one year from the expiry of the time so specified, be executed-
(a) as a decree for money of a Civil Court under the Code, or
(b) as an order for payment of fine made by a Magistrate under the Code of Criminal Procedure, 1898 (Act V of 1898), and on such execution the decretal amount recovered shall be paid to the decree-holder.
(3A) For the purpose of execution of a decree under sub-section (3)(a), the Court shall be deemed to be a Civil Court and shall have all the powers of such Court under the Code.
(3B) For the purpose of execution of a decree under sub-section (3)(b), the Judge of the Family Court shall be deemed to be a Magistrate of the first class and shall have all the powers of such Magistrate under the Code of Criminal Procedure, 1898 (Act V of 1898), and he may issue a warrant for levying the decretal amount due in the manner provided in that Code for levying fines, and may sentence the judgment debtor, for the whole or any part of the decretal amount remaining unpaid after the execution of the warrant, to imprisonment for a term which may extend to three months or until payment if sooner made.
(3C) When a decree does not relate to payment of money, it shall be executed as a decree, other than a decree for money of a Civil Court and for that purpose the Court shall be deemed to be a Civil Court and shall have all the powers of such Court under the Code.

(4) The decree shall be executed by the Family Court passing it or by such other Family Court to which the decree may be transferred for execution by the Court passing it and in executing such a decree the Court to which it is transferred shall have all powers of the Family Court passing the decree as if the decree were passed by it.

(5) The Court may, if it so deems fit, direct that any money to be paid under a decree passed by it be paid in such instalments as it deems fit.

Interim order by Family Courts

16A. Where, at any stage of a suit, the Family Court is satisfied by affidavit or otherwise, that immediate action should be taken for preventing any party from frustrating the purpose of the suit, it may make such interim order as it deems fit.

Appeal

17. (1) Subject to the provisions of sub-section (2), an appeal shall lie from a judgment, decree or order of a Family Court to the Court of District Judge.

(2) No appeal shall lie from a decree passed by a Family Court-

(a) for dissolution of marriage, except in the case of dissolution for reasons specified in section 2(viii)(d) of the Dissolution of Muslim Marriages Act, 1939 (VIII of 1939);

(b) for dower not exceeding five thousand taka.

(3) An appeal under this section shall be preferred within thirty days of the passing of the judgment, decree or order excluding the time required for obtaining copies thereof:

Provided that the Court of District Judge may, for sufficient cause, extend the said period.

(4) An appeal shall-

(a) be in writing;

(b) set out the grounds on which the appellant seeks to challenge the judgment, decree or order;

(c) contain the names, description and addresses of the parties; and

(d) bear the signature of the appellant.

(5) A certified copy of the judgment, decree or order of the Court from which the appeal is preferred shall be attached with the appeal.

(6) Any order passed by the Court of District Judge shall, as soon as may be, be communicated to the Family Court which shall modify or amend the judgment, decree or order accordingly and shall also make necessary entries to that effect in the appropriate column in the register of decrees.

(7) The District Judge may transfer an appeal to the Court of an Additional District Judge or a Subordinate Judge for hearing and disposal and may withdraw any such appeal form such Court.

Power of Family Court to summon witnesses

18. (1) A Family Court may issue summons to any person to appear and give evidence, or to produce or cause the production of any document:

Provided that-

(a) no person who is exempt from personal appearance in a Court under section 133(1) of the Code, shall be required to appear in person;

(b) a Family Court may refuse to summon a witness or to enforce a summons already issued against a witness when, in the opinion of the Court, the attendance of the witness cannot be procured without such delay, expense or inconvenience as in the circumstances would be unreasonable.

(2) If any person to whom a Family Court has issued summons to appear and give evidence or to cause the production of any document before it wilfully disobeys such summons, the Court may take cognizance of such disobedience, and after giving such person an opportunity to explain, sentence him to a fine not exceeding one hundred taka.

Contempt of Family Courts

19. A person shall be guilty of contempt of the Family Court if he, without lawful excuse,-

(a) offers any insult to the Family Court;

(b) causes an interruption in the work of the Family Court;

(c) refuses to answer any question put by the Family Court, which he is bound to answer; or

(d) refuses to take oath to state the truth or to sign any statement made by him in the Family Court; and the Family Court may forthwith try such person for such contempt and sentence him to a fine not exceeding two hundred taka.

Application and non-application of certain laws

20. (1) Save as otherwise expressly provided by or under this Ordinance, the provisions of the Evidence Act, 1872 (I of 1872), and of the Code except sections 10 and 11 shall not apply to proceedings before the Family Courts.

(2) The Oaths Act, 1873 (X of 1873), shall apply to all proceedings before the Family Courts.

Appearance through agents

21. If a person required under this Ordinance to appear before a Family Court, otherwise than as a witness, is a *pardahnashin* lady, the Family Court may permit her to be represented by a duly authorised agent.

Court-fee

22. The Court-fees to be paid on any plaint presented to a Family Court shall be twenty-five taka for any kind of suit.

Ordinance VIII of 1961 not affected

23. (1) Nothing in this Ordinance shall be deemed to affect any of the provisions of the Muslim Family Laws Ordinance, 1961 (VIII of 1961), or the rules made there under.

(2) Where a Family Court passes a decree for the dissolution of a marriage solemnised under the Muslim Law, the Court shall, within seven days of the passing of the decree, send by registered post a certified copy of the same to the appropriate Chairman referred to in section 7 of the Muslim Family Laws Ordinance, 1961 (VIII of 1961), and upon receipt of such copy, the Chairman shall proceed as if he had received an intimation of *talaq* required to be given under the said Ordinance.

(3) A decree passed by a Family Court for the dissolution of a marriage solemnised under the Muslim Law shall-

(a) not be effective until the expiration of ninety days from the day on which a copy thereof has been received under sub-section (2) by the Chairman; and

(b) be of no effect if within the period specified in clause (a) a reconciliation has been effected between the parties in accordance with the provisions of the Muslim Family Laws Ordinance, 1961 (VIII of 1961).

Family Court deemed to be a District Court for purposes of Act VIII of 1890

24. (1) A Family Court shall be deemed to be a District Court for the purposes of the Guardians and Wards Act, 1890 (VIII of 1890), and notwithstanding anything contained in this Ordinance, shall, in dealing with matters specified in that Act, follow the procedure specified in that Act.

(2) Notwithstanding anything contained in the Guardians and Wards Act, 1890 (VIII of 1890), an appeal from an order made by a Family Court as District Court under that Act shall lie to the Court of District Judge, and the provisions of section 17 shall apply to such appeal.

Transfer and stay of suits and appeals

25. (1) The High Court Division may, either on the application of any party or of its own accord, by an order in writing,-

(a) transfer any suit under this Ordinance from one Family Court to another Family Court in the same district or from a Family Court of one district to a Family Court of another district;

(b) transfer any appeal under this Ordinance from the Court of District Judge of one district to the Court of District Judge of another district.

(2) A District Judge may, either on the application of any party or of his own accord, by an order in writing, transfer any suit under this Ordinance from one Family Court to another Family Court within the local limits of his jurisdiction.

(3) Notwithstanding anything contained in this Ordinance, a District Judge may transfer an appeal pending before him under this Ordinance to any Court of Additional District Judge or Subordinate Judge under his administrative control and may also retransfer such appeal from such Court to his own Court.

(4) Any Court to which a suit or appeal is transferred under this section, shall, notwithstanding anything contained in this Ordinance, have the jurisdiction to dispose it of in the manner as if it were instituted or filed before it:

Provided that on the transfer of a suit, it shall not be necessary to commence the proceedings before the succeeding Judge de novo unless the Judge, for reasons to be recorded in writing, directs otherwise.

(5) A District Judge may, by an order in writing, stay any suit pending before a Family Court within the local limits of his jurisdiction.

(6) The High Court Division may, by an order in writing, stay any suit or appeal pending before any Family Court or Court of District Judge.

Power to make rules

26. The Government may, by notification in the official Gazette, make rules for carrying out the purposes of this Ordinance.

Provisions relating to pending cases

27. Notwithstanding anything contained in this Ordinance, all suits, appeals and other legal proceedings relating to, or arising out of, any of the matters specified in section 5 pending in any Court immediately before the commencement of this Ordinance shall continue in the same Court and shall be heard and disposed of by that Court as if this Ordinance had not been made.

ACT RELATING TO COMMUNITY DISPUTES RESOLUTION

(C) *Village Courts Act 2006*[4] (Act XIX of 2006)

Section 4-Constitution of village courts: when a case is, under this Act, triable by a Village Court, any party to the dispute may, in the prescribed manner and on payment of the prescribed fee, apply to the Chairman of the Union *Parishad* (Council) concerned for the constitution of a Village Court for the trial of the case. If the Chairman rejects the application, he shall record the reason in writing and the person aggrieved by the order of rejection for constitution of a Village Court may, on the ground that the order is mala fide or substantially unjust, submit application against the order to the Assistant Judge having jurisdiction.

Section 5-Composition of village courts: (1) a Village Court shall consist of a Chairman and two members to be nominated by each of the parties to the dispute and amongst the two members to be nominated by each party one should be a member of the concerned Union *Parishad* (Council).

(2) The Chairman of the Union *Parishad* (Council) shall be the Chairman of the Village Court, but where he is, for any reason, unable to act as Chairman or his impartiality is challenged by any party to the dispute, any member of the Union *Parishad* (Council) other than those mentioned under sub-section (1) of section 5 appointed in the prescribed manner, shall be the Chairman of the Village Court.

(3) If either party to the dispute consists of more than one person, the Chairman shall call upon the persons constituting that party to nominate two members on their behalf, and if they fail to do so, the Chairman shall authorise any one of them to nominate such members.

(4) With permission of the Chairman, any party to dispute may nominate any person other than the members of the Union *Parishad* (Council) as members of the Village Court. If the members cannot be nominated within the prescribed time, the Village Court shall be deemed to have been validly constituted without such members, and it shall be legally competent to continue with the proceedings.

---

[4] Source: Baseline survey report on village court in Bangladesh, UNDP; available at <http://www.villagecourts.org/Publication/Baseline%20Survey%20Report.pdf>

Section 13 Quasi-formal procedure: (1) Except some cases provided by this Act, the provisions of the Evidence Act, 1872 (Act No. I of 1872), the Code of Criminal Procedure and the Code of Civil Procedure, shall not apply to the proceedings before any Village Court.

(2) However, section 8, 9, 10 and 11 of the Oaths Act, 1873 (Act No. X of 1873) shall apply to all proceedings before Village Courts.

Section 14 No appointment of lawyers: no party shall be permitted to engage any legal practitioner to conduct his case before any Village Court.

APPENDIX IV
UNITED STATES OF AMERICA

INDIANA RULES OF COURT

Rules for Alternative Dispute Resolution[1]

Including Amendments Received Through January 1, 2011

RULE 2. MEDIATION

Rule 2.1. Purpose
Mediation under this section involves the confidential process by which a neutral, acting as a mediator, selected by the parties or appointed by the court, assists the litigants in reaching a mutually acceptable agreement. The role of the mediator is to assist in identifying the issues, reducing misunderstanding, clarifying priorities, exploring areas of compromise, and finding points of agreement as well as legitimate points of disagreement. Any agreement reached by the parties is to be based on the autonomous decisions of the parties and not the decisions of the mediator. It is anticipated that an agreement may not resolve all of the disputed issues, but the process can reduce points of contention. Parties and their representatives are required to mediate in good faith, but are not compelled to reach an agreement.

Rule 2.2. Case Selection/Objection
At any time fifteen (15) days or more after the period allowed for peremptory change of judge under Trial Rule 76(B) has expired, a court may on its own motion or upon motion of any party refer a civil or domestic relations case to mediation. After a motion referring a case to mediation is granted, a party may object by filing a written objection within seven (7) days in a domestic relations case or fifteen (15) days in a civil case. The party must specify the grounds for objection. The court

[1] Source: <http://www.in.gov/judiciary/rules/adr/index.html>

shall promptly consider the objection and any response and determine whether the litigation should then be mediated or not. In this decision, the court shall consider the willingness of the parties to mutually resolve their dispute, the ability of the parties to participate in the mediation process, the need for discovery and the extent to which it has been conducted, and any other factors which affect the potential for fair resolution of the dispute through the mediation process. If a case is ordered for mediation, the case shall remain on the court docket and the trial calendar.

Rule 2.3. Listing of Mediators: Commission Registry of Mediators

Any person who wishes to serve as a registered mediator pursuant to these rules must register with the Indiana Supreme Court Commission for Continuing Legal Education (hereinafter "Commission") on forms supplied by the Commission. The registrants must meet qualifications as required in counties or court districts (as set out in Ind. Administrative Rule 3(A)) in which they desire to mediate and identify the types of litigation which they desire to mediate. Two or more persons individually who are qualified under A.D.R. Rule 2.5 may register as a mediation team. All professional licenses must be disclosed and identified in the form which the Commission requires.

The registration form shall be accompanied by a fee of $50.00 for each registered area (Civil or Domestic). An annual fee of $50.00 shall be due the second December 31st following initial registration. Registered mediators will be billed at the time their annual statements are sent. No fee shall be required of a full-time, sitting judge.

The Commission shall maintain a list of registered mediators including the following information: (1) whether the person qualified under A.D.R. Rule 2.5 to mediate domestic relations and/or civil cases; (2) the counties or court districts in which the person desires to mediate; (3) the type of litigation the person desires to mediate; and (4) whether the person is a full-time judge.

The Commission may remove a registered mediator from its registry for failure to meet or to maintain the requirements of A.D.R. Rule 2.5 for non-payment of fees. A registered mediator must maintain a current business and residential address and telephone number with the Commission. Failure to maintain current information required by these rules may result in removal from the registry.

For the billing of calendar year 2011, when this Rule becomes effective, registered mediators must pay the $50.00 annual fee and a one-time fee of $25.00 for the time period July 1, 2011-December 31, 2011, for a total of $75.00 per registration area. The annual fee shall be $50.00 per calendar year per registration area thereafter.

On or before October 31 of each year, each registered mediator will be sent an annual statement showing the mediator's educational activities that have been approved for mediator credit by the Commission.

Rule 2.4. Selection of Mediators
Upon an order referring a case to mediation, the parties may within seven (7) days in a domestic relations case or within fifteen (15) days in a civil case: (1) choose a mediator from the Commission's registry, or (2) agree upon a non-registered mediator, who must be approved by the trial court and who serves with leave of court. In the event a mediator is not selected by agreement, the court will designate three (3) registered mediators from the Commission's registry who are willing to mediate within the Court's district as set out in Admin. R. 3 (A). Alternately, each side shall strike the name of one mediator. The side initiating the lawsuit will strike first. The mediator remaining after the striking process will be deemed the selected mediator.
A person selected to serve as a mediator under this rule may choose not to serve for any reason. At any time, a party may request the court to replace the mediator for good cause shown. In the event a mediator chooses not to serve or the court decides to replace a mediator, the selection process will be repeated.

Rule 2.5. Qualifications of Mediators
(A) Civil Cases: Educational Qualifications.
(1) Subject to approval by the court in which the case is pending, the parties may agree upon any person to serve as a mediator.
(2) In civil cases, a registered mediator must be an attorney in good standing with the Supreme Court of Indiana.
(3) To register as a civil mediator, a person must meet all the requirements of this rule and must have either: (1) taken at least forty (40) hours of Commission approved civil mediation training in the three (3) years immediately prior to submission of the registration application, or (2) completed forty (40) hours of Commission approved civil mediation training at any time and taken at least six (6) hours of approved Continuing Mediation Education in the three (3) years immediately prior to submission of the registration application.
(4) However, a person who has met the requirements of A.D.R. Rule 2.5(B)(2)(a), is registered as a domestic relations mediator, and by December 31 of the second full year after meeting those requirements completes a Commission approved civil crossover mediation training program may register as a civil mediator.
(5) As part of a judge's judicial service, a judicial officer may serve as a

mediator in a case pending before another judicial officer.
(B) Domestic Relations Cases: Educational Qualifications.
(1) Subject to approval of the court, in which the case is pending, the parties may agree upon any person to serve as a mediator.
(2) In domestic relations cases, a registered mediator must be either: (a) an attorney, in good standing with the Supreme Court of Indiana; (b) a person who has a bachelor's degree or advanced degree from an institution recognized by a U.S. Department of Education approved accreditation organization, e.g. The Higher Learning Commission of the North Central Association of Colleges and Schools. Notwithstanding the provisions of (2)(a) and (b) above, any licensed professional whose professional license is currently suspended or revoked by the respective licensing agency, or has been relinquished voluntarily while a disciplinary action is pending, shall not be a registered mediator.
(3) To register as a domestic relations mediator, a person must meet all the requirements of this rule and must have either: (1) taken at least forty (40) hours of Commission approved domestic relations mediation training in the three (3) years immediately prior to submission of the registration application, or (2) taken at least forty (40) hours of Commission approved domestic relations mediation training at any time, and taken at least six (6) hours of approved Continuing Mediation Education in the three (3) years immediately prior to submission of the registration application.
(4) However, if a person is registered as a civil mediator and by December 31 of the second full year after meeting those requirements completes a Commission approved domestic relations crossover mediation training program (s)he may register as a domestic relations mediator.
(5) As part of a judicial service, a judicial officer may serve as a mediator in a case pending before another judicial officer.
(C) Continuing Mediation Education ("CME") Requirements for All Registered Mediators. A registered mediator must complete a minimum of six hours of Commission approved continuing mediation education anytime during a three-year educational period. A mediator's initial educational period commences January 1 of the first full year of registration and ends December 31 of the third full year. Educational periods shall be sequential, in that once a mediator's particular three-year period terminates, a new three-year period and six hour minimum shall commence. Mediators registered before the effective date of this rule shall begin their first three-year educational period January 1, 2004.
(D) Basic and Continuing Mediation Education Reporting Requirements. Within thirty (30) days of presenting a Commission approved basic or continuing mediation education training course, the sponsor of that course

must forward a list of attendees to the Commission. This list shall include for each attendee: full name; attorney number (if applicable); residence and business addresses and phone numbers; and the number of mediation hours attended. A course approved for CME may also qualify for CLE credit, so long as the course meets the requirements of Admission and Discipline Rule 29. For courses approved for both continuing legal education and continuing mediation education, the sponsor must additionally report continuing legal education, speaking and professional responsibility hours attended.

(E) Accreditation Policies and Procedures for CME.

(1) Approval of courses. The Commission shall approve the course, including law school classes, if it determines that the course will make a significant contribution to the professional competency of mediators who attend. In determining if a course, including law school classes, meets this standard the Commission shall consider whether:

(a) the course has substantial content dealing with alternative dispute resolution process;

(b) the course deals with matters related directly to the practice of alternative dispute resolution and the professional responsibilities of neutrals;

(c) the course deals with reinforcing and enhancing alternative dispute resolution and negotiation concepts and skills of neutrals;

(d) the course teaches ethical issues associated with the practice of alternative dispute resolution;

(e) the course deals with other professional matters related to alternative dispute resolution and the relationship and application of alternative dispute resolution principles;

(f) the course deals with the application of alternative dispute resolution skills to conflicts or issues that arise in settings other than litigation, such as workplace, business, commercial transactions, securities, intergovernmental, administrative, public policy, family, guardianship and environmental, and,

(g) in the case of law school classes, in addition to the standard set forth above the class must be a regularly conducted class at a law school accredited by the American Bar Association.

(2) Credit will be denied for the following activities:

(a) Legislative, lobbying or other law-making activities.

(b) In-house program. The Commission shall not approve programs which it determines are primarily designed for the exclusive benefit of mediators employed by a private organization or mediation firm. Mediators within related companies will be considered to be employed by the same

organization or law firm for purposes of this rule. However, governmental entities may sponsor programs for the exclusive benefit of their mediator employees.
(c) Programs delivered by these methods: satellite, microwave, video, computer, internet, telephone or other electronic methods. To be approved courses must provide a discussion leader or two-way communication, classroom setting away from the mediator's offices, opportunity to ask questions, and must monitor attendance.
(d) Courses or activities completed by self-study.
(e) Programs directed to elementary, high school or college student level neutrals.
(3) Procedures for Sponsors. Any sponsor may apply to the Commission for approval of a course. The application must:
(a) be submitted to the Commission at least thirty (30) days before the first date on which the course is to be offered;
(b) contain the information required by and be in the form approved by the Commission and available upon request or at the Commission's web site: www.in.gov/judiciary/cle: and
(c) be accompanied by the written course outline and brochure used to furnish information about the course to mediators.
(4) Procedure for Mediators. A mediator may apply for credit of a live course either before or after the date on which it is offered. The application must:
(a) contain the information required by and be in the form approved by the Commission and available upon request or at the Commission's web site: www.in.gov/judiciary/cle;
(b) be accompanied by the written course outline and brochure used to furnish information about the course to mediators; and,
(c) be accompanied by an affidavit of the mediator attesting that the mediator attended the course together with a certification of the course Sponsor as to the mediator's attendance. If the application for course approval is made before attendance, this affidavit and certification requirement shall be fulfilled within thirty (30) days after course attendance.

(F) Procedure for Resolving Disputes. Any person who disagrees with a decision of the Commission and is unable to resolve the disagreement informally, may petition the Commission for a resolution of the dispute. Petitions pursuant to this Section shall be considered by the Commission at its next regular meeting, provided that the petition is received by the Commission at least ten (10) business days before such meeting. The person filing the petition shall have the right to attend the Commission meeting at which the petition is considered and to present relevant evidence and arguments to the Commission. The rules of pleading and practice in civil cases shall not apply, and the proceedings shall be informal as directed by the Chair. The determination of the Commission shall be final subject to appeal directly to the Supreme Court.

(G) Confidentiality. Filings with the Commission shall be confidential. These filings shall not be disclosed except in furtherance of the duties of the Commission or upon the request, by the mediator involved, or as directed by the Supreme Court.

(H) Rules for Determining Education Completed.

(1) Formula. The number of hours of continuing mediation education completed in any course by a mediator shall be computed by:

(a) Determining the total instruction time expressed in minutes;

(b) Dividing the total instruction time by sixty (60); and

(c) Rounding the quotient up to the nearest one-tenth (1/10).

Stated in an equation the formula is:

$$\frac{\text{Total Instruction time (in minutes)}}{\text{Sixty (60)}} = \text{Hours completed (rounded up the nearest 1/10)}$$

(2) Instruction Time Defined. Instruction time is the amount of time when a course is in session and presentations or other educational activities are in progress. Instruction time does not include time spent on:

(a) Introductory remarks;

(b) Breaks; or

(c) Business meetings

(3) A registered mediator who participates as a teacher, lecturer, panelist or author in an approved continuing mediation education course will receive credit for:

(a) Four (4) hours of approved continuing mediation education for every hour spent in presentation.

(b) One (1) hour of approved continuing mediation education for every four (4) hours of preparation time for a contributing author who does not make a presentation relating to the materials prepared.

(c) One (1) hour of approved continuing mediation education for every hour the mediator spends in attendance at sessions of a course other than those in which the mediator participates as a teacher, lecturer or panel member.

(d) Mediators will not receive credit for acting as a speaker, lecturer or panelist on a program directed to elementary, high school or college student level neutrals, or for a program that is not approved under Alternative Dispute Resolution Rule 2.5(E).

Rule 2.6. Mediation Costs
Absent an agreement by the parties, including any guardian ad litem, court appointed special advocate, or other person properly appointed by the court to represent the interests of any child involved in a domestic relations case, the court may set an hourly rate for mediation and determine the division of such costs by the parties. The costs should be predicated on the complexity of the litigation, the skill levels needed to mediate the litigation, and the litigants' ability to pay. The mediation costs shall be paid within thirty (30) days after the close of each mediation session.

Rule 2.7. Mediation Procedure
(A) Advisement of Participants. The mediator shall:
(1) advise the parties of all persons whose presence at mediation might facilitate settlement; and
(2) in child related matters, ensure that the parties consider fully the best interests of the children and that the parties understand the consequences of any decision they reach concerning the children; and
(3) inform all parties that the mediator (a) is not providing legal advice, (b) does not represent either party, (c) cannot assure how the court would apply the law or rule in the parties' case, or what the outcome of the case would be if the dispute were to go before the court, and (d) recommends that the parties seek or consult with their own legal counsel if they desire, or believe they need legal advice; and
(4) explain the difference between a mediator's role and a lawyer's role when a mediator knows or reasonably should know that a party does not understand the mediator's role in the matter; and
(5) not advise any party (i) what that party should do in the specific case, or (ii) whether a party should accept an offer.
(B) Mediation Conferences.
(1) The parties and their attorneys shall be present at all mediation sessions involving domestic relations proceedings unless otherwise agreed. At the discretion of the mediator, non-parties to the dispute may also be present.
(2) All parties, attorneys with settlement authority, representatives with settlement authority, and other necessary individuals shall be present at each mediation conference to facilitate settlement of a dispute unless excused by the court.
(3) A child involved in a domestic relations proceeding, by agreement of the parties or by order of the court, may be interviewed by the mediator

out of the presence of the parties or attorneys.
(4) Mediation sessions are not open to the public.
(C) Confidential Statement of Case. Each side may submit to the mediator a confidential statement of the case, not to exceed ten (10) pages, prior to a mediation conference, which shall include:
(1) the legal and factual contentions of the respective parties as to both liability and damages;
(2) the factors considered in arriving at the current settlement posture; and
(3) the status of the settlement negotiations to date.
A confidential statement of the case may be supplemented by damage brochures, videos, and other exhibits or evidence. The confidential statement of the case shall at all times be held privileged and confidential from other parties unless agreement to the contrary is provided to the mediator. In the mediation process, the mediator may meet jointly or separately with the parties and may express an evaluation of the case to one or more of the parties or their representatives. This evaluation may be expressed in the form of settlement ranges rather than exact amounts.

(D) Termination of Mediation. The mediator shall terminate mediation whenever the mediator believes that continuation of the process would harm or prejudice one or more of the parties or the children or whenever the ability or willingness of any party to participate meaningfully in mediation is so lacking that a reasonable agreement is unlikely. At any time after two (2) sessions have been completed, any party may terminate mediation. The mediator shall not state the reason for termination except when the termination is due to conflict of interest or bias on the part of the mediator, in which case another mediator may be assigned by the court. According to the procedures set forth herein, if the court finds after hearing that an agreement has been breached, sanctions may be imposed by the court.

(E) Report of Mediation: Status.
(1) Within ten (10) days after the mediation, the mediator shall submit to the court, without comment or recommendation, a report of mediation status. The report shall indicate that an agreement was or was not reached in whole or in part or that the mediation was extended by the parties. If the parties do not reach any agreement as to any matter as a result of the mediation, the mediator shall report the lack of any agreement to the court without comment or recommendation. With the consent of the parties, the mediator's report may also identify any pending motions or outstanding legal issues, discovery process, or other action by any party which, if resolved or completed, would facilitate the possibility of a settlement.

(2) If an agreement is reached, in whole or in part, it shall be reduced to writing and signed by the parties and their counsel. In domestic relations matters, the agreement shall then be filed with the court. If the agreement is complete on all issues, a joint stipulation of disposition shall be filed with the court. In all other matters, the agreement shall be filed with the court only by agreement of the parties.
(3) In the event of any breach or failure to perform under the agreement, upon motion, and after hearing, the court may impose sanctions, including entry of judgment on the agreement.
(F) Mediator's Preparation and Filing of Documents in Domestic Relations Cases.
At the request and with the permission of all parties in a domestic relations case, a Mediator may prepare or assist in the preparation of documents as set forth in this paragraph (F).

The Mediator shall inform an unrepresented party that he or she may have an attorney of his or her choosing (1) be present at the mediation and/or (2) review any documents prepared during the mediation. The Mediator shall also review each document drafted during mediation with any unrepresented parties. During the review the Mediator shall explain to unrepresented parties that they should not view or rely on language in documents prepared by the Mediator as legal advice. When the document(s) are finalized to the parties' and any counsel's satisfaction, and at the request and with the permission of all parties and any counsel, the Mediator may also tender to the court the documents listed below when the mediator's report is filed.

The Mediator may prepare or assist in the preparation of only the following documents:
(1) A written mediated agreement reflecting the parties' actual agreement, with or without the caption in the case and "so ordered" language for the judge presiding over the parties' case;
(2) An order approving a mediated agreement, with the caption in the case, so long as the order is in the form of a document that has been adopted or accepted by the court in which the document is to be filed;
(3) A summary decree of dissolution, with the caption in the case, so long as the decree is in the form of a document that has been adopted or accepted by the court in which the document is to be filed and the summary decree reflects the terms of the mediated agreement;
(4) A verified waiver of final hearing, with the caption in the case, so long as the waiver is in the form of a document that has been adopted or accepted by the court in which the document is to be filed;

(5) A child support calculation, including a child support worksheet and any other required worksheets pursuant to the Indiana Child Support Guidelines or Parenting Time Guidelines, so long as the parties are in agreement on all the entries included in the calculations;
(6) An income withholding order, with the caption in the case, so long as the order is in the form of a document that has been adopted or accepted by the court in which the document is to be filed and the order reflects the terms of the mediated agreement.

Rule 2.8. Rules of Evidence
With the exception of privileged communications, the rules of evidence do not apply in mediation, but factual information having a bearing on the question of damages should be supported by documentary evidence whenever possible.

Rule 2.9. Discovery
Whenever possible, parties are encouraged to limit discovery to the development of information necessary to facilitate the mediation process. Upon stipulation by the parties or as ordered by the court, discovery may be deferred during mediation pursuant to Indiana Rules of Procedure, Trial Rule 26(C).

Rule 2.10. Sanctions
Upon motion by either party and hearing, the court may impose sanctions against any attorney, or party representative who fails to comply with these mediation rules, limited to assessment of mediation costs and/or attorney fees relevant to the process.

Rule 2.11. Confidentiality
Mediation shall be regarded as settlement negotiations as governed by Ind.Evidence Rule 408. For purposes of reference, Evid.R. 408 provides as follows:

Rule 408. Compromise and Offers to Compromise
Evidence of (1) furnishing or offering or promising to furnish, or (2) accepting or offering or promising to accept a valuable consideration in compromising or attempting to compromise a claim, which was disputed as to either validity or amount, is not admissible to prove liability for or invalidity of the claim or its amount. Evidence of conduct or statements made in compromise negotiations is likewise not admissible. This rule does not require exclusion when the evidence is offered for another purpose, such as proving bias or prejudice of a witness, negating a contention of undue delay, or proving an effort to obstruct a criminal investigation or prosecution. Compromise negotiations encompass

alternative dispute resolution.

Mediation sessions shall be closed to all persons other than the parties of record, their legal representatives, and other invited persons.

Mediators shall not be subject to process requiring the disclosure of any matter discussed during the mediation, but rather, such matter shall be considered confidential and privileged in nature. The confidentiality requirement may not be waived by the parties, and an objection to the obtaining of testimony or physical evidence from mediation may be made by any party or by the mediators.

Rule 7. Conduct and Discipline for Persons Conducting ADR

Rule 7.0. Purpose
This rule establishes standards of conduct for persons conducting an alternative dispute resolution ("ADR") process recognized by ADR Rule 1, hereinafter referred to as "neutrals."

Rule 7.1. Accountability And Discipline
A person who serves with leave of court or registers with the Commission pursuant to ADR Rule 2.3 consents to the jurisdiction of the Indiana Supreme Court Disciplinary Commission in the enforcement of these standards. The Disciplinary Commission, any court or the Continuing Legal Education Commission may recommend to the Indiana Supreme Court that a registered mediator be removed from its registry as a sanction for violation of these rules, or for other good cause shown.

Rule 7.2. Competence
A neutral shall decline appointment, request technical assistance, or withdraw from a dispute beyond the neutral's competence.

Rule 7.3. Disclosure and Other Communications
(A) A neutral has a continuing duty to communicate with the parties and their attorneys as follows:
(1) notify participants of the date, time, and location for the process, at least ten (10) days in advance, unless a shorter time period is agreed by the parties;
(2) describe the applicable ADR process or, when multiple processes are contemplated, each of the processes, including the possibility in nonbinding processes that the neutral may conduct private sessions;
(3) in domestic relations matters, distinguish the ADR process from therapy or marriage counselling;
(4) disclose the anticipated cost of the process;

(5) advise that the neutral does not represent any of the parties;
(6) disclose any past, present or known future
(a) professional, business, or personal relationship with any party, insurer, or attorney involved in the process, and
(b) other circumstances bearing on the perception of the neutral's impartiality;
(7) advise parties of their right to obtain independent legal counsel; and
(8) advise that any agreement signed by the parties constitutes evidence that may be introduced in litigation.
(B) A neutral may not misrepresent any material fact or circumstance nor promise a specific result or imply partiality.
(C) A neutral shall preserve the confidentiality of all proceedings, except where otherwise provided.

Rule 7.4. Duties
(A) A neutral shall observe all applicable statutes, administrative policies, and rules of court.
(B) A neutral shall perform in a timely and expeditious fashion.
(C) A neutral shall be impartial and shall utilize an effective system to identify potential conflicts of interest at the time of appointment. After disclosure pursuant to ADR Rule 7.3(A)(6), a neutral may serve with the consent of the parties, unless there is a conflict of interest or the neutral believes the neutral can no longer be impartial, in which case a neutral shall withdraw.
(D) A neutral shall avoid the appearance of impropriety.
(E) A neutral may not have an interest in the outcome of the dispute, may not be an employee of any of the parties or attorneys involved in the dispute, and may not be related to any of the parties or attorneys in the dispute.
(F) A neutral shall promote mutual respect among the participants throughout the process.

Rule 7.5. Fair, Reasonable and Voluntary Agreements
(A) A neutral shall not coerce any party.
(B) A neutral shall withdraw whenever a proposed resolution is unconscionable.
(C) A neutral shall not make any substantive decision for any party except as otherwise provided for by these rules.

Rule 7.6. Subsequent Proceedings
(A) An individual may not serve as a neutral in any dispute on which another neutral has already been serving without first ascertaining that the current neutral has been notified of the desired change.

(B) A person who has served as a mediator in a proceeding may act as a neutral in subsequent disputes between the parties, and the parties may provide for a review of the agreement with the neutral on a periodic basis. However, the neutral shall decline to act in any capacity except as a neutral unless the subsequent association is clearly distinct from the issues involved in the alternative dispute resolution process. The neutral is required to utilize an effective system to identify potential conflict of interest at the time of appointment. The neutral may not subsequently act as an investigator for any court-ordered report or make any recommendations to the Court regarding the mediated litigation.
(C) When multiple ADR processes are contemplated, a neutral must afford the parties an opportunity to select another neutral for the subsequent procedures.
Rule 7.7 Remuneration
(A) A neutral may not charge a contingency fee or base the fee in any manner on the outcome of the ADR process.
(B) A neutral may not give or receive any commission, rebate, or similar remuneration for referring any person for ADR services.

Rule 8. Optional Early Mediation

Preamble.
The voluntary resolution of disputes in advance of litigation is a laudatory goal. Persons desiring the orderly mediation of disputes not in litigation may elect to proceed under this Rule.

Rule 8.1. Who May Use Optional Early Mediation.
By mutual agreement, persons may use the provisions of this Rule to mediate a dispute not in litigation. Persons may participate in dispute resolution under this Rule with or without counsel.

Rule 8.2. Choice of Mediator.
Persons participating in mediation under this Rule shall choose their own mediator and agree on the method of compensating the mediator. Mediation fees will be shared equally unless otherwise agreed. The mediator is governed by the standards of conduct provided in Alternative Dispute Resolution Rule 7.

Rule 8.3. Agreement to Mediate.
Before beginning a mediation under this Rule, participants must sign a written Agreement To Mediate substantially similar to the one shown as Form A to these rules. This agreement must provide for confidentiality in accordance with Alternative Dispute Resolution Rule 2.11; it must

acknowledge judicial immunity of the mediator equivalent to that provided in Alternative Dispute Resolution Rule 1.5; and it must require that all provisions of any resulting mediation settlement agreement must be written and signed by each person and any attorneys participating in the mediation.

Rule 8.4. Preliminary Considerations.
The mediator and participating persons should schedule the mediation promptly. Before beginning the mediation session, each participating person is encouraged to provide the mediator with a written confidential summary of the nature of the dispute, as outlined in Alternative Dispute Resolution Rule 2.7(c).

Rule 8.5. Good Faith.
In mediating their dispute, persons should participate in good faith. Information sharing is encouraged. However, the participants are not required to reach agreement.

Rule 8.6. Settlement Agreement.
If an agreement is reached, to be enforceable, all agreed provisions must be put in writing and signed by each participant. This should be done promptly as the mediation concludes. A copy of the written agreement shall be provided to each participant.

Rule 8.7. Subsequent ADR and Litigation.
If no settlement agreement is reached, put in writing, and signed by the participants, the participants may thereafter engage in litigation and/or further alternative dispute resolution.

Rule 8.8. Deadlines Not Changed.
WARNING: Participation in optional early mediation under this Rule does not change the deadlines for beginning a legal action as provided in any applicable statute of limitations or in any requirement for advance notice of intent to make a claim (for example, for claims against government units under the Indiana Tort Claims Act).

APPENDIX V
AUSTRALIA

(A) *Family Law Act 1975*[1]

Part IIIB—Court's powers in relation to court and non-court based family services

Division 1—Introduction

13A Objects of this Part

(1) The objects of this Part are:

(a) to facilitate access to family counselling:

(i) to help married couples considering separation or divorce to reconcile; and

(ii) to help people adjust to separation or divorce; and

(iii) to help people adjust to court orders under this Act; and

(b) to encourage people to use dispute resolution mechanisms (other than judicial ones) to resolve matters in which a court order might otherwise be made under this Act, provided the mechanisms are appropriate in the circumstances and proper procedures are followed; and

(c) to encourage people to use, in appropriate circumstances, arbitration to resolve matters in which a court order might otherwise be made, and to provide ways of facilitating that use; and

(d) to give the court the power to require parties to proceedings under this Act to make use of court or non-court based family services appropriate to the needs of the parties.

[1] Source: <http://www.austlii.edu.au/au/legis/cth/consol_act/fla1975114/>

(2) The object mentioned in paragraph (1)(b) also lies behind the general requirement in section 60I for family dispute resolution services to be used before applications for orders under Part VII are made.

Division 2—Help with reconciliation

13B Court to accommodate possible reconciliations

(1) A court exercising jurisdiction in:

(a) proceedings for a divorce order; or

(b) financial or part VII proceedings instituted by a party to a subsisting marriage;

must consider, from time to time, the possibility of a reconciliation between the parties to the marriage.

(2) If, during the proceedings, the court considers, from the evidence in the proceedings or the attitude of the parties to the marriage, that there is a reasonable possibility of a reconciliation between the parties, the court may adjourn the proceedings to give the parties the opportunity to consider a reconciliation.

(3) If the court adjourns the proceedings under subsection (2), the court must advise the parties to attend family counselling, or use the services of another appropriate person or organisation.

Note: Before advising the parties, the court must consider seeking the advice of a family consultant about the services appropriate to the parties' needs (see section 11E).

(4) If, after an adjournment under subsection (2), either of the parties requests that the proceedings resume, the court must resume the proceedings as soon as practicable.

Division 3—Referrals to family counselling, family dispute resolution and other family services

13C Court may refer parties to family counselling, family dispute resolution and other family services

(1) A court exercising jurisdiction in proceedings under this Act may, at any stage in the proceedings, make one or more of the following orders:

(a) that one or more of the parties to the proceedings attend family counselling;

(b) that the parties to the proceedings attend family dispute resolution;

(c) that one or more of the parties to the proceedings participate in an appropriate course, program or other service.

Note 1: Before making an order under this section, the court must consider seeking the advice of a family consultant about the services appropriate to the parties' needs (see section 11E).

Note 2: The court can also order parties to attend, or arrange for a child to attend, appointments with a family consultant (see section 11F).

(2) The court may suggest a particular purpose for the attendance or participation.

(3) The order may require the party or parties to encourage the participation of specified other persons who are likely to be affected by the proceedings.

Note: For example, the participation of children, grandparents or other relatives may be encouraged.

(4) The court may make any other orders it considers reasonably necessary or appropriate in relation to the order.

(5) The court may make orders under this section:

- (a) on its own initiative; or
- (b) on the application of:
  - (i) a party to the proceedings; or
  - (ii) a lawyer independently representing a child's interests under an order made under section 68L.

13D Consequences of failure to comply with order under section 13C

(1) If a party fails to comply with an order of a court under section 13C, the family counsellor, family dispute resolution practitioner or provider of the course, program or other service must report the failure to the court.

(2) On receiving the report, the court may make any further orders it considers appropriate.

(3) The court may make orders under subsection (2):

- (a) on its own initiative; or
- (b) on the application of:
  - (i) a party to the proceedings; or
  - (ii) a lawyer independently representing a child's interests under an order made under section 68L.

COMMUNITY MEDIATION, NSW, AUSTRALIA

(B) *Community Justice Centres Act 1983*[2]

SECTION 21
Conduct of mediation sessions

21 Conduct of mediation sessions

(1) The procedure for commencing and conducting a mediation session at a Community Justice Centre is to be as determined by the Director.

(2) Mediation sessions shall be conducted with as little formality and technicality, and with as much expedition, as possible.

(3) The rules of evidence do not apply to mediation sessions.

(4) A party to a mediation session may be accompanied by or represented by another person.

(5) The Director or the mediator conducting a mediation session may exclude a person (other than a party to the mediation session) from attending, or continuing to attend the mediation session if, in the Director's or mediator's opinion, the presence of the person may frustrate the purpose or conduct of the mediation session.

---

[2] Source: http://www.austlii.edu.au/au/legis/nsw/consol_act/cjca1983302/s21.html

COMMUNITY MEDIATION, NSW, AUSTRALIA

(C)Issues Paper 23 (2003) - Community Justice Centres NSW Law Reform Commission[3]

TERMS OF REFERENCE

1.1 In a letter to the Commission received on 2 October 2002, the Attorney General, the Hon R J Debus MP asked the Commission to review the *Community Justice Centres Act 1983* (NSW) including:

(a) The role of Community Justice Centres as a state wide conflict management and mediation service;

(b) Whether the current structure of Community Justice Centres sufficiently meets the needs of the indigenous community of New South Wales;

(c) The role and entitlements of mediators; and

(d) Any related matter.

BACKGROUND

1.2 Community Justice Centres ("CJCs") were established to provide a means of settling the sort of disputes that conventional court-based procedures are unable to resolve satisfactorily. The disputes envisaged were basically within a relatively narrow range of domestic or neighbourhood disputes where the disputing parties had, or once had, an ongoing relationship.[1] Such disputes could include disputes between family members, partners, friends, workmates, members of social groups and other community organisations, neighbours, landlords and tenants, flatmates and so on.[2]

---

[3] Source: NSW Law Reform Commissions

1.3 In handling disputes CJCs make use of mediation. Mediation is defined by the National Dispute Resolution Advisory Council ("NADRAC") as being:

> A process in which the parties to a dispute, with the assistance of a neutral third party (the mediator), identify the disputed issues, develop options, consider alternatives and endeavour to reach an agreement. The mediator has no advisory or determinative role in regard to the content of the dispute or the outcome of its resolution, but may advise on or determine the process of mediation whereby resolution is attempted.[3]

1.4 However, there is not complete agreement about what constitutes mediation and there has been debate about some of its features. In practice mediators are sometimes more active than merely facilitating the settling of an agreement. There are a number of styles of mediation, some of which involve a greater degree of mediator intervention than others.[4]

1.5 The key point often emphasised, particularly in relation to community-based mediation, is that the mediators do not make decisions or impose outcomes on the parties to a dispute, rather, the parties make any settlement themselves.

1.6 Mediation differs from other methods of alternative dispute resolution such as conciliation and arbitration. Conciliation is somewhat similar to mediation except that the conciliator has a more active advisory role than the mediator, NADRAC notes that a conciliator, unlike a mediator, "may have an advisory role on the content of the dispute or the outcome of its resolution" but, like a mediator, still not have a "determinative role".[5] Arbitration, on the other hand, is an adversarial process where, following submissions, one or more arbitrators impose an award that is binding on the parties.[6]

1.7 The mediation services that CJCs provide to disputing parties are available free of charge. The mediations are conducted by mediators who provide their services on a voluntary basis (receiving small remuneration) and who are, at least in theory, drawn from the communities where the services are provided. Any changes to the type or level of service provided by CJCs will, therefore, have resource implications for the Government.

APPENDIX VI
UNITED KINGDOM

FAMILY PROCEEDINGS
Senior Courts of England and Wales, Country Courts, England and Wales Magistrate Courts, England and Wales

The Family Procedure Rules 2010[1]

PART 35
MEDIATION DIRECTIVE

Scope and Interpretation

35.1.—(1) This Part applies to mediated cross-border disputes that are subject to Directive 2008/52/EC of the European Parliament and of the Council of 21 May 2008 on certain aspects of mediation in civil and commercial matters ("the Mediation Directive").

(2) In this Part—

"cross-border dispute" has the meaning given by article 2 of the Mediation Directive;

"mediation" has the meaning given by article 3(a) of the Mediation Directive;

"mediation administrator" means a person involved in the administration of the mediation process;

"mediation evidence" means evidence regarding information arising out of or in connection with a mediation process;

"mediator" has the meaning given by article 3(b) of the Mediation Directive; and

"relevant dispute" means a cross-border dispute that is subject to the Mediation Directive.

---

[1] Source:<http://www.legislation.gov.uk/uksi/2010/2955/contents/made>

Relevant disputes: applications for consent orders in respect of financial remedies

35.2.—(1) This rule applies in relation to proceedings for a financial remedy where the applicant, with the explicit consent of the respondent, wishes to make an application that the content of a written agreement resulting from mediation of a relevant dispute be made enforceable by being made the subject of a consent order.

(2) The court will not include in a consent order any matter which is contrary to the law of England and Wales or which is not enforceable under that law.

(3) The applicant must file two copies of a draft of the order in the terms sought.

(4) Subject to paragraph (5), the application must be supported by evidence of the explicit consent of the respondent.

(5) Where the respondent has written to the court consenting to the making of the order sought, the respondent is deemed to have given explicit consent to the order and paragraph (4) does not apply.

(6) Paragraphs (1)(b) and (2) to (6) of rule 9.26 apply to an application to which this rule applies.

Mediation evidence: disclosure and inspection

35.3.—(1) Where a party to proceedings seeks disclosure or inspection of mediation evidence that is in the control of a mediator or mediation administrator, that party must first obtain the court's permission to seek the disclosure or inspection, by an application made in accordance with Part 18.

(2) The mediator or mediation administrator who has control of the mediation evidence must be named as a respondent to the application and must be served with a copy of the application notice.

(3) Evidence in support of the application must include evidence that—

(a) all parties to the mediation agree to the disclosure or inspection of the mediation evidence;

(b) disclosure or inspection of the mediation evidence is necessary for overriding considerations of public policy, in accordance with article 7(1)(a) of the Mediation Directive; or

(c) the disclosure of the content of an agreement resulting from mediation is necessary to implement or enforce that agreement.

(4) Where this rule applies, Parts 21 to 24 apply to the extent they are consistent with this rule.

Mediation evidence: witnesses and depositions

35.4.—(1) This rule applies where a party wishes to obtain mediation evidence from a mediator or mediation administrator by–

(a) a witness summons;

(b) cross-examination with permission of the court under rule 22.8 or 23.4;

(c) an order under rule 24.7 (evidence by deposition);

(d) an order under rule 24.9 (enforcing attendance of witness);

(e) an order under rule 24.10(4) (deponent's evidence to be given orally); or

(f) an order under rule 24.12 (order for the issue of a letter of request).

(2) When applying for a witness summons, permission under rule 22.8 or 23.4 or order under rule24.7, 24.9, 24.10(4) or24.12, the party must provide the court with evidence that-

(a) all parties to the mediation agree to the obtaining of the mediation evidence;

(b) obtaining the mediation evidence is necessary for overriding considerations of public
policy in accordance with article 7(1)(a) of the Mediation Directive; or

(c) the disclosure of the content of an agreement resulting from mediation is necessary to implement or enforce that agreement.

(3) When considering a request for a witness summons, permission under rule 22.8 or 23.4 or order under rule 24.7, 24.9, 24.10(4) or 24.12, the court may invite any person, whether or not a party, to make representations.

(4) Where this rule applies, Parts 21 to 24 apply to the extent they are consistent with this rule.

BIBLIOGRAPHY

Abramson, Harold I. 2004, *Mediation representation: Advocating in a problem-solving process*, National Institute for Trial Advocacy, Louisville.

Acland, Andrew F. 1995, *Resolving Disputes without Going to Court,* Century Books, London.

Adair, Wendi, Brett, Jeanne, Lempere, Alain, Okumura, Tetsushi, Shikhirev, Peter, Tinsley, Catherine and Lytle, Anne 2004, 'Culture and negotiation strategy', *Negotiation Journal*, vol. 20, no.1, pp. 87-111.

Adamopoulos, John and Kashima, Yoshihisa 1999, *Social psychology and cultural context*, Sage, Thousand Oaks.

AG-AGD 2009, *A strategic framework for access to justice in the federal civil justice system*, Australian Government-Attorney General's Department, Barton, ACT.

Agarwal, Archana 2009, 'Lok Adalot and judicial reform in India', in Singh, Anita and Nasir, Zahid A. (eds.), *Strengthening governance through access to justice*, PHI, New Delhi.

Akhter, Salma 2000, 'Changing role and status of working women in urban Bangladesh: A study of Dhaka city', *Social Science Review*, vol. 17, no. 1, pp. 233-45.

Alam, Shah M. 2000, 'A possible way out of backlog in our judiciary', *The Daily Star*, 16 April.

Alberta Law Reform Institute 1994, *Court-connected family mediation programs in Canada*, Alberta Law Reform Institute, Edmonton, Alberta.

Aldous, Jules 2008, *Making and breaking the law*, Macmillan Education Australia Private Limited, South Yarra.

Alexander, Nadja 2004, 'Visualising ADR landscape', *ADR Bulletin*, vo.7, no.3, pp.1-3.

—. 2006, *Global trends in mediation*, 2nd edn, Kluwer Law International, Hague.

Alfini, James J. 1991, 'Trashing, bashing, and hashing it out: is this the end of a good mediation', *Florida State University Law Review,* vol. 19, pp. 47-75.

—. 'Evaluative Versus Facilitative Mediation: A Discussion', *Florida*

State University Law Review vol. 24, pp. 919 -935.
—. 2006, *Mediation theory and practice*, 2nd edn, LexisNexis/Matthew Bender, Newark, New Jersey.
Alim, Mohammod and Ali, Tariq 2007, 'NGO-shalish and justice-seeking behaviour in rural Bangladesh', *SOCIAL, BRAC Research Report*, BRAC Research and Evaluation Division, BRAC, Dhaka.
Alschuler, Albert W. 1986, 'Mediation with a mugger: The shortage of adjudicative services and the need for a two-tier trial system in civil cases', *Harvard Law Review*, vol. 99, no. 8, pp. 1808-59.
Altobelli, Tom 1995, 'Family lawyers as mediators', *Australian Journal of Family Law*, vol. 10, no.1, pp.222-33.
Ambrus, Attila, Field, Erica and Torero, Maximo 2008, 'Muslim family law, prenuptial agreements and the emergence of dowry in Bangladesh', in Working Paper, Harvard University.
Ameen, Nusrat 2005a, 'Dispensing justice to the poor: The village court, arbitration council *vis-a-vis* NGO', *The Dhaka University Studies Part F*, vol. 16, no. 2, pp. 103-22.
—. 2005b, *Wife abuse in Bangladesh: An unrecognized offence*, The University Press Limited, Dhaka.
Ammicchino, Pasquale 2010, 'Beyond art', Ninth Law and Religion in the Culture Wars before the European Court of Human Rights', paper presented to Law and Religion Scholars Network (LARSN) Conference, Cardiff, 11 May, 2010.
Anderson, Siwan 2007, 'Why the marriage squeeze cannot cause dowry inflation', *Journal of Economic Theory*, vol. 137, no. 1, pp. 140-52.
Appel, Gabriela and Lantolf, James P. 1994, 'Speaking as mediation: A study of L1 and L2 text recall tasks', *The Modern Language Journal*, vol. 78, no. 4, pp. 437-52.
Armstrong, Susan 2006, 'Women's legal services and family law reform', PhD thesis, University of Sydney.
Arriaga, Manuel P. 2006, *The modernist-postmodernist quarrel on philosophy and justice: A possible Levinasian mediation*, Lexington Books, Lanham.
Asian Development Bank 2002, *Asian Development Outlook*-2002-Bangladesh, Asian Development Bank, viewed 4 November 2009, <http://www.adb.org/documents/books/ado/2002/ban.asp>.
—. 2004, *Bangladesh: Gender, Poverty and MGDs 2004*, Asian Development Bank, viewed 15 February 2010, <http://www.adb.org/Documents/Reports/Country-Gender-Assessments/ban.asp>.
Astor, Hilary 1990, 'Domestic violence and mediation', *Australian Dispute*

Resolution Journal, vol. 1, no. 3, pp. 143-53.
—. 1991a, *Position paper on mediation,* National Committee on Violence against Women, Office of the Status of Women, Canberra.
—. 1991b, 'Feminist issues in ADR', *Law Institute Journal,* vol.65, pp. 69-71.
—. 1991c, 'Position Paper on Mediation', *National Committee on Violence against Women,* office of the Status of Women, Commonwealth Government of Australia, Canberra.
—. 1992, *Guidelines for use of mediating in cases involving violence against women*, National Committee on Violence against Women, Office of the Status of Women, Canberra.
—. 1994a, 'Swimming against the tide: Keeping violent men out of mediation', in Stubbs, Julie (ed.) *Women, male violence and the law*, Institute of Criminology, Sydney, pp. 147-73.
—. 1994b, 'Violence and family mediation policy', *Australian Journal of Family Law*, vol. 8, no. 1, pp. 3-21.
—. 1995, 'The weight of silence: Talking about violence in family mediation', in Thornton, Margaret (ed.), *Public and private: Feminist legal debates*, Oxford University Press, Melbourne, pp. 174-96.
—. 1997, 'Elizabeth's story: Mediation, violence and the legal academy', *Flinders Journal of Law Reform,* vol.2, pp. 13-29
—. 2000a, 'Rethinking neutrality: A theory to inform practice - part I', *Australian Dispute Resolution Journal*, vol. 11, no. 1, pp. 73-83.
—. 2000b, 'Rethinking neutrality: A theory to inform practice - part II', *Australian Dispute Resolution Journal*, vol. 11, no. 1, pp. 145-54.
—. 2001, *Quality in court connected mediation programs: An issues paper*, Australian Institute of Judicial Administration, Carlton, Victoria.
—. 2002, *Dispute Resolution in Australia*, 2nd edn, Butterworth, Sydney.
—. 2003, 'Language, power and mediation', *Australian Dispute Resolution Journal*, vol. 14, no. 2, pp. 130-41.
—. 2005, 'Some contemporary theories in mediation: A primer for the puzzled practitioner', *Australian Dispute Resolution Journal*, vol. 16, no 1, pp. 30-39.
—. 2007, 'Mediator neutrality: making sense of theory and practice', *Social & Legal Studies*, vol. 16, no. 2, pp. 221-39.
—. 2008, 'Making a genuine effort in family dispute resolution: What does it mean?' *Australian Journal of Family Law,* vol. 22, no.2, pp. 102-22.
Astor, Hilary and Chinkin, Cristine M. 1992, *Dispute Resolution in Australia*, Butterworths, Sydney.

Atkinson, Roslyn 2004, 'Access to justice: Rhetoric or reality', paper presented to Australian Law Reform Agencies Conference, Wellington, 13-16 April, 2004.

Augsberger, David W. 1992, Conflict mediation across cultures: pathways and patterns John Knox Press, Kentucky.

Australia Family Law Council 1991, *Family mediation*, Family Law Council, Barton, ACT.

Australian Bureau of Statistics (ABS) 1996, *Women's safety Australia*, Australian Bureau of Statistics, Canberra.

Australian Institute of Criminology (AIC) 2004, *Women's experience of male violence: Findings from the Australian component of the international violence against women survey*, Australian Institute of Criminology, Canberra.

Avruch, Kevin 1998, *Culture and Conflict Resolution,* United States Institute of Peace Press, Washington DC.

Bacigal, Ronald J. 1988, 'An empirical case study of informal alternative dispute resolution', *Ohio State Journal on Dispute Resolution,* vol. 4, no.1, pp. 1-28.

Bagshaw, Dale 2001, 'The three M's-mediation, postmodernism, and the new millennium', *Mediation Quarterly*, vol. 18, no. 3, pp. 205-28.

—. 2009, Mediation of disputes in the Australian family law system, in Swain, Phillip and Rice, Simon *in the shadow of the law*, The Federation Press, Sydney.

Bagshaw, Dale and Porter, Elisabeth 2009, *Mediation in the Asia-Pacific region transforming conflicts and building peace*, Routledge, London.

Bailey, James R. and Eastman, Wayne 1998, 'Mediation in moderation', *Organization Science*, vol. 9, no. 2, pp. 250-1.

Bangladesh Bureau of Statistics 1996, *Report of survey on marriage, divorce and separation in Bangladesh*, Bangladesh Bureau of Statistics, Dhaka.

—. 2006, *Statistical pocket book-2006*, Bangladesh Bureau of Statistics, Dhaka.

—. 2007a, *Population census 2001,* Bangladesh Bureau of Statistics, Dhaka.

—. 2007b, *Report of the Household income & expenditure survey 2005*, Bangladesh Bureau of Statistics, Dhaka.

—. 2008, *Statistical pocket book-2008*, Bangladesh Bureau of Statistics, viewed 11 March 2010, <http://www.bbs.gov.bd/dataindex/pby/pk_book_08.pdf>

Bangladesh Legal Aid and Services Trust (BLAST) 2006, *Government Legal Aid Act 2000*, Bangladesh Legal Aid and Services Trust, Dhaka.

—. 2007, *Annual report 2007*, Bangladesh Legal Aid and Services Trust, Dhaka.

Bangladesh National Women Lawyers' Association (BNWLA) 2005, *Violence against women in Bangladesh 2004*, Bangladesh National Women Lawyers' Association, Dhaka.

Barendrecht, Maurits, Mulder, Jose and Giesen, Ivo 2006, *How to measure the price and quality of access to justice*, Social Science Research Network, viewed 10 February 2010, <http://papers.ssrn.com/sol3/papers.cfm?abstract_id=949209>

Bergoglio, Maria I. 2003, 'Argentian: the effects of democratic institutionalization', in Friedman, Lawrence M. and Perez-Perdomo, Rogelio (eds.), *Legal culture in the age of globalization: Latin America and Latin Europe*, Stanford University Press, California.

Barskey, Allen E. 1993, 'When advocates and mediators negotiate', *Negotiation Journal*, vol. 9, no.2, pp. 115-22.

Batagol, Becky 2008, 'Bargaining in the shadow of the law? The case of family mediation', PhD thesis, Monash University, Victoria.

Baxi, Upendra 1987, 'On the shame of not being an activist: Thoughts of judicial activism', in Tiruchelvam, Neelan & Coomaraswamy, Radhika (eds), *The role of the judiciary in plural societies*, Frances Printer, London, pp. 168-77.

Beardsley, Kyle C., Quinn, David M., and Wilkenfeld, Jonathan 2006, 'Mediation style and crisis Outcomes', *The Journal of Conflict Resolution*, vol. 50, no. 1, pp. 58-86.

Beauchamp, Tom L. 1980, 'Distributive justice and the difference principle', in Blocker, Gene H. and Smith, Elizabeth H. (eds), *John Rawls' Theory of Social Justice: An introduction*, Ohio University Press, Athens.

Beck, Connie J. and Sales, Bruce D. 2001, *Family mediation: Facts, myths, and future prospects*, The law and public policy, American Psychological Association, Washington, DC.

Beer, Jennifer E. 1986, *Peacemaking in your neighbourhood: Reflections on an experiment in community mediation*, New Society Publishers, Philadelphia.

Begum, Hamida A. 2005, 'Combating domestic violence through changing knowledge and attitude of males: An experimental study in three villages of Bangladesh', *Empowerment*, vol. 12, no.1, pp. 53-69.

Begum, Nahar 1999, 'Population control policy & women in Bangladesh', *Social Science Review*, vol. 16, no. 2, pp. 47-54.

Behrendt, Larissa and Kelly, Loretta 2008, *Resolving indigenous disputes: land conflict and beyond*, The Federation Press, Sydney.

Behrens, Juliet 1993, 'Domestic violence and property adjustment: A critique of no-fault discourse', *Australian Journal of Family Law*, vol. 7, no. 1, pp. 9-28.

Benjamin, Robert D. 1990, 'The physics of mediation: reflections of scientific theory in professional mediation practice', *Mediation Quarterly,* vol. 8, no. 2, pp. 91-113.

Bevan, Alexander 1992, *Alternative dispute resolution: A lawyer's guide to mediation and other forms of dispute resolution*, Sweet & Maxwell, London.

Bhushan, Jamila B. 1980, *Muslim women in purdah and out of it*, University Press Limited, Dhaka.

Bickerman, John 1996, 'Evaluative Mediator Responds', *Alternatives to High Cost Litigation, vol.* 14, pp. 70.

Bienenfeld, Florence 1983, *Child custody mediation: Techniques for counsellors, attorneys, and parents*, Science and Behaviour Books, Palo Alto, Calif.

Blades, Joan 1985, *Family mediation: Cooperative divorce settlement*, Prentice-Hall, Englewood Cliffs, N.J.

Blankenburg, Erhard 1997, *Lawyers' lobby and the welfare state: The political economy of legal aid*, Oxford University Press, Edinburgh.

Blazejowska, Louise 1994, 'Sorting the myths and reality of domestic violence', *Law Society Journal*, vol. 32, no. 1, pp. 41-67.

Blocker, Gene H. and Smith, Elizabeth H. (eds) 1976, *John Rawls' theory of social justice an introduction*, Ohio University Press, Athens.

Blunch, Niels-Hugo and Das, Maitreyi B. 2007, *Changing norms about gender inequality in education: Evidence from Bangladesh*, The World Bank, South Asia Region, Sustainable Development Department, 12 April 2008.

Bogue, Ronald and Cornis-Pope, Marcel 1996, *Violence and mediation in contemporary culture*, SUNY series, the margins of literature, State University of New York Press, Albany.

Bohmer, Carol and Ray, Marilyn L. 1994-95, 'Effects of different dispute resolution methods on women and children after divorce', *Family Law Quarterly*, vol. 28, no.2, pp. 223-46.

Bolton, John 2006, *The mediation handbook: A practical guide for lawyers on the art of mediation*, Chusid, Melbourne.

Boo, Lawrence 1997, 'Singapore', in Michael Pryles (ed.), Dispute resolution in Asia, pp. 207-250.

Bordow, Sophy and Gibson, Janne 1994, *Evaluation of the family court mediation service*, Family Court Research and Evaluation Unit, Australia Family Court.

Borisoff, Deborah and Victor, David A. 1989, *Conflict management: A communication skills approach,* Prentice-Hall, Englewood Cliffs, NJ.

Boserup, Hans 2007, *Mediation: Six ways in seven days: Special part of the mediation process*, DJØF Publication, Copenhagen.

Boulle, Laurence 1996, *Mediation: Principles, process, practice*, Butterworths, Sydney.

—. 2001, *Mediation: Skills and techniques*, , Butterworths, Sydney.

—. 2005, *Mediation: Principles, process, practice*, 2nd edn, Butterworths, Sydney.

—. 2011, *Mediation: principles, process, practice*, 3rd edn, Butterworths, Sydney.

Bowen, Murray 1978, *Family therapy in clinical practices*, J. Aronson, New York.

Bozzomo, James W. and Scolieri, Gregory 2004, 'A survey of united family courts', *Family Court Review*, vol. 42, no. 1, pp. 12-38.

Brager, Marshall J. 2001, 'The administrative dispute resolution act of 1996 and the private practitioner', in Breger, Marshall J., Schatz, Gerald S. and Laufer, Deborah S. (eds.), *Federal Administrative Dispute Resolution Deskbook*, American Bar Association, Chicago.

Brams, Steven J. and Taylor, Alan D. 1996, *Fair division: From cake cutting to dispute resolution,* Cambridge University Press, Cambridge.

Brazil, Wayne D. 2002, 'Court ADR 25 years after Pound: Have we found a better way? *Ohio State Journal on Dispute Resolution,* vol.18, no.1, pp. 93-150.

Bretherton, Diane 1997, *A mediation process for Sri Lanka*, Australian National University. Peace Research Centre, Canberra.

Brodie, Donald W. 1989, 'Gender and dispute resolution: The court studies arbitration framework', *Journal of Contemporary Legal Issues,* vol. 3, pp.75-100.

Brown, Jennifer G. and Ayres, Ian 1994, 'Economic rationales for mediation', *Virginia Law Review*, vol. 80, no. 2, pp. 323-402.

Brown, Scott, Cervenak, Christine and Fairman, David 1998, *Alternative dispute resolution practitioners guide*, Center for Democracy and Governance, USAID, Washington, DC.

Bryan, Penelope E. 1992, 'Killing us softly: Divorce mediation and the politics of power', *Buffalo Law Review*, vol. 40, no.2, pp. 441-523.

Bush, Robert AB. 1989, 'Defining quality in dispute resolution: Taxonomies and anti-taxonomies of quality arguments', *Denver University Law Review*, vol. 66, no. 3, pp. 335-80.

—. 1996, 'Review: The unexplored possibilities of community Mediation: A comment on Merry and Milner', *Law & Social Inquiry*, vol. 21, no. 3, pp. 715-36.

—. 2002, 'Substituting mediation for arbitration: the growing market for evaluative mediation, and what it means for the ADR field', *Pepperdine Dispute Resolution Law Journal,* vol.3, no.1, pp.111-31.

Bush, Robert AB. and Folger, Joseph P. 1994, *The promise of mediation: Responding too conflict through empowerment and recognition*, Jossey-Bass, San Francisco.

—. 2005, *The promise of mediation: The transformative approach to conflict*, rev. edn, Jossey-Bass, San Francisco.

Buttram, Robert T., Folger, Robert and Sheppard, BH. 1995, 'Equity, equality and need: Three faces of social justice', in Bunker, Barbara B. and Deutsch, Morton (eds), *Conflict, cooperation, and justice: Essays inspired by the work of Morton Deutsch*, Jossey-Bass Inc. San Francisco.

Calleros, Juan C. 2009, *The unfinished transition to democracy in Latin America*, Routledge, New York.

Cappelletti, Mauro 1981, 'Access to justice as a focus of reserch', *Windsor Yearbook of Access to Justice*', vol. 1, pp. ix-xxv.

—. 1993, 'Alternative dispute resolution processes within the framework of world-wide access-to-justice movement', *Modern Law Review*, vol. 56, no. 2, pp. 282-96.

Cappelletti, Mauro and Garth, Bryant 1978, 'Access to justice: The newest wave in the worldwide movement to make rights effective', *Buffalo Law Review,* vol. 27, no. 2, pp. 181–92.

Caputo, Chiara-Marisa 2007, 'Lawyers' participation in mediation', *Australian Dispute Resolution Journal*, vol. 18, no. 2, pp. 84-91.

Carney, Terry 1989, 'Client assessment of Victoria's guardianship and administration board', *Monash University Law Review*, vol. 15, no. 3&4, pp. 229-52.

Carney, Terry and Tait, David 1997, *The adult guardianship experiment: Tribunals and popular justice*, Federation Press, Sydney.

Carolyn, Schwarz D. 2004, 'Unified family courts', *Family Court Review*, vol. 42, no. 2, pp. 304-20.

Carrington, Paul D. 1995, 'ADR and future adjudication: A primer on dispute resolution', *Review of Litigation,* vol.15, no.3, pp. 485-502.

Carroll, Lucy 1985, 'Recent Bangladeshi legislation affecting women: Child marriage, dowry, cruelty to women', Islamic and Comparative Law Quarterly, vol. 5, no. 3-4, pp.255-64.

—. 1986, 'Fatima in the House of Lords', *The Modern Law Review*, vol.

49, pp. 776-81.

Casper, Jonathan D. 1978, 'Having their day in court: Defendant evaluations of the Fairness of their treatment', *Law & Society Review*, vol. 12, no. 2, pp. 237-51.

Casper, Karen L. and Kamal, Sultana 1995, *Evaluation report: Community legal services conducted by family planning NGOs*, The Asia Foundation, Dhaka.

Caspi, Sandra 1998, 'Mediation in the family courts of Australia: Rhetoric versus reality', PhD thesis, Monash University.

Centre for Muslim-Jewish Engagement 2009, *Partial translation from Sunan Abu-Dawud*, University of Southern California, viewed 3 January 2009, <http://www.usc.edu/schools/college/crcc/engagement/resources/texts/muslim/hadith/abudawud/011.sat.html>

Charlton, Ruth and Dewdney, Micheline 1995, *The mediator's handbook: Skills and strategies for practitioners*, Law Book Company, Sydney.

Cheater, Angela 1999, 'Power in the post-modern era', in Cheater, Angela (ed.), *The anthropology of power: Empowerment and disempowerment in changing structures*, Routledge, London, pp.1-12.

Cheema, Shabbir G. 2005, Building democratic institutions: governance reform in developing countries, Kumarian Press Inc., Bloomfield.

Chen, Bee G. 2002, *Law without lawyers, justice without courts: on traditional Chinese mediation*, Ashgate, Barlington.

Chernick, Richard 2003, 'ADR comes of age: What can we expect in the future', *Pepperdine Dispute Resolution Law Journal,* vol. 4, no. 2, pp. 187-94.

Chisholm, Richard 1991, 'Mediation services for the family court: Something new under the sun?', *Australian Journal of Family Law*, vol. 5, no. 3, pp. 277-80.

Chornenki, Genevieve A. 1999, 'Mediation: Entry point not destination', *Windsor Year Book of Access to Justice*, vol.17, pp. 261-70.

Choudhury, Alimuzzaman 1983, *Mahomedan Law* Interline Publisher, Dhaka.

Chowdhury, Jamila A. 1999a, 'Where do we stand today with regard to inheritance', *The Independent*, 9 April, p. 12.

—. 1999b, 'Dower: a matrimonial right of women', *The Independent*, 2 July, p. 12.

—. 2000, 'Offences that affect the dignity of women', *The Independent*, 7 April, p. 12.

—. 2001, 'Polygamy: an assault on women's dignity', The Independent, 24 August, p. 12.

—. 2002, 'Status of women in Bangladesh', *The Independent*, 15 November, p. 12.

—. 2003, 'Rights in law and in practice: the case of Bangladesh', *Hurights Osaka*, Asia-Pacific human rights information centre, vol. 32, pp. 14-15.

—. 2004, 'Achievements of and obstacles to effective in-court mediation in Bangladesh: a perspective on family disputes', *The Chittogong University Journal of Law*, vol. 9, no. 1, pp. 96-124.

—. 2005, *Women's access to justice in Bangladesh through ADR in family disputes,* Modern Book Shop, Mansoura, Egypt.

—. 2006a, 'Women's access to justice', *International Journal of Women, Social Justice and Human Rights*, vol. 1, no. 2, pp. 161-84.

—. 2006b, 'Power imbalance and its impact on mediation of family disputes involving family violence: Australian perspective', *The Dhaka University Studies Part F*, vol. 17, no. 2, pp. 173-92.

—. 2008a, 'Gender, power and mediation: post-structural power in social antiquity', *Pakistan Journal of Women's Studies: Alam-e-Niswan*, vol. 15, no. 2, pp. 101-116.

—. 2008b, 'Family court ADR in Egypt and some exemplary provisions for other Muslim countries', DIAC Journal, vol. 2, no. 2, pp. 49-72.

Chowdhury, Obaidul H. 2005, *Handbook of Muslim family laws*, 6th edn, Dhaka Law Reports, Dhaka.

Clark, Theodore R. 1974, *Coping with mediation, fact finding, and interest arbitration*, International Personnel Management Association, Chicago.

Cloke, Ken and Goldsmith, Joan 2000, *Resolving personal and organisational conflict: Stiries of transformation and forgiveness*, Jossey-Bass, San Francisco.

Cobb, Sara 1993, 'Empowerment and mediation: A narrative perspective', *Negotiation Journal*, vol. 9, no. 3, pp. 245-67.

Cobb, Sara and Rifkin, Janet 1991, 'Practice and paradox: Deconstructing neutrality in mediation', *Law & Social Inquiry*, vol. 16, no. 1, pp. 35-62.

Cochran, William G. 1963, *Sampling techniques*, 2nd edn, John Wiley & Sons, New York.

Cohen, Louis, Manion, Lawrence and Morrison, Keith 2003, *Research methods in education*, Routledge, New York.

Cohen, Richard 1995, 'Mediation standards', *Australasian Dispute Resolution Journal,* vol. 6, no. 1, pp. 25-32.

Cole, Sarah R., Rogers, Nancy H and McEwen, Craig A 1994, *Mediation: Law, policy, practice*, 2nd edn, Trial practice series, West Group, St. Paul, Minn.

Coogler, OJ. 1978, *Structured mediation in divorce settlement: A handbook for marital mediators*, Lexington Books, Lexington, Mass.

Coogler, OJ., Weber, Ruth E. and McKenry, Patrick C. 1979, 'Divorce mediation: A means of facilitating divorce and adjustment', *The Family Coordinator*, vol. 28, no. 2, pp. 255-59.

Cook, Harold and Smothergill, Daniel 1971, 'Verbal mediation and satiation in young children', *Child Development*, vol. 42, no. 6, pp. 1805-12.

Cook, Karen S. and Hegtvedt Karen A. 1983, 'Distributive justice, equity, and equality', *Annual Review of Sociology*, vol.9, pp.217-41.

Cooley, John W. 1996, *Mediation advocacy*, National Institute for Trial Advocacy, Notre Dame, Ind.

—. 2006, *The mediator's handbook: advanced practice guide for civil litigation*, National Institute for Trial Advocacy, Louisvillle.

Cooley, John W. and Hubet, Steven 2003, *Arbitration advocacy*, National Institute for Trial Advocacy, South Bend.

Cooks, Leda M. and Hale, Claudia L. 1994, 'The construction of ethics in mediation', *Mediation Quarterly*, vol. 12, pp. 55-76.

Cooper, Donna and Brandon, Mieke 2007, 'How can family lawyers effectively represent their clients in mediation and conciliation processes?', *Australian Journal of Dispute Resolution*, vol. 21, no.3, pp. 288-308.

Cooper, Donna and Field, Rachael 2008, 'The family dispute resolution of parenting matters in Australia: an analysis of the notion of an independent practitioner', *Queensland University of Technology Law and Justice Journal,* vol. 8, no. 1, pp. 158-75.

Copeland, Roger 1990, 'The presence of mediation', *TDR*, vol. 34, no. 4, pp. 28-44.

Coulson, Robert 1996, *Family mediation: Managing conflict, resolving disputes*, 2nd edn, Jossey-Bass, San Francisco, Calif.

Council of Europe 2000, '*Family mediation in Europe*', proceedings of the 4th European Conference on Family Law, Strasbourg, Europe, 1-2 October, 1998.

Craver, Charles B. 1990, 'The impact of gender on clinical negotiating achievement', *Ohio State Journal on Dispute Resolution*, vol. 6, no. 1, pp. 1-18.

Cremin, Hilary 2007, *Peer mediation*, McGraw Hill, Maidenhead, England.

Crime Facts Info 2003, Australian Institute of Criminology, Melbourne, viewed 20 November 2009, <www.aic.gov.au>

Crosby, Faye J. 1995, 'Aspects of confidentiality in mediation: a matter of balancing competing public interests', *Commercial Dispute Resolution Journal* , vol. 2, no. 1, pp. 51.

Crosby, Faye J., Stockdale, Margaret S., and Ropp, Ann, S. 2007, Sex discrimination in the workplace: multidisciplinary perspectives, Blackwell Publishing Ltd., Oxford.

Cross, Frank B. and Miller, Roger L. 2007, West's legal environment of business: text and cases, Thomson, Ohio.

Crowley, Thomas E. 1994, *Settle it out-of-court: How to resolve business and personal disputes using mediation, arbitration, and negotiation*, J. Wiley, New York.

Csaszar, Fruzsina 2005, 'Understanding the concept of power', in Alsop, Ruth (ed.), *Power, rights and poverty: Concepts and connections*, The World Bank, Washington DC, pp. 137-46.

Dana, Daniel 2001, *Conflict resolution: Mediation tools for everyday work life*, McGraw-Hill, New York.

Danzig, Richard and Lowy, Michael J. 1975, 'Everyday disputes and mediation in the United States: A reply to professor Felstiner', *Law & Society Review*, vol. 9, no. 4, pp. 675-94.

Datta, Prabhat and Datta, Chandan 2002, 'The panchayet system in west Bengal', in Palanithurai, Ganapathy, *Dynamics of new panchayet raj system in India*, Concept publishing company, New Delhi.

David, Flynn 2005, 'The social worker as family mediator: Balancing power in cases involving family violence', *Australian Social Work*, vol. 58, no. 4, pp. 407-18.

David, Shichor and Sechrest, Dale K. 1998, 'A comparison of mediated and non-mediated juvenile offender cases in California', *Juvenile and Family Court Journal*, vol. 49, no. 2, pp. 27-40.

Davis, Aeron 2007, *The mediation of power: A critical introduction*, Routledge, London , New York.

Davis, Albie M. and Salem, Richard A. 1984, 'Dealing with power imbalances in the mediation of interpersonal disputes', *Mediation Quarterly*, vol.6, no. 4, pp. 17-26.

Davis, Gwynn and Roberts, Marian 1988, *Access to agreement: A consumer study of mediation in family disputes*, Open University Press, Milton Keynes, Philadelphia, PA.

Delgado, Richard, Dunn, Chris, Brown, Pamela, Lee, Helena and Hubbert, David 1985, 'Fairness and formality: Minimising the risk of prejudice in alternative dispute resolution', *Wisconsin Law Review,* vol. 65, no.6, pp. 1359-1404.

Delhi Mediation Centre 2012, 'History', *Delhi Mediation Centre*, at <http://www.delhimediationcentre.gov.in/history.htm>

DeMarco, Joseph P. 1980, 'Rawls and Marx' in Blocker, Gene H. and Smith, Elizabeth H. (eds.) *John Rawls' theory of social Justice an introduction*, Ohio University Press, Athens.

Denning, Alfred 1993, *What next in the law*, Butterworths, New Delhi.

Department for International Development 2001, *Making government work for poor people: Building state capability*, DFID, London.

Devolve, Piere 2000, 'General report', in *Proceedings for multilateral conference,* Lisbon, 31 May-2 June, Council of Europe Publishing, Cedex, pp. 13-34.

Dickson, Brian 1989, 'Access to justice', *Windsor Review of Legal and Social Issues*, vol. 1, pp. 1-4.

Dienes, Thomas 1970, 'Judges, legislators, and social change, *The American Behavioral Scientist*, vol. 13, no. 4, pp. 511-22.

Dignan, James, Sorsby, Angela and Hibbert, Jeremy 1996, *Neighbour disputes : Comparing the cost-effectiveness of mediation and alternative approaches*, Centre for Criminological and Legal Research, University of Sheffield, Sheffield.

Dingwall, Robert and Eekelaar, John 1988, *Divorce mediation and the legal process*, Oxford socio-legal studies, Clarendon Press, Oxford.

Dinovitzer, Ronit and Leon, Jeffrey S. 2001, 'When long becomes too long: Legal culture and litigators' view on long civil trials', *Windsor Year Book of Access to Justice*, vol.19, pp. 106-60.

Dobash, Russell P., Dobash, Emerson R. Wilson, Margo and Daly, Martin 1992, 'Social Problems', *The myth of Sexual Symmetry in Marital Violence*, vol. 39, no. 1, pp. 71-91.

Doherthy, Nora and Guyler, Marcelas 2008, *The essential guide to workplace mediation & conflict resolution*, Kogan Page Ltd. Philadelphia.

Donnelly, Jack 1989, *Universal human rights in theory and practice*, Cornell University Press, London.

Douglas, Susan 2008, 'Neutrality in mediation: a study of mediator perceptions', *Queensland University of Technology Law and Justice Journal*, vol. 8, no. 1, pp. 139-157.

Dreyfus, Hubert L. and Rabinow, Paul 1982, *Michel Foucault: Beyond structuralism and hermeneutics*, University Chicago Press, Chicago.

Dror, Yehezkel 1970, 'Law as a tool of directed social change', *The American Behavioral Scientist*, vol. 13, no. 4, pp. 533-61.

Druckman, Daniel and Mitchell, Christopher 1995, 'Flexibility in negotiation and mediation', *Annals of the American Academy of Political and Social Science*, vol. 542, pp. 10-23.

Duffy, Karen G., Grosch, James W. and Olczak, Paul V. 1991, *Community mediation: A handbook for practitioners and researchers*, Guilford Press, New York.

Eadie, William F. and Nelson, Paul E. 2001, *The Language of Conflict resolution,* Sage Publications, Thousand Oaks.

Egle, Gilbert R. 1983, 'Divorce mediation: An innovative approach to family dispute resolution', *Land and Water Law Review*, vol. 18, no. 2, pp. 693-711.

Ellis, Amanda, Blackden, Mark, Cutura, Jozefina, MacCulloch, Fiona and Seebens, Holer 2007, Gender and economic growth in Tanzania: creating opportunities for women, The World Bank, Washington DC.

Emery, Robert E. 1994, *Renegotiating family relationships: Divorce, child custody and mediation*, Guilford Press, New York.

—. 1995, 'Divorce mediation: Negotiating agreements and renegotiating relationships', *Family Relations*, vol. 44, no. 4, pp. 377-83.

Eribon, Didier (1991), *Michel Foucault*, Wing, Betsy (trans.), Harvard University Press, Cambridge.

Erickson, Stephen K. and Erickson, Marilyn SM. 1988, *Family mediation casebook: Theory and process*, frontiers in couples and family therapy, Brunner, New York.

Erll, Astrid and Rigney, Ann 2009, *Mediation, remediation, and the dynamics of cultural memory*, Walter de Gruyter, Berlin.

Estey, Willard Z. 1985, 'The changing role of the judiciary', *Law Institute Journal*, vol. 59, pp.1071-76.

Eyben, Rosalind 2005, 'Linking power and poverty reduction', in Alsop, Ruth (ed.), *Power, rights and poverty: Concepts and connections*, The World Bank, Washington DC, pp. 15-28.

Feerick, John, Izumi, Carol, Kovach, Kimberlee, Love, Lela, Moberly, Robert, Riskin, Leonard and Sherman E 1995, 'Symposium: Standards of Professional Conduct in Alternative Dispute Resolution, *Journal of Dispute Resolution,* vol. 1, pp. 95-128.

Fehlberg, Belinda and Behrens, Juliet 2008, *Australian family law: The contemporary context*, Oxford University Press, Melbourne.

Felicity, Kaganas and Piper, Christine 1994, 'Domestic violence and divorce mediation', *Journal of Social Welfare and Family Law*, vol. 16, no. 3, pp. 265-78.

Felstiner, William LF. 1974, 'Influences of social organization on dispute processing', Law *and Society Review*, vol. 9, no. 1, pp. 63-94.

Felstiner, William LF. and Williams, Lynne A. 1978, 'Mediation as an alternative to criminal prosecution: Ideology and limitations', *Law and Human Behaviour*, vol. 2, no. 3, pp. 223-44.

Field, Rachael M. 1996, 'Mediation and the art of power (im) balancing',

Queensland University *Technology Law Journal*, vol. 12, pp. 264-73.

—. 2004, 'A model of family mediation that supports the participation of victims of domestic violence', paper presented at the True Walking, Forward Walking – 7th Bi-annual Mediation Conference, Darwin, 30 June, 2004.

—. 2006, 'Using the feminist critique of mediation to explore 'the good, the bad and the ugly' implications for women of the introduction of mandatory family dispute resolution in Australia', *Australian Journal of Family Law*, vol. 20, no. 1, pp. 45-78.

—. 2007, 'A mediation profession in Australia: an improved framework for mediation ethics' *Australian Dispute Resolution Journal*, vol. 18, pp. 178-85.

Finn, Janet L. 2000, 'Walls and bridges: Cultural mediation and the legacy of Ella Deloria', *Frontiers: A Journal of Women Studies*, vol. 21, no. 3, pp. 158-82.

Fisher Linda and Brandon Mieke 2002, *Mediating with families, making the difference*, Pearson Education, Sydney.

Fisher, Harry M. 1993, 'Judicial mediation: How it works through pre-trial conference', *The University of Chicago Law Review*, vol. 10, no. 4, pp. 453-65.

Fisher, Roger 1983, 'Negotiating power', *American Behavioral Scientist*, vol. 27, no. 2, pp. 149-66.

Fisher, Roger, Ury, William and Patton, Bruce 1991, *Getting to yes - Negotiating an agreement without giving in*, 2nd edn, Penguin, New York.

Fisher, Ronald J. and Keashly, Loraleigh 1991, 'The potential complementarily of mediation and consultation within a contingency model of third party intervention', *Journal of Peace Research*, vol. 28, no. 1, pp. 29-42.

Fogarty, Thomas 1976, System concepts and dimensions of self, in Guerin, Philip (ed.) Family therapy: theory and practice, Gradner, New Yorik, pp. 144-153.

Folberg, Jay and Taylor, Alison 1984, *Mediation: A comprehensive guide to resolving conflicts without litigation*, Jossey-Bass, San Francisco.

Folberg, Jay, Milne, Ann and Salem, Peter 2004, *Divorce and family mediation: Models, techniques, and applications*, Guilford Press, New York.

Foucault, Michel 1980, *Power/Knowledge: Selected interviews and other writings 1972-1977*, Gordon, Colin, Marshall, Leo, Mepham, John and Soper, Kate (trans.), Gordon, Colin (ed.), The Harvester Press Limited, Brighton, Sussex.

—. 1989, *The archaeology of knowledge and the discourse on language*, Smith, Sheridan AM. (trans.), Routledge Classics, London and New York.

Fox, Erica A. 2004, 'Bringing peace into the room', *Negotiation Journal,* vol.20, no.3, pp. 461-69.

Fraser, Nancy 1981, 'Foucault on modern power: Empirical insights and normative confusions', *Praxis International*, vol.1, no.1, pp. 272-87.

Frederico, Margarita, Cooper, Brian and Picton, Cliff 1998, *Mediation and cultural values: A model of culturally sensitive mediation*, Dept. of Immigration and Multicultural Affairs, Belconnen, ACT.

Freedom House 2010, *Countries at the coss roads 2010*, Rowman & Littlefield Publishers Inc., Maryland.

Frey, Martin A. 2001, 'Does ADR offer second class justice', *Tulsa Law Journal,* vol. 36, no. 4, pp. 727-66.

Friedman, Gary J. and Himmelstein, Jack 1993, *A guide to divorce mediation: How to reach a fair, legal settlement at a fraction of the cost*, Workman Publishing, New York.

Fries, Horace S. 1945, 'Mediation in cultural perspective', *American Journal of Economics and Sociology*, vol. 4, no. 4, pp. 449-60.

Fuller, Lon L. 1979, 'The forms and limits of adjudication', *Harvard Law Review*, vol. 92, no.2, pp. 353-409.

Fulton, Maxwell J. 1989, *Commercial alternative dispute resolution*, The Law Book Co., Sydney.

Fyzee, Asaf A 1974, *Outlines of Muhammadan law*, 4th edn, Oxford University Press, New Delhi.

—. 2008, *A modern approach to Islam,*, Oxford University Press, USA.

Gaffal, Margit 2010, *Psychological and legal perspectives of marital breakdown: with special emphasis on Spain*, Springer, Heidelberg.

Gagnon, Andree G. 1992, 'Ending mandatory divorce mediation for battered women', *Harvard Women's Law Journal*, vol. 15, pp. 272-94.

Galanter, Marc 1981, 'Justice in many rooms', in Cappelletti, Mauro (ed.), *Access to justice and the welfare state*, Le Monnier, Florence, pp. 147-81.

—. 1985, 'A settlement judge, not a trial judge: Judicial mediation in the United States', *Journal of Law and Society*, vol. 12, no. 1, pp. 1-18.

Geirbo, Hanne C. and Imam, Nuzhat 2006, 'The motivations behind giving and taking dowry', *Research Monograph Series*, no. 28, viewed 12 January 2010, <http://www.bracresearch.org/monographs/Monograph_Series_28.pdf>

Glaser, Daniel 1957, 'A Note on differential mediation of social perception as a correlate of social adjustment', *Sociometry*, vol. 20, no. 2, pp. 156-

60.
Goh, Bee C. 2002, '*Law Without lawyers, justice without courts: On traditional Chinese mediation*', Aldershot: Ashgate.
Gold, Lois 2009, *The healthy divorce: keys to ending your marriage while preserving your emotional well-being*, Sourcebook Inc., Illinois.
Goldberg, Stephen B. 2003, *Dispute resolution: Negotiation, mediation, and other processes*, 4th edn, Aspen Publishers, New York.
Golub, Stephen 2000a, 'From the Village to the University: Legal Activism in Bangladesh' in McClymont, Mary and Golub, Stephen (eds) *Many roads to Justice: The law-related work of Ford Foundation grantees around the world,* Ford Foundation, USA, pp. 127-53.
—. 2000b, 'Non lawyers as legal resources' in McClymont, Mary and Golub, Stephen (eds) *Many roads to Justice: The law-related work of Ford Foundation grantees around the world,* Ford Foundation, USA, pp. 297-313.
—. 2003, *Non-state Justice system in Bangladesh and Philippines* , viewed 18 August 2009,<http://www.gsdrc.org/docs/open/DS34.pdf>
Goodman, Ellen 1986, 'Dispute resolution in family law: Is "Conciliatory Procedure" the answer?', *Australian Journal of Family Law*, vol. 1, no.1, pp. 28-49.
Gouda, Frances 1993, 'Review: No paradise for women', *The Women's Review of Books*, vol. 10, no. 7, pp. 22-3.
Gramberg, Bernadine V. 2006, Managing workplace conflict: Alternative dispute resolution in Australia, The Federation Press, Annandale, NSW.
Gray, John, Halliday, Moira and Woodgate, Andrew 2002, *Responding to community conflict: A review of neighbourhood mediation*, the Joseph Rowntree Foundation, York.
Graycar, Regina 1989, 'Family law and social security: The child support connection', *Australian Journal of Family Law,* vol. 3, no. 1, pp. 70-92.
—. 1992, 'Before the high court: Women's work: Who cares' *Sydney Law Review,* vol. 14, no. 1, pp.86-105.
Graycar, Regina and Morgan, Jenny 1990, *The hidden gender of law*, Federation Press, Annandale, NSW.
—. 2002, *The hidden gender of Law*, 2nd edn, Federation Press, Annandale, NSW.
Greatbatch, David and Dingwall, Robert 1989, 'Selective facilitation: some preliminary observations on a strategy used by divorce mediators', *Law and Society Review*, vol. 23, pp. 613–41.
—. 1997, 'Argumentative talk in divorce mediation sessions', *American Sociological Review*, vol. 62, no. 1, pp. 151-70.

Greenberg, Melanie C., Barton, John H. and McGuinness, Margaret E. 2000, *Words over war: Mediation and arbitration to prevent deadly conflict*, Carnegie Commission on Preventing Deadly Conflict series., Rowman & Littlefield Publishers, Lanham.

Greenhouse, Carol J. 1985, 'Mediation: A comparative approach', *Man*, vol. 20, no. 1, pp. 90-114.

Greenstone, James L., Leviton, Sharon C and Fowler, Craig M 1994, 'Mediation advocacy: A new concept in the dispute resolution arena', *Mediation Quarterly,* vol. 11, no.3, pp. 293-99.

Gribben, Susan 1992, 'Mediation of family disputes', *Australian Journal of Family Law*, vol. 6, no. 2, pp. 126-43.

Grillo, Trina 1991, 'The mediation alternative: Process dangers for women', *The Yale Law Journal*, vol. 100, no. 6, pp. 1545-610.

Guhathakurta, Meghna 1985, 'Gender violence in Bangladesh: The role of the state', *Journal of Social Studies*, vol. 30, pp.77-90.

Gupta, Ramchandra and Sarkar, Sadhanchandra 1982, *Overview of Indian legal and constitutional history*, Surjeet Publications, Delhi.

Gutting, Gary 2005, *Foucault: A very short introduction*, Oxford University Press, Oxford.

Hadi, Abdullahel 2000, 'Prevalence and correlates of the risk of marital sexual violence in Bangladesh', *Journal of Interpersonal Violence*, vol.15, pp.787-805.

Haley, Jay 1991, *Problem-solving therapy*, Jossey-Bass, San Francisco.

Halim, Mohammod A. 2008, *The Legal System of Bangladesh*, 3rd edn, CCB Foundation, Dhaka.

Hall, Kermit L. (ed.) 2002, The Oxford companion to American law, Oxford University Press, Oxford.

Hamid, Shamim 1996, *Why women count: Essays on women in development in Bangladesh*, The University Press Limited, Dhaka.

Hammond, Matthew B. 1917, 'Compulsory arbitration in Australia and New Zealand', *Proceedings of the Academy of Political Science in the City of New York*, vol. 7, no. 1, pp. 19-30.

Hansen, James C. and Crebe, Sarah C. 1985, *Divorce and family mediation*, The Family therapy collections, Aspen Systems Corp., Rockville.

Haq, Jahanara 1995, *Empowerment of women in Bangladesh: Neirobi to Beijing*, Woemn for women, Dhaka.

Harrington, Christine B. and Merry, Sally E. 1988, 'Ideological production: The making of community mediation', *Law & Society Review*, vol. 22, no. 4, pp. 709-35.

Harrold, Daphne K. 2007, *Legal empowerment strategies in Bangladesh:*

Empowering women and poor people through legal means, Bangladesh Rural Advancement Committee (BRAC), Dhaka.

Hart, Barbara J. 1990, 'Gentle jeopardy: The further endangerment of battered women and children in custody Mediation', *Mediation Quarterly*, vol. 7, no. 4, pp. 317-30.

Hasan, Mohammod K. 2001, 'A report on mediation in the family courts: Bangladesh experience', paper presented to 25th Anniversary Conference of the Family Courts of Australia, Sydney, 26-29 July.

—. 2002, 'Mediation in the family courts: Bangladesh experience', paper presented at the *First South Asian Regional Judicial Colloquium on Access to Justice*, New Delhi, 1-3 November.

—. 2005, 'Alternative dispute resolution', in Rahman, Waliur & Shahabuddin, Mohammod (eds), *Judicial training in the new millennium: An anatomy of BILIA judicial training with difference*, Bangladesh Institute of Law and International Affairs, Dhaka, pp. 123-36.

—. 2008, 'A report on mediation in the family courts: Bangladesh experience' , in Islam, Soma & Shahiduzzaman, Mohammod (eds), *Reviewing the Family Courts Ordinance 1985,* Bangladesh Legal Aid and Services Trust, Dhaka, pp. 7-16.

Hasan, Manzoor 2002, *'Corruption in Bangladesh' surveys: An overview*, Transparency International, Bangladesh, viewed 15 August 2009, <http://www.ti-bangladesh.org>

Haugaard, Mark 1997, *The constitution of power*, Manchester University Press, New York.

Hauser, Joyce 1995, *Good divorces, bad divorces: A case for divorce mediation*, University Press of America, Lanham.

Haynes, John M. and Charlesworth, Stephanie 1996, *The fundamentals of family mediation*, Federation Press, Leichhardt, NSW.

Haynes, John M., Haynes, Ggetchen L and Fong, Larry S 2004, *Mediation: Positive conflict management*, SUNY series in transpersonal and humanistic psychology, State University of New York Press, Albany.

Helmke, Gretchen and Rios-Figueroa, Julio 2011, *Courts in Latin America*, Cambridge University Press, Cambridge.

Hermann, Margaret S. 1989, 'ADR in context: Linking our past, present and possible future', Journal *of Contemporary Legal Issues,* vol.3, pp. 37-58.

—. 2006, *The Blackwell handbook of mediation: Bridging theory, research, and practice*, Blackwell Publication, Malden, USA.

Hermann, Michele G. 1989, 'The dangers of ADR: A three-tiered system of justice', *Journal of Contemporary Legal Issues,* vol.3, pp. 117-24.

Hill, Eve 1990, 'Alternative dispute resolution in a feminist voice', *Ohio State Journal on Dispute Resolution,* vol. 5, no.2, pp. 337-80.

Hodges, Joseph L. and Lehmann, Erich L. 1970, *Basic concepts of probability and statistics*, Society for Industrial and Applied Mathematics, Holden-Day, San Francisco.

Hoffman, Ben 1993, Win-win competitiveness made in Canada: how to be competitive using the consensus approach, Captus Press Inc, Ontario.

Hofstede, Geert 2001, *Culture's consequences: comparing values, behaviors, institutions and organizations across nations*, SAGE, Thousand Oaks.

Holland, Kenneth M. 1991, *Judicial activism in comparative perspective*, McMillan, London.

Hosain, Sahara and Begum, Dilara 1999, *Marriage, divorce and women rights (Beie, bibaho-bichched & mohila odikhar)*, Women for Women, Dhaka.

Hualing, Fu 2010, Access to justice in China: potentials, limits and alternativies, in John Gillespie and Albert H.Y. Chen, Legal reforms in China and Vietnam: A comparison of Asian communist regimes, Routledge, Ney York.

Hughes, Dolores S. and Walsh, John F. 1971, 'Effects of syntactical mediation, age, and modes of representation on paired-associate learning', *Child Development*, vol. 42, no. 6, pp. 1827-36.

Hughes, Patricia 2001, 'Mandatory mediation: Opportunity or subversion?', *Windsor Year Book of Access to Justice*, vol.19, pp. 161-202.

Hughes, Scott H. 1995, 'Elizabeth's story: Exploring power imbalances in divorce mediation', *Georgetown Journal of Legal Ethics*, vol. 8, no.3, pp. 553-95.

Human Rights Watch 1998, *Behinds bars in Brazil*, Human Rights Watch, New York.

Huq, Mohammod 2005, 'Courts system of Bangladesh', in Rahman, Waliur & Shahabuddin, Mohammod (eds), *Judicial training in the new millennium: An anatomy of BILIA judicial training with difference*, Bangladesh Institute of Law and International Affairs, Dhaka, pp. 100-04.

Husain, Sheikh A. 1976, *Marriage customs among Muslims in India: A sociological study of Shia marriage customs*, Sterling Publishers Pvt. Ltd., New Delhi.

Hutchinson, Allan C. 1990, *Access to civil Justice*, Carcwell, Toronto.

Hydén, Margareta 2001, 'For the child's sake: Parents and social workers discuss conflict-filled parental relations after divorce', *Child & Family Social Work*, vol. 6, no. 2, pp. 115-28.

Hyman, Herbert H. 1975, *Interviewing in social research*, University of Chicago Press, Chicago.

Iacobucci, Dawn 2008, *Mediation analysis*, Quantitative applications in the social sciences, Sage, Los Angeles.

Ikram, Khalid 2006, *The Egyptian economy 1952-2000: performance, policies, and issues*, Routledge, New York.

Ingleby, Richard 1993, 'Court sponsored mediation: The case against mandatory participation', *The Modern Law Review*, vol. 56, no. 3, pp. 441-51.

Inglehart, Ronald and Welzel, Christian 2005, *Modernization, cultural change, and democracy: the human development sequence*, Cambridge University Press, Cambridge.

Institute for Civil Engineers (ICE) 2007, Construction law handbook, Thomas Telford Publishing, London.

Institute for the Study and Development of Legal Systems (ISDLS) 2005, 'Bangladesh Civil Justice Reform'. 27 July 2007, viewed <http://www.isdls.org/projects_bangladesh.html>

Institute of Arbitrators & Mediators Australia 2003, *The practitioner's certificate in mediation and conciliation: Handbook*, Institute of Arbitrators & Mediators Australia, Melbourne.

International Centre for Diarrheal Disease Research Centre, Bangladesh (ICDDR,B) 2006, 'Domestic violence against women in Bangladesh' *Health and Science Bulletin*, vol. 4, no. 2, pp.1-6.

International Institute for Conflict Prevention Resolution (CPR) 1994, *Mediation*, CPR Institute for Dispute Resolution, New York.

International Monetary Fund (IMF) 2011, 'Rwanda-poverty reduction strategy paper-progress report', *IMF country report*, no. 11/154, IMF, Washington DC.

International Women's Rights Action Watch (IWRAW) 2002, 'Baseline report on violence against women in Bangladesh', International Women Rights Action Watch, Asia Pacific, Kuala Lumpur.

Irving, Howard H. 1980, *Divorce mediation: The rational alternative*, Personal Library Publishers, Toronto.

Irving, Howard H. and Benjamin, Michael 1995, *Family mediation: Contemporary issues*, Sage Publications, Thousand Oaks.

Islam, Formanul 2002, *The Madaripur model of mediation: A new dimension in the field of dispute resolution in rural Bangladesh*, Dhaka, unpublished research paper.

Iwai, Nobuaki 1991, 'Alternative dispute resolution in court: The Japanese experience', *Ohio State Journal on Dispute Resolution,* vol. 6, no. pp. 201-41.

Jahan, Roushan 1994, *Hidden danger: Women and family violence in Bangladesh*, Women for Women, Dhaka.

Jahan, Roushan and Islam, Mahmuda 1997, *Violence against women in Bangladesh*, Women for Women, Dhaka.

Jain, Mahabir P. 1999, *Outline of Indian legal history*, Tripathy, Bombay.

Jeffrey, Bob 2003, 'Countering learner 'Instrumentalism' through creative mediation', *British Educational Research Journal*, vol. 29, no. 4, pp. 489-503.

Jenkins, James J. and Palermo, David S. 1964, 'Mediation processes and the acquisition of linguistic structure', *Monographs of the Society for Research in Child Development*, vol. 29, no. 1, pp. 141-69.

Jia, Wenshan 2002, 'Chinese Mediation and Its Cultural Foundation' in Guo-Ming Chen and Ringo Ma (eds.), *Chinese conflict management and resolution*, Ablex Publishing, Westport, 2002, pp. 289-295.

Johnson, Earl 1993, Toward equal justice, where the united states stand two decades later, Maryland Journal of Contemporary Legal Issues, vol. 5-6, pp. 199-221.

Johnson, Michael P. 1995, 'Patriarchal terrorism and common couple violence: Two forms of violence against women', *Journal of Marriage and the Family*, vol. 57, no. 2, pp. 283-94.

Jones, Hardy 1980, 'A Rawlasian discussion of discrimination', in Blocker, Gene H. and Smith, Elizabeth H. (eds), *John Rawls' Theory of Social Justice*, Ohio University Press, Athens.

Joseph, Suad and Najmabadi, Afsanes 2003, Encyclopaedia of women and Islamic cultures: family, law and politics, Brill, Leiden.

Kaganas, Felicity and Piper, Christine 1993, 'Towards a definition of abuse', *Family Mediation,* vol. 3, no.2, pp 7-8.

—. 1994, 'Domestic violence and divorce mediation', *Journal of Social Welfare and Family Law*, vol. 16, no. 3, pp. 265-78.

Kalowski, Joanna 1996, 'In a manner of speaking: A cross-cultural view of mediation', *Commercial Dispute Resolution Journal*, vol. 2, no. 3, pp. 201-9.

Kamal, Mustafa 2002, 'Introducing ADR in Bangladesh: Practical model', paper presented at the seminar on *alternative dispute resolution: In quest of a new dimension in civil justice system in Bangladesh*, Dhaka, 31 October, 2002.

—. 2005, 'Alternative dispute resolution', in Rahman, Waliur & Shahabuddin, Mohammod (eds), *Judicial training in the new millennium: An anatomy of BILIA judicial training with difference*, Bangladesh Institute of Law and International Affairs, Dhaka, pp. 137-43.

Kamal, Sultana 1995, 'Law as an instrument of women's empowerment', in Jahan, Rowshan, Begum, Afroza Huq, Jahan(eds), *Empowerment of women: Nairobi to Beijing (1985-1995),* Women for Women, Dhaka, pp. 68-85.

Kapsos, Steven 2008, *The gender wage gap in Bangladesh*, International Labour Organization, viewed March 2 2010, <http://www.oit.org/wcmsp5/groups/public/asia/bangkok/documents/publication/wcms_098063.pdf>

Keith, Hodkinson 1984, Muslim family law, Croom Helm, London.

Kelly, Joan B. 1995, 'Power imbalance in divorce and interpersonal mediation: Assessment and intervention', *Mediation Quarterly*, vol. 13, no. 2, pp. 85-98.

—. 2000, 'Issues facing the family mediation field', *Piperidine Dispute Resolution Law Journal*, vol.1, pp.37-44.

Kelsen, Hans 2000, *What is Justice?, The Lawbook Exchange, Ltd.,* Union, New Jersey.

Khair, Sumaiya 1998, 'Understanding sexual harassment in Bangladesh: Dynamics of male control and female subordination', *Journal of the Faculty of Law*, vol. 9, no. 1, pp. 87-110.

—. 2004, 'Alternative dispute resolution: How it works in Bangladesh', *The Dhaka University Studies, Part F*, vol. 15, no. 1, pp. 59-92.

—. 2008, *Legal empowerment for the poor and the disadvantaged: Strategies Achievements and Challenges: Experiences from Bangladesh*, CIDA, Dhaka.

Khan, Sarfaraz A. 2006, *Lok Adalot: an effective alternative dispute resolution mechanism*, Chaman Enterprises, New Delhi.

Khanum, Rashida A. 2008, 'Feminism, Status of Women and Islam', *Empowerment*, vol. 15, pp. 67-78.

Klaming, Laura and Giesen, Ivo 2008, *Access to justice: The quality of the procedure*, Social Science Research Network, viewed 10 January 2010, <http://papers.ssrn.com/sol3/papers.cfm?abstract_id=1091105>

Kochan, Thomas A. and Jick, Todd 1978, 'The public sector mediation process: A Theory and Empirical Examination', *Journal of Conflict Resolution*, vol. 22, no. 2, pp. 209-40.

Koenig, Michael A., Ahmed, Saifuddin, Hossain, Mian B. and Mozumder, Khorshed A. 2003, 'Women's status and domestic violence in rural Bangladesh: Individual- and community – level effects', *Demography*, vol. 40, no. 2, pp. 269-88.

Konow, James 2005, 'Which is the fairest one of the all? A positive analysis of justice theories', *Journal of Economic Literature*, vol. 41, no. XLI, pp.1188-1239.

Koroscik, Judith S., Osman, Abla H. and DeSouza, Isabel 1988, 'The function of verbal mediation in comprehending works of art: A comparison of three cultures', *Studies in Art Education*, vol. 29, no. 2, pp. 91-102.

Koshi, Yamazaki and Chowdhury, Jamila A. 2005, 'Violation of human rights in Bangladesh: are Islamic values liable? ', *The Journal of Law and Politics*, vol. 37, no. 3-4, pp. 143-77.

Kottler, Jeffrey A. 1994, *Beyond blame: A new way of resolving conflict in relationships*, Jossey-Bass Publishers, San Francisco.

Kovach, Kimberlee K. 1994, *Mediation: Principles and practice*, West Publication Co., St. Paul, Minn.

Kovach, Kimberlee K. and Love, Lela P. 1996, '"Evaluative" mediation is an oxymoron', *Alternatives to High Cost Litigation*, vol. 14, pp. 31.

Kreisberg, Louis 1998, *Constructive Conflicts: From Escalation to Resolution.* Rowman & Littlefield Publishers, Inc., Lanham.

Kressel, Kenneth and Pruitt, Dean G. 1989, *Mediation research: The process and effectiveness of third-party intervention*, Jossey-Bass, San Francisco.

Kriesberg, Louis 1982, *Social conflicts*, Prentice-Hall, Inc., Englewood Cliffs, NJ.

Kulshreshth, Visheshwar D. 1995, *Landmarks in Indian legal and constitutional history*, 8th edn, Eastern Book Company, Lucknow.

Kydd, Andrew 2003, 'Which side are you on? Bias, credibility, and mediation', *American Journal of Political Science*, vol. 47, no. 4, pp. 597-611.

Landau, Barbara, Bartoletti, Mario D. and Mesbur, Ruth 1987, *Family mediation handbook*, Butterworths, Toronto.

Landis, Jean M. and Goodstein, Lynne 1986, 'When is justice fair? An integrated approach to the outcome versus procedure debate', *American Bar Foundation Research Journal*, vol. 11, no. 4, pp. 675-707.

Langstaff, Deborah and Christie, Jane 2000, *Trauma care: a team approach*, Butterworth, Heinemann, Oxford.

Law Commission Bangladesh 2008, *A Final report on the proposed law of domestic violence along with a draft bill namely, the domestic violence Act,* Law Commission of Bangladesh, Dhaka, viewed 8 September 2009,<http://www.lawcommissionbangladesh.org/reports/71.pdf>

Lawson, Fred H. 1987, 'Review: Analysis of mediation', *Journal of Palestine Studies*, vol. 16, no. 4, pp. 135-9.

LeBaron, Michell 2001, *Conflict and Culture: A literature review and bibliography*, rev. edn, Institute for Dispute Resolution, University of Victoria, Victoria.

Lee, Joel and Hwee, Teh H. 2009, 'The quest for an "Asian" perspective in mediation', in Lee, Joel and Hwee, Teh H. (eds.), *An Asian perspective on mediation*, Academy Publishing, Singapore, pp. 3-20.

Legal and Judicial Capacity Building Project (LJCBP) 2004, *Final report: Improving mechanism for delivering legal aid*, Unpublished report, Ministry of Law and Parliamentary Affairs, Dhaka.

LeResche, Diane 1992, 'Comparison of the American mediation process with a Korean-American harmony restoration process', *Mediation Quarterly*, vol. 9, no. 4, pp. 323-39.

Lerman, Lisa G. 1984, 'Mediation of wife abuse cases: The adverse impact of informal dispute resolution on women', *Harvard Journal of Law and Gender*, vol. 7, pp. 57-114.

Liebmann, Marian 2000, *Mediation in context*, Jessica Kingsley Publishers, London.

Lim, Lan Y. 1999, The theory & practice of mediation, FT Law & Tax Asia Pacific, Singapore.

Limparangsri, Sorawit and Yuprasert, Prachya 2005, 'Arbitration and mediation in ASEAN: laws and practice from a Thai perspective', paper presented in *The ASEAN Law Association 25th anniversary commemorative session*, Manila, 24-27 November 2005.

Longan, Patrick E. 1994, 'Bureaucratic Justice Meets ADR: The Emerging Role for Magistrates as Mediators', *Nebraska Law Review,* vol. 73, no.3, pp. 712-55.

Lowry Randolph L. 2004, 'Evaluative mediation', in Folberg, Jay, Milne, Ann L. and Saem, Peter (eds.), *Divorce and family mediation: models, techniques, and applications*, The Gilford Press, New York.

Luban, David 1989, 'The quality of justice', *Denver University Law Review,* vol, 66, no. 3, pp. 381-418.

Lucy, William 2005, 'The Possibility of Impartiality', *Oxford Journal of Legal Studies,* vol. 25, pp. 3-31.

—. 2009, 'Abstraction of rule of law', *Oxford Journal of Legal Studies*, 29, no.3, pp. 481-509.

Lyotard, Jean-Francois 1984, *The postmodern condition: A report on knowledge*, G. Bennington & B. Massumi (trans.), University Minnesota Press, Minneapolis.

Macdonald, Roderick A. 1990, 'Access to Justice and Law Reform', Windsor Year of Access to Justice, vol. 10, pp. 287-300.

Macfarlane, Julie 1997, *Rethinking disputes: The mediation alternative*, Cavendish Publication, London.

Mack, Kathy 1995, 'Alternative dispute resolution and access to justice for women', *Adelaide Law Review*, vol. 17, no.1, pp. 123-46.

MacKinnon, Catharine A. 1991, 'Reflections on sex equality under law', *Yale Law Journal*, vol. 100, no.6, pp.1282-1328.

Madaripur Legal Aid Association (MLAA) 2004, *Mediation manual*, MLAA, Madaripur.

Madonik, Barbara G. 2001, *I hear what you say, but what are you telling me? The strategic use of nonverbal communication in mediation*, Jossey-Bass, San Francisco.

Maggiolo, Walter A. 1985, *Techniques of mediation*, Oceana Publications, New York.

Mahmood, Syed T. 1980, *The Muslim law of India*, 2nd edn, Law Book Co., Allahabad.

—. 1983, *Muslim personal law: Role of the state in the Indian subcontinent*, 2nd edn, Diwan Press, Nagpur.

Makuto, Kubo and Chowdhury Jamila A. 2005, 'Women's rights and discrimination in Bangladesh: achievements made and challenges remaining for the 21st century', *Osaka Sangyo University Journal of Economics*, vol. 6, no. 2, pp. 47-86.

Malia, Julia A., Cunningham, Jo L., MacMillan, Elsa and Wynn, Elaine 1995, 'Expanding the policy infrastructure for resolving family-related disputes: Mediation as a technology', *Family Relations*, vol. 44, no. 1, pp. 19-27.

Manchanda, Shiv C. 1973, *The Law and practice of divorce*, 4th edn, Law Book Co., Allahabad.

Mansnerus, Laura 2001, 'A Brake on the Wheels of Justice; Shortage of Lawyers for the Poor Plagues the Courts', *The New York Times*, 17 January, viewed 10 July,2010, <http://www.nytimes.com/2001/01/17/nyregion/brake-wheels-justice-shortage-lawyers-for-poor-plagues-courts.html?pagewanted=1?pagewanted=1>.

Marcus, Mary G., Walter, Marcus, Stilwell, Nancy A. and Neville, Doherty 1999, 'To mediate or not to mediate: Financial outcomes in mediated versus adversarial divorces', *Mediation Quarterly*, vol. 17, no. 2, pp. 143-52.

Margolis, Joseph 1967, 'Perception, inference, and mediation', *The Journal of Philosophy*, vol. 64, no. 4, pp. 119-23.

Marlow, Lenard and Sauber, Richard S 1990, *The handbook of divorce mediation*, Plenum, New York.

Marquis, Bessie L and Huston. Carol J 2009, *Leadership roles and management functions in nursing: theory and application*, Wolters Kluwer Health, Philadelphia.

Marthaler, Dennis 1989, 'Successful mediation with abusive couples', *Mediation Quarterly*, vol 23, pp. 53-66.

Maxwell, Albert E. 1971, *Analyzing qualitative data*, John Wiley & Sons, New York

May, Todd 1993, *Between genealogy and epistemology: Psychology, politics, and knowledge in the thought of Michel Foucault*, Pennsylvania State University Press, University Park.

—. 1995, *The moral theory of post structuralism*, Pennsylvania State University Press, University Park.

—. 2006, *The Philosophy of Foucault*, Acumen Publishing Limited, Chesham.

Mayer, Bernard 1987, 'The dynamics of power in mediation and negotiation', *Mediation Quarterly*, vol. 16, no. 1, pp. 75-86.

—. 1998 *Beyond Neutrality - Confronting the Crisis in Conflict Resolution,* Jossey-Bass, San Francisco.

—. 2000, *The dynamics of conflict resolution*, Jossey-Bass, San Francisco.

Mazzarella, William 2004, 'Culture, globalization, mediation', *Annual Review of Anthropology*, vol. 33, pp. 345-67.

McCold, Paul 2006, 'The recent history of restorative justice: mediation, circles and conferencing', in Sullivan, Dennis, and Tifft, Larry (eds.), Handbook of restorative justice: a global perspective, London, Routledge, pp. 23-51.

McEwen, Craig A. and Maiman, Richard J. 1984, 'Mediation in small claims court: Achieving compliance through consent', *Law & Society Review*, vol. 18, no. 1, pp. 11-49.

McEwen, Craig A., Mather, Lynn and Maiman, Richard J 1994, 'Lawyers, mediation, and the management of divorce practice', *Law & Society Review*, vol. 28, no. 1, pp. 149-86.

McGillis, Daniel 1997, Community mediation programs: development and challenges, National Institute of Justice, US Department of Justice, Washington D.C.

Meene, Ineke V and Rooij, Benjamin V. 2008, *Access to justice and legal empowerment: making the poor central in legal development co-operation*, Leiden University Press, Amsterdam.

Menkel-Meadow, Carrie 1991, 'Pursuing settlement in adversary culture: A tale of innovation co-opted or the law of ADR', *Florida State University Law Review,* vol. 19, no. 1, pp. 1-46.

—. 1992, *Mediation & alternative dispute resolution*, National Institute for Dispute Resolution, Washington, DC.

—. 1993, 'Lawyer negotiations: Theories and realities: What we learn from mediation', *The Modern Law Review*, vol. 56, no. 3, pp. 361-79.

—. 1995, 'The many ways of mediation: The transformations of traditions, ideologies, paradigms, and practices', Negotiation *Journal,* vol. 11, no. 3, pp. 217-42.

—. 1999, 'Ethics and Professionalism in Non-Adversarial Lawyering', *Florida State University Law Review,* vol. 27, no. 1, pp. 153-92.

—. 2002a, 'Practicing in the interests of justice' in the twenty-first century: Pursuing peace as justice', *Fordham Law Review,* vol. 70, no. 5, pp. 1761-74.

—. 2002b, The lawyer as consensus builder: Ethics for a new practice', *Tennessee Law Review,* vol. 70, no. 1, pp. 63-119.

Menski, Werner F. 1988, 'English family law and ethnic laws in Britain', *Kerala Law Times*, vol.1, pp.556-66.

Miller, Richard E. and Sarat, Austin 1980-81, 'Grievances, claims and disputes: Assessing the adversary culture', *Law & Society Review,* vol. 15, no.3, pp. 525-65.

Milne, Ann L., Folberg, Jay and Salem, Peter 2004, 'The evolution of divorce and family mediation: an overview', in Folberg, Jay, Milne, Ann L. and Saem, Peter (eds.), *Divorce and family mediation: models, techniques, and applications*, The Gilford Press, New York, pp. 3-28.

Milner, Neal 1996, 'Review: Mediation and political theory: A critique of Bush and Folger', *Law & Social Inquiry*, vol. 21, no. 3, pp. 737-59.

Mnookin, Robert H. and Kornhauser, Lewis 1979, 'Bargaining in the shadow of the law: The case of divorce', *Yale Law Journal*, vol. 88, no. 5, pp. 950-97.

Moberly, Robert B. 1997, 'Mediator gag rules: is it ethical for mediators to evaluate or advise?' *South Texas Law Review,* vol. 38, no. 2, pp. 669-79.

Monsoor, Taslima 1999, *From patriarchy to gender equity: Family law and its impact on women in Bangladesh*, The University Press Limited, Dhaka.

—. 2008a, *Gender Equity and Economic Empowerment: Family Law and Women in Bangladesh*, British Council, Dhaka.

—. 2008b, *Management of gender relations: Violence against women and criminal justice system in Bangladesh,* British Council, Dhaka.

Moore, Christopher W. 1986, *The mediation process: Practical strategies for resolving conflict*, Jossey-Bass social and behavioral science series, Jossey-Bass, San Francisco.

Morrill, Calvin and Facciola, Peter C. 1992, 'The power of language in adjudication and mediation: Institutional contexts as predictors of social evaluation', *Law & Social Inquiry*, vol. 17, no. 2, pp. 191-212.

Morris, Catherine 1999, 'The moulding of lawyers: ADR and legal education, *Windsor Year Book of Access to Justice*, vol.17, pp. 271-79.

Morrison, Andrew S. 1987, 'Is divorce mediation the practice of law? A matter of perspective', *California Law Review*, vol. 75, no. 3, pp. 1093-1155.

Moser, Michael J. 1997, 'Peoples republic of China', in Michael Pryles (ed.), Dispute Resolution in Asia, Kulwer Law International, London.

Moshinsky, Ada, Cyngler, James, Keon-Cohen, CS. and Street, Patrick 1995, *Court based mediation initiative: Court perspective to the mediation process*, Seminar papers Leo Cussen Institute, Leo Cussen Institute, Melbourne, Victoria.

Nader, Laura 1980, *No access to law: Alternatives to the American judicial system,* Academic Press, New York.

Nasir, Jamal J. 1990, *The status of women under Islamic law and under modern Islamic legislation*, Graham and Trotman, London.

Nasir, Rasheda I. 1991, 'Role and status of urban working women', *Social Science Review*, vol. 8, no. 1&2, pp. 135-50.

National Alternative Dispute Resolution Advisory Council (NADRAC) 2002, Terminology: a discussion paper, National Alternative Dispute Resolution Advisory Committee, Canberra.

—. 2004, Federal civil justice system strategy paper, National Alternative Dispute Resolution Advisory Committee, Canberra.

National Alternative Dispute Resolution Advisory Council (NADRAC) & Attorney-General's Department 1999, *A fair say: Managing differences in mediation and conciliation: A guide for all involved*, Commonwealth of Australia, Canberra.

National Institute of Justice 1997, *National Institute of Justice: research in action*, National Institute of Justice, Department of Justice, Washington DC.

National Mediator Accreditation System (NMAS) 2007, *Practice Standards,* Federal Court of Australia, Sydney.

Nedelsky, Jennifer 1997, 'Embodied Diversity and Challenges to Law', *McGill Law Journal*, vol 42, p. 91 - 117.

Nelson, Dorothy W. 2004, 'Which way to true justice: Appropriate dispute resolution (ADR) and adversarial legalism', *Nebraska Law Review,* vol. 83, no.1, pp. 167-78.

Neumann, Diane 1992, 'How mediation can effectively address the male-female power imbalance in divorce', *Mediation Quarterly*, vol. 9, no. 3, pp. 227-39.

New South Wales Law Reform Commission 2004, *Mediation and community justice centres : An empirical study*, NSW Law Reform Commission, Sydney, NSW.

New York State Unified Court System 2003, *Dispute resolution centers program: Annual report for the fiscal year 2002-03*, Office of alternative dispute resolution, Division of court operations, Albany, NY.

NGO Committee on Beijing Plus Five, Bangladesh (NCBPF) 2001, *Stop violence against women,* Women for Women, Dhaka.

Nichols, Michael P. and Schwartz, Richard C. 1991, Family therapy: concepts and methods, 2nd ed. Allen and Bacon, Boston.

Nietzsche, Friedrich W. 1967, *The will to power*, in W. Kaufman & R. J. Hollingdale (trans.), W. Kaufman (ed.), Random House, New York.

Nolan-Haley, Jacqueline 1998, 'Lawyers, clients, and mediation', *Notre Dame Law Review* 73, no.5, pp. 1369-90.

—. 1999, 'Informed consent in mediation: A guiding principle for truly educated decision-making', *Notre Dame Law Review,* vol. *74*, no.3, pp. 775-840.

Noone, Michael 1996, *Mediation: Essential legal skills*, Cavendish Publication, London.

Nyquist, Linda V. and Spence, Janet T. 1986. Effects of dispositional dominance and sex role expectations on leadership behaviors. Journal of Personality and Social Psychology, vol. 50, no. 1, pp. 87–93.

O'Barr, William M. and Conley, John M. 1988, 'Lay expectations of the civil justice system', *Law & Society Review*, vol. 22, no. 1, pp. 137-162.

O'Connor, Maureen, Gutek, Barbara A., Stockdale, Margaret., Geer, Tracey M. and Melancon, Renee 2004, 'Explaining sexual harassment judgments: Looking beyond gender of the ratter', *Law and Human Behaviour*, vol. 28, no. 1, pp. 69-95.

Oppenheim, Abraham N. 1986, *Questionnaire design and attitude measurement*, Henry Holt and Co., New York.

Palenski, Joseph E. and Launer, Harold M. 1986, *Mediation : Contexts and challenges*, C.C. Thomas, Springfield.

Palmer, Michael 1988, 'The revival of mediation in the People's Republic of China' in Butler, William E. (ed.), Yearbook on Socialist Legal Systems: 1987, Transnational Publishers, Inc., Dobbs Ferry, New York, pp. 220.

Palmer, Michael and Roberts, Simon 2005, *Dispute processes: ADR and the primary forms of decision making,* Cambridge University Press,

Cambridge.

Paras, Eric 2006, *Foucault 2.0: Beyond power and knowledge*, Other Press, New York.

Parkinson, Lisa 1997, Family Mediation, Sweet & Maxell, London.

Paul, Madan C. 1986, *Dowry and Position of Women in India: A Study of Delhi Metropolis*, Inter-India Publications, New Delhi.

Pearson, Jessica 1997, *Divorce mediation and domestic violence*, Center for Policy Research, New York.

Pearson, Jessica and Thoennes, Nancy 1984, 'Mediating and litigating custody disputes: a longitudinal evaluation', *Family Law Quarterly*, vol.17, no.4, pp. 497-533.

Peterson, Brooks 2004, *Cultural intelligence: A guide to working with people from other cultures*, Intercultural Press, Yarmouth.

Phillips, Ruth 2006, 'Undoing an activist response: Feminism and the Australian government's domestic violence policy', *Critical Social Policy*, vol. 26, no. 1, pp. 192-219.

Picard, Cheryl A. 2002, *Mediating interpersonal and small group conflict*, Dundurn Press Ltd., Canada.

Pinzon, Luis A. 1996, 'The production of power and knowledge in mediation', *Mediation Quarterly*, vol.14, no. 1, pp. 3-20.

Piper, Christine 1993, *The responsible parent: a study of divorce mediation*, London: Harvester Wheatsheaf.

Podell, Jerome E. and Knapp, William M. 1969, 'The effect of mediation on the perceived firmness of the opponent', *The Journal of Conflict Resolution*, vol. 13, no. 4, pp. 511-20.

Pryles, Michael C. 2006, *Dispute resolution in Asia*, Kulwer Law International, Bedfordshire.

Pruitt, Dean G., Peirce, Robert S., McGillicuddy, Neil B., Welton, Gary L and Castrianno, Lynn M 1993, 'Long-term success in mediation', *Law and Human Behavior*, vol. 17, no. 3, pp. 313-30.

Pusey, Michael and Young, Robert E. 1979, *Control and knowledge : The mediation of power in institutional and educational settings*, Education Research Unit, Research School of Social Sciences, ANU, Canberra.

Putnam, Linda 1994, 'Challenging the assumptions of traditional approaches to mediation', *Negotiation Journal,* vol. 10, no.4, pp. 337-45.

Rack, Philip 1983, *Race, Culture and Mental Disorder*, J.W. Arrowsmith Ltd. Bristol.

Raftesath, Gerald and Thaler, Sue 1999, *Cases for mediation*, LBC Information Services, Sydney.

Rahman, Fazlur 1998, 'Post-divorce maintenance for Muslim women in

Pakistan and India', *Bangladesh Journal of Law*, vol.2, no. 1, pp. 26-52.

Rahman, Gazi S. 1997, *Bangladesher Ainer Itihash* [Legal History of Bangladesh] Dhaka.

Rahman, Waliur and Shahabuddin, Mohammad (eds) 2005, *Judicial training in the new millennium,* Bangladesh Institute of Law and International Affaris, Dhaka.

Rajchman, John 1985, *Michel Foucault: The freedom of Philosophy*, Columbia University Press, New York.

Rao, Chandra P and Sheffield, William (eds) 1997, *Alternative dispute resolution – what it is and how it works*, International Centre for Alternative Dispute Resolution, New Delhi.

Rao, Vijayendra 1993, 'The rising price of husbands: A hedonic analysis of dowry increases in rural India', *Journal of Political Economy*, vol. 101, no. 4, pp. 666-77.

Rashid, Syed K. 2004, *Muslim law*, 4th edn, Eastern Book Company, New Delhi.

Rawls, John 1971, *A theory of justice*, Harvard University Press, Cambridge.

—. 1999, *The law of peoples,* Harvard University Press, Cambridge.

Ray, Larry 1997, 'Community mediation centers: delivering first class services to low-income people for the past twenty years', Mediation Quarterly, vol. 15, no. 1. pp. 71-77.

Rayburn, Jill 1995, 'Neighborhood justice centers: Community use of ADR - Does it really work? ', *University of Memphis Law Review,* vol. 26, no. 3, pp. 1197-1228.

Rhoades, Helen, Astor, Hilary and Sanson, Ann 2009, 'A study of inter-professional relationships in a changing family law system', *Australian Journal of Family Law*, vol. 23, no. 1, pp. 10-29

Rhoades, Helen, Graycar Regina and Harrison, Margaret 2000, The Family Law Reform Act 1995: The first three years, University of Sydney & Family Court of Australia, Sydney.

Rhode, Deborah L. 2000-01, 'Access to justice', *Fordham Law Review*, vol. 69, no. 5, pp. 1785-1811.

—. 2003-04, 'Access to Justice: Connecting principles to practice', *Georgetown Journal of Legal Ethics*, vol. 17, no. 3, pp. 369-422.

Riskin, Leonard L. 1985, 'The special place of mediation in alternative dispute processing Alternative methods of dispute resolution: An overview', *University of Florida Law Review*, vol. 37, no.1, pp. 19-27.

—. 1995, 'Many doors? Closing doors? Alternative dispute resolution and adjudication', *Ohio State Journal on Dispute Resolution,* vol. 10, no.2, pp. 211-65.

—. 1996, 'Understanding mediators' orientations, strategies, and techniques: A grid for the perplexed', *Harvard Negotiation Law Review*, vol 1, no 7, pp. 7-51.

Riskin Leonard L. and Westbrook, James E. 2005, *Dispute Resolution and Lawyers*, 3rd edn, Thomson/West Publishing Co., St. Paul, Minnesota. 1987.

Robbins, Stephen P., Judge Timothy A., Odendaal, A. and Roodt G. 2009, *Organisational behaviour: global and Southern African perspectives*, Pearson Education, Cape Town.

Roberts, Marian 2008, *Mediation in family disputes: Principles of practice*, 3rd edn, Ashgate Publishing Limited, Aldershot.

Roberts, Simon 1983, 'Mediation in family disputes', *The Modern Law Review*, vol. 46, no. 5, pp. 537-57.

Ross, William H. and Conlon, Donald E. 2000, 'Hybrid forms of third-party dispute resolution: Theoretical implications of combining mediation and arbitration', *The Academy of Management Review*, vol. 25, no. 2, pp. 416-27.

Rothfield, Jonathan 2001, 'What (I think) I do as the mediator' *Australasian Dispute Resolution Journal* , vol. 12, no. 4, pp.240-47.

Rovine, Arthur W. 2009, *Contemporary issues in international arbitration and mediation*, Martinus Nijhoff Publishers, Leiden.

Rozdeiczer, Lukasz and Campa, Alejandro A. (eds) 2006, *Alternative dispute resolution manual: Implementing commercial mediation*, SME Department, The World Bank Group.

Russo, Thomas A. and Katzal, Aaron J. 2010, The 2008 crisis and its aftermath: Confronting the next debt challenge, working draft.

Sabatino, Jack M. 1998, 'ADR as litigation lite: Procedural and evidentiary norms embedded within alternative dispute resolution', *Emory Law Journal,* vol. 47, no.4, pp. 1289-1350.

Sainsbury, Richard and Genn, Hazel 1995, 'Access to justice: Lessons from tribunals', in Zuckerman, A A S and Cranston, Ross (eds), *Reform of civil procedure: Essays on 'access to justice'*, Clarendon Press, Oxford, pp. 413–29.

Samovar, Lary A., Porter, Richard E and McDaniel, Edwin R 2012, Intercultural communication: a reader, 13th ed, Wadsworth, Boston.

Sanchez, Valerie A. 2003, 'Back to the future of ADR: Negotiation justice and human needs', *Ohio State Journal on Dispute Resolution*, vol. 18, no. 3, pp. 669-76.

Sandel, Michael J. 1982, *Liberalism and the Limits of Justice,* Cambridge University Press, Cambridge.

Sander, Frank EA 1985, 'Alternative methods of dispute resolution: An overview', *University of Florida Law Review*, vol. 37, no.1, pp. 1-18.

Sarkar, Sudipto 2002, *Sarkar on Code of Civil Procedure*, 10th edn, Wadhwa and Company, Nagpur.

Sattar, Rana P. 2007, *Existing ADR framework and practices in Bangladesh: A rapid assessment*, Bangladesh Legal Reform Project, Dhaka.

Schacht, Joseph 1982, *An Introduction to Islamic Law*, Oxford University Press, New York.

Scheb, John M. and Scheb II, John M 2011, Criminal law & procedure, Wodsworth, Belmont.

Schuler, Sidney R., Hashemi Syed M., Riley Ann P. and Akhter Shireen 1996, 'Credit programs, patriarchy and men's violence against women in rural Bangladesh', *Social Science and Medicine*, vol. 43, no. 12, pp. 1729-42.

Sember, Brette 2006, *No-fight divorce: Spend less money, save time, and avoid conflict using mediation*, McGraw-Hill, New York.

Sen, Amartya K. 1984, 'Family and food: Sex bias in poverty', in Sen, Amartya K. (ed.), *Resources, Values and Development*, Basil Blackwell, Oxford.

—. 1995, 'Gender inequality and theories of justice', in Nassbaum, Martha C. & Glover, Jonathon (eds), *Women, culture and development: A study on human capabilities*, Clarendon Press, Oxford, pp. 259-73.

Senft, Louise P. and Savage, Cynthia A. 2003, 'ADR in the courts: Progress, problems and possibilities', *Penn State Law Review,* vol. 108, no.1, pp. 327-48.

Shabbir, Mohammad 1988, *Muslim Personal Law and Judiciary*, Law Book Co., Allahabad.

Sharma, Mukundakam 2012, 'Conciliation and Mediation', *Delhi Mediation Center: articles*, at <http://www.delhimediationcentre.gov.in/articles.htm>

Sheehan, Grania and Smyth, Bruce 2000, 'Spousal violence and post-separation financial outcomes', *Australian Family Law Journal*, vol. 14, no. 2, pp. 102-18 .

Siddiqi, Dina M. 1999, 'Informed consent in mediation: A guiding principle for truly educated decision making', *Notre Dame Law Review,* vol. *74*, no.3, pp. 775-840. 2006a, *Shalish and the quest for gender justice: an assessment of strategic interventions in Bangladesh*, Research Initiative Bangladesh, Dhaka.

—. 2006, *Shalish and the quest for gender justice: An assessment of strategic interventions in Bangladesh*, Research Initiative Bangladesh,

Dhaka.

Siddiqua, Begum A. 2005, *The family courts of Bangladesh: An appraisal of Rajshahi sadar family court and the gender issues*, Bangladesh Freedom Foundation, Dhaka.

Siddiqui, Kamal 2005, *Local government in Bangladesh*, The University Press Limited, Dhaka.

Siegel, Larry J. 2011, *Essentials of criminal justice,* Wadsworth, Belmont.

Simpson, Carolyn 1998, *Coping through conflict resolution and peer mediation*, The Rosen Publishing Group, New York.

Singer, Jana B. 2009, 'Dispute resolution and the post divorce family: Implications of a paradigm shift', *Family Court Review*, vol. 47, no. 3, pp. 363-70.

Singer, Linda R. 1994, *Settling disputes: conflict resolution in business, families, and the legal system*, Westview Press, Oxford.

Singh, Anita and Zahid, Nasir A. 2002, *Strengthening Governance through Access to Justice*, PHI, New Delhi.

Sinha, Arvind K. 2004, *Panchayet raj and empowerment of women*, Northern Book Centre, New Delhi.

Smith, Belinda 2008, 'It's time –for a new approach to equality', *Federal Law Review,* vol. 36, no. 2, pp. 117-44.

Smolicz, Jerzy J. and Margaret, Secombe J. 2003, 'Sociology as a Science of culture, linguistic pluralism in Australia and Belarus', in Rafael, Eliezer B., *Sociology and Ideology*, Brill, Leiden.

Sobhan, Salma 2005, 'Violence against women: Laws, implementation and reforms', in Rahman, Waliur & Shahabuddin, Mohammod (eds), *Judicial training in the new millennium: An anatomy of BILIA judicial training with difference*, Bangladesh Institute of Law and International Affairs Dhaka.

Sommerlad, Hilary 2004, 'Some reflections on the relationship between citizenship, access to justice, and the reform of legal aid', *Journal of Law and Society*, vol. 31, no. 3, pp. 345.

Sourdin, Tania 1999, 'Informed consent in mediation: A guiding principle for truly educated decision making', *Notre Dame Law Review,* vol. *74*, no.3, pp. 775-840. 2006, 'Mediation in Australia: Impacts on litigation', in Alexander, Nadja M. *Global Trends in Mediation,* Kulwer Law International, Bedfordshire.

—. 2005, *Alternative dispute resolution*, Law Book Co., 2nd edn, Pyrmont, NSW.

—. 2008, *Alternative dispute resolution*, Law Book Co., 3rd edn, Pyrmont, NSW.

Spegel, Nadja., Rogers, Bernadette and Buckley, Ross 1998, *Negotiation:*

theory and techniques, Butterworts, Sydney.

Spencer David 2002, Essentials of dispute resolution, Cavendish Publishing Limited, London.

—. 2011, *Principles of dispute resolution*, Thomson Reuters Australia, Limited, Rozelle, NSW.

Spencer, David and Brogan, Michael C. 2006, *Mediation law and practice*, Cambridge University Press, Cambridge.

Spencer, David, Spencer, David and Hardy, Samantha 2009, *Dispute resolution in Australia: Cases, commentary and materials*, 2nd edn, Thomas Reuters, Sydney.

Spencer, Maleson J. and Zammit, Joseph P. 1976, 'Mediation-arbitration: A proposal for private resolution of disputes between divorced or separated parents', *Duke Law Journal*, vol. 1976, no. 5, pp. 911-39.

Stahler, Gerald J., DuCette, Jesoph P. and Povich, Edna 1990, 'Using mediation to prevent child maltreatment: An exploratory study', *Family Relations*, vol. 39, no. 3, pp. 317-22.

Stallone, Dianna R. 1984, 'Decriminalization of violence in the home: Mediation in wife battering cases', *Law and Inequality Journal,* vol. 2, no. 2 pp. 493-519.

Stark, James H. 1997, 'The ethics of mediation evaluation: some troublesome questions and tentative proposals from a lawyer mediator', *South Texas Law Review,* vol. 38, pp. 769-800.

Stempel, Jeffrey W. 1997, 'Beyond formalism and false dichotomies: the need for institutionalizing a flexible concept of the mediator's role' *Florida State University Law Review,* vol. 24, 949-984.

Stephenson, Geoffrey D., Elder, Anthony, Cyngler, James, Golvan, George H., Alter, March and Leo Cussen Institute 1995, *Court based mediation initiative: The role of the legal profession in mediation*, Seminar papers, Leo Cussen Institute, Melbourne.

Sternlight, Jean R. 1999, 'Lawyer's representation of clients in mediation: Using economics and psychology to structure advocacy in a non-adversarial setting', *Ohio State Journal on Dispute Resolution*, vol. 14, no. 2, pp. 269-90.

Stintzing, Heike 1994, *Mediation - a necessary element in family dispute resolution? A comparative study of the Australian model of alternative dispute resolution for family disputes and the situation in German law*, Peter Lang, Frankfurt am Main.

Stipanowich, Thomas J. 2004, 'ADR and the vanishing trial: The growth and impact of alternative dispute resolution', Journal *of Empirical Legal Studies,* vol.1, no. 3, pp. 843-912.

Stitt, Allan 2004, *Mediation: A practical guide*, Cavendish Publishing,

London.

Strasser, Freddie and Randolph, Paul 2004, *Mediation a psychological insight into conflict resolution*, Cronwell Press Ltd., London.

Street, Laurence and Jacobs, Marcus 1991, *Mediation and arbitration*, Young Lawyers Section, Law Society of New South Wales, Sydney.

Stulberg, Joseph B. 1996-97, 'Facilitative versus evaluative mediator orientations: piercing the 'Grid' lock', *Florida State University Law Review*, vol. 24, pp. 985-1005.

—. 1998, *'Fairness and mediation'*, *Australian Dispute Resolution Journal*, vol. 13, no.3, pp. 909-45.

Sultana, Nahar 2004, 'Polygamy and divorce in rural Bangladesh', *Empowerment*, vol. 11, pp. 75-96.

—. 2006, 'Two conceptions of procedural fairness', *Social Research*, vol. 73, no. 2, pp. 619-46.

Sunstein, Cass R. 1996, ' Social norms and social rules', *Columbia Law Review*, vol. 96, no. 2, pp. 903-68.

Supreme Court of Bangladesh 2008, *Annual report of the judiciary, 2007*, Supreme Court of Bangladesh, Dhaka.

Susskind, Laurance, McKearnan, Sarah and Thomas-Larner, Jenifer 1999, *The consensus building handbook: A comprehensive guide to reaching agreement*, Sage, New Delhi.

Suvanpanich, Thawatchai 1997, 'Thailand', in Pryles, Michael (ed.), Dispute resolution in Asia, pp. 261-292.

Tamanaha, Brian Z. 2001, *A general jurisprudence of law and society*, Oxford University Press, Oxford.

Tarpley, Joan R. 2001, 'ADR, jurisprudence and myth', *Ohio State Journal on Dispute Resolution,* vol. 17, no. 1, pp. 113-44.

Tate, Shepherd S. 1979, 'Access to justice', *American Bar Association Journal*, vol. 65, no. 6, pp. 904-7.

Taylor, Alison 1997, 'Concepts of neutrality in family mediation: Contexts, ethics, influence, and transformative process', *Mediation Quarterly*, vol. 14, no. 3, pp. 215-36.

—. 2002, *The handbook of family dispute resolution: Mediation theory and practice*, Jossey-Bass, San Francisco.

Termini, Michael J. 2007, Walking the talk: pathways to leadership, Society of Manufacturing Engineers, Michigan.

Terris, Lesley G. and Maoz, Zeev 2005, 'Rational mediation: A theory and a test', *Journal of Peace Research*, vol. 42, no. 5, pp. 563-83.

Tertilt, Michele 2005, 'Polygamy, Fertility, and Savings', *Journal of Political Economy*, vol. 113, no. 6, pp. 1341-70.

The Asia Foundation 2002a, *Access to justice: Best practices under the*

Democracy Partnership, The Asia Foundation, Dhaka.
—. 2002b, *The democracy partnership*, The Asia Foundation, Dhaka.
The Change Makers 2002, 'Justice for all', *Review,* vol.4, no.1, pp. 45-51.
The Daily Star 2002, 'Fundamental changes in judicial system', *The Daily Star*, 31 October.
—. 2003, 'Mediatory system to reduce pressure on judiciary:5 lakh civil suits pending, Moudud tells workshop', The Daily Star, National, 26 July.
Thomas, Roosevelt R. 1992, *Beyond race and gender: unleashing the power of your total work* AMACOM, New York.
Tillett, Gregory and French, Brendan 2006, Resolving conflict: a practical approach, Oxford university press, oxford.
Tom Beauchamp 1980, 'Distributional justice and the difference principle' in Blocker, Gene H. and Smith, Elizabeth H. (eds), *John Rawls' theory of social justice an introduction,* Ohio University Press, Athens.
Tomlinson, John 1991, *Cultural imperialism: A critical introduction*, Continuum, London.
Transparency International Bangladesh (TIB) 1997, *Survey on corruption in Bangladesh*, TIB, Dhaka, (Unpublished).
—. 2002, Corruption in South Asia: Insights and benchmarks from citizen feedback', viewed 18 June 2009, <http://unpan1.un.org/intradoc/groups/public/documents/APCITY/UNPAN019883.pdf>
—. 2007, Global corruption report 2007, Transparency International.
Trubek, David M., Sarat, Austin, Felstiner, William LF., Kritzer, Herbert M and Grossman, Joel B 1983, 'The costs of ordinary litigation', *UCLA Law Review*, vol. 31, no.1, pp. 72-127.
Tyler, Tom 1984, 'The role of perceived injustice in defendants' evaluations of their courtroom experience', *Law and Society Review*, vol. 18, no. 1, pp. 51-74.
—. 1988, 'What is procedural justice? Criteria used by citizens to assess the fairness of legal procedures', *Law and Society Review*, vol. 22, no.1, pp. 103-36.
—. 1989, 'The quality of dispute resolution procedures and outcomes: Measurement, problems and possibilities', *Denver University Law Review,* vol. 66, no. 3, pp. 419-36.
United Nations 1994, *International convent on civil and political rights*, viewed 12 October 2008, <http://www.hrweb.org/legal/cpr.html>
United Nations Development Programme (UNDP) 1998, *ADR practitioners 'guide*, Centre for Democracy and Governance, Dhaka.

—. 2002, *Human security in Bangladesh: In search of justice and dignity*, UNDP, Dhaka.

United Nations High Commissioner for Refugees (UNHCR) 2000, *Basic principles on the role of lawyers*, viewed 10 March 2010, <http://www.unhchr.ch/html/menu3/b/h_comp44.htm>

United States Agency for International Development (USAID) 1998, 'Alternative dispute resolution practitioners guide', *Technical Publication Series*, Office of Democracy and Governance, Bureau for Democracy, Conflict and Humanitarian assistance, US Agency for International Development, Washington D.C.

University of Massachusetts Social Justice Mediation Institute (UMASS) 2012, 'Social justice mediation institute', University of Massachutes at Amherst, at <http://people.umass.edu/lwing/>

University of Southern California 2007-08, *Partial translation from Sunan Abu-Dawud*, Book 11, Centre for Muslim-Jewish Engagement, University of Southern California, viewed 25 June 2009, <http://www.usc.edu/schools/college/crcc/engagement/resources/texts/muslim/hadith/abudawud/011.sat.html>

Upadhya, Carol B. 1990, 'Dowry and women's property in coastal Andhra Pradesh', *Contributions to Indian Sociology*, vol. 24, no. 1, pp. 29-59.

US Senate 1990, 'Women and violence' hearings before the US Senate Judiciary Committee, August 29 and December 11, 1990, Senate Hearing 101-939, pt. 1, p. 12.

Vanderkool, Lois and Pearson, Jessica 1983, 'Mediating divorce disputes: Mediator behaviors, styles and roles', *Family Relations*, vol. 32, no. 4, pp. 557-66.

Verghese, Jamila 1980, *Her gold and her body*, Vikas Publishing House, New Delhi.

Wade, John 1997, 'Four evaluative studies of family mediation services in Australia', *Australian Journal of Family Law,* vol. 11, no. 3, pp. 343-48.

Wahrhaftig, Paul 1978. 'Citizens dispute resolution: a blue chip investment in community growth', *Pre-trial Services Annual Journal*, pp. 1-8.

Waldman, Ellen A. 1997, 'Identifying the role of social norms in mediation: A multiple model approach', *Hastings Law Journal*, vol. 48, no.4, pp. 703-69.

—. 1998, 'The evaluative-facilitative debate in mediation: Applying the lens of therapeutic jurisprudence ', *Marquette Law Review,* vol. 82, no. 1, pp. 155-70.

—. 2011, *Mediation ethics: cases and commentaries*, Jossey Bass, San Francisco.

Walker, Jeffery T. 1999, *Statistics in criminal justice: Analysis and interpretation*, Aspen Publishers, Inc., Maryland.

Walker, Mary and Ettinger, Geri 1992, *Mediation: An option to consider*, Young Lawyers, Law Society of New South Wales, Sydney.

Wall, James A. 1981, 'Mediation: An analysis, review, and proposed research', *The Journal of Conflict Resolution*, vol. 25, no. 1, pp. 157-80.

Wall, James A. and Callister, Rhonda R. 1999, 'Malaysian community mediation', *Journal of Conflict Resolution*, vol. 43, no. 3, pp.343-65.

Wall, James A. and Lynn, Ann 1993, 'Mediation: A current review', *The Journal of Conflict Resolution*, vol. 37, no. 1, pp. 160-94.

Wall, James A., Stark, John B. and Standifer, Rhetta L. 2001, 'Mediation: A current review and theory development', *The Journal of Conflict Resolution*, vol. 45, no. 3, pp. 370-91.

Watnik, Webster 2003, *Child custody mde simple: understanding the laws of child custody and child support*, Single Parent Press, Claremont.

Watson, Carol 1994, 'Gender versus power as a predictor of negotiation behaviour and outcomes', *Negotiation Journal*, vol. 10, no. 2, pp. 117-27.

Weinstein, Rebecca J. 2001, *Mediation in the workplace: a guide for training, practice and administration*, Quorum Books, Westort.

Wendt, Sarah and Brian, Cheers 2004, 'Rural cultures, domestic violence, and stories from a rural region', *Women against Violence Journal*, vol. 15, pp. 4-11.

Westen, Peter 1982, 'The Empty idea of equality', *Harvard Law Review*, vol. 95, no. 3, pp. 537-96.

—. 1983, 'The meaning of equality in law, science, math, and morals: A reply', *Michigan Law Review*, vol. 81, no. 3, pp. 604-61.

Wikipedia 2009, *Divisions of Bangladesh*, viewed 10 January 2010, <http://en.wikipedia.org/wiki/File:LocMap_Bangladesh_Dhaka.png>

Wing, Leah 2008, 'Wither neutrality? Mediation in the 21st Century', in Trujillo, Mary Adams, Myers, Linda J., Richards, Phillip M. and Roy, Beth. *Re-Centering culture and knowledge in conflict resolution practice*, Syracuse University Press, New York.

Winslade, John and Monk, Gerald 2001, *Narrative mediation: A new approach to conflict resolution,* Calif: Jossey-Bass, San Francisco.

Wissler, Roselle L. 1995, 'Mediation and adjudication in the small claims court: The effects of process and case characteristics', *Law & Society Review*, vol. 29, no. 2, pp. 323-58.

Wood, Julia T. 2011, *Communication in our lives*, Wadsworth Cengage learning, Boston.

Woods, Laurie 1985, 'Mediation: A backlash to women's progress on family law issues', *Clearinghouse Review* , vol. 19, no.4, pp. 431-36.

Woolf, Lord 1995, *Access to Justice: Interim Report to the Lord Chancellor on the Civil Justice System in England and Wales,* London, HMSO.

World Bank 2004, *Legal/judicial reform projects approved, identified, or under preparation 2004*, The World Bank, viewed 10 July 2011, <http://www1.worldbank.org/publicsector/legal/legalprojects.htm>

—. 2006, World Development Report, The World Bank, Washington DC.

Wubbolding, Robert E. 2009, 'Applying family systems therapy in schools', in Christner, Ray W. and Mennuti, Rosemary B. (eds.), School based mental health: a practitioner's guide to comparative practices, Routledge, New York.

Zahir, Mohammod 1988, *Delay in courts and court management*, Bangladesh Institute of Law and International Affairs, Dhaka.

Zander, Michael and Trust, Hamlyn 2000, The state of justice, Sweet & Maxwell, London.

Zant, Eric V. 2005, 'Moudud Ahmed, the Bangladesh Minister of Law, Justice, and Parliamentary Affairs, explains his efforts to reform the country's justice system', *ADB Review,* vol. 37, no. 2, pp.24-25.

Zartman, William 2002, 'Cowardly lions: Missed ppportunities for dispute settlement', *Ohio State Journal on Dispute Resolution,* vol. 18, no.1, pp. 1-26.

Zondervan, Deborah B. 2000, 'Community mediation in the USA: current developments', in Marian Liebmann, Mediation in context, Jessica Kingsley Publishers, Ltd., Philadelphia.

Zumeta, Zena 2000, 'Styles of Mediation: Facilitative, Evaluative, and Transformative Mediation', at <http://www.mediate.com/articles/zumeta.cfm>

INDEX